D0206019

WITHDRAWN

ISLAMIC
FUNDAMENTALISM

ISLAMIC FUNDAMENTALISM

An Introduction
Revised and Updated Edition

Lawrence Davidson

Greenwood Press
Westport, Connecticut • London

Library of Congress Cataloging-in-Publication Data

Davidson, Lawrence, 1945–
    Islamic fundamentalism : an introduction / Lawrence Davidson.—Rev. and updated ed.
      p. cm.
    Includes bibliographical references and index.
    ISBN 0–313–32429–8 (alk. paper)
    1. Islamic fundamentalism. 2. Islam—20th century. I. Title. II. Series.
BP60.D38 2003
320.5′5′0917671—dc21   2002075343

British Library Cataloguing in Publication Data is available.

Library of Congress Catalog Card Number: 2002075343
ISBN: 0–313–32429–8

First published in 2003

Greenwood Press, 88 Post Road West, Westport, CT 06881
An imprint of Greenwood Publishing Group, Inc.
www.greenwood.com

Printed in the United States of America

The paper used in this book complies with the
Permanent Paper Standard issued by the National
Information Standards Organization (Z39.48–1984).

10 9 8 7 6 5 4 3 2 1

Contents

A photographic essay follows page 60

Preface

Islam is one of the most rapidly growing religions in the world, and Islamic fundamentalism is one of its more forceful manifestations. The violent activities and pronouncements of a small number of Islamic fundamentalists often appear in our newspapers, news magazines, and television reports, yet it is a phenomenon that continues to be little understood. Perhaps because this is so, it is increasingly feared. This book seeks to give a clearer picture of what Islamic fundamentalism is by explaining its history and identifying its adherents over time. It also seeks to analyze what Islamic fundamentalists believe and what they want.

Chapter 1 presents a brief history of the Muslim people, for one of the basic factors shaping the perceptions and goals of all Islamic fundamentalists is their reading of their common Muslim history. This chapter also describes how Islamic fundamentalists see their contemporary situation and what reforms they want to bring about.

With this foundation laid, Chapter 2 describes the first successful modern Islamic fundamentalist organization, the Society of the Muslim Brothers. In many ways, this organization has inspired most of today's Islamic fundamentalists, as well as providing them with lessons on what can be expected when Islamic reformers come up against hostile and resistant governments.

Chapters 3 and 4 examine two cases of functioning Islamic states. The first is the Islamic Republic of Iran. Established by a revolution in 1979, the subsequent evolution of Iranian society has been influenced not only by the application of strong fundamentalist Muslim norms and values but also by a pronounced anti-Western orientation. The case of Iran is then compared to that of Saudi Arabia. Saudi Arabia is a nonrevolutionary, conservative society but also of Islamic fundamentalist character. Where Iran is a republic, Saudi Arabia is a monarchy, and where Iran is suspicious of and hostile toward the West, Saudi Arabia's relations with countries such as the United States are strong and stable. These examples are designed to let the reader see that Islamic fundamentalism is not a monolithic affair. There are many differences among Islamic fundamentalist movements and states in terms of forms of governance, the application of Islamic values, and attitudes toward the West.

Chapter 5 presents a review of Western attitudes and perceptions, concentrating mainly on the issues of democracy and women's rights. These are issues which seem to separate Islamic civilization from the West. The questions are asked: can Islam support democratic values and practices, and can gender equality be achieved within an Islamic context?

Chapter 6 addresses the issues of violence and terrorism, as well as supplying information on various Islamic groups. Many people in the West look at the activities of Islamic fundamentalists with apprehension, and now associate them with violent attacks on the United States. Some even claim that there is little or no room for peaceful relations with movements that often appear to hold values so different from those in the West. Whether this point of view is accurate or exaggerated poses an important question, with serious policy implications for the Western world.

This book also contains a documents section and brief biographies of leading Islamic fundamentalists. The documents give the reader a sample of the writings of a number of Islamic fundamentalists, as well as relevant sections of the Quran and sayings of the prophet Muhammad. These serve to illustrate and elaborate on the points and arguments made in the various chapters. The reader is encouraged to become familiar with these documents and refer to them often. The biographies give additional important information on most of the personalities taken up in the chapters, as well as other fundamentalist leaders. As with most historical figures, knowing something of their background can help make their beliefs and actions more understandable.

Finally, the book contains a chronology of events, a glossary of terms, and an annotated bibliography. The reader should briefly go through the chronology as an introduction to the history given in Chapter 1. An effort has been made to explain unfamiliar terms as they appear in the text, but their meanings can also be found in the glossary. A wealth of additional information is available on Islamic fundamentalists, Muslims in general, and the religion of Islam. The bibliography will lead the interested reader to books, videos, and Internet sources that can broaden his or her understanding of this important subject.

I would like to acknowledge the patient and skillful editing and many good suggestions of Randall Miller of St. Joseph's University in Philadelphia. His hard work is much appreciated.

Chronology of Events

1744   Muhammad ibn Saud of Diriyah in Arabia allies with Muhammad
            ibn abd al-Wahhab, an early Islamic fundamentalist reformer. This
            alliance creates a movement known as Wahhabism—an austere form
            of Sunni Islam which forms the basis of today's Saudi Arabian so-
            ciety.

1798   Napoleon invades Egypt. This is the first serious Western military
            intrusion into the Middle East and anticipates the pattern of impe-
            rialism that will evolve in the nineteenth century.

1802   The Wahhabis occupy Mecca and Medina.

1819–1822   The Ottoman Empire sponsors a military campaign that destroys the
            early Saudi-Wahhabi movement as a political and military force. It
            will reappear in the twentieth century.

1830   French military forces arrive in Algeria. The French now begin a
            long process of conquest and occupation that will soon spill over into
            other North African lands.

1869   The Suez Canal opens. With the opening of the canal, Egypt becomes
            a site of great importance to European and particularly British trade.

1871   Jamal al-Din 'al-Afghani arrives in Egypt. Through his teaching and
            writing, Egyptian consciousness of the implications of Western
            domination is given a deeper intellectual foundation.

1875   Khedive Isma'il, the leader of Egypt, sells his shares in the Suez
            Canal Company to the British government. This gives the British a

direct stake in the Suez Canal and thus in the associated policies of the Egyptian government.

1878   The British and the French agree to establish dual financial control in Egypt. A pattern of Western intrusion into Egyptian economic/political policy making begins.

1879   Jamal al-Din al-Afghani is expelled from Egypt.

1881   A consortium of European powers takes over the debt administration of the Ottoman Empire. This gives the Europeans great power over the Ottoman economy. Elsewhere, France occupies Tunis.

1881–1885   Muhammad Ahmad declares himself the "Mahdi" (the divinely guided one or precursor of Judgment Day) and leads a revolt against Egyptian and British control of the Sudan.

1882   Britain militarily occupies Egypt and suppresses a nationalist revolution led by the Egyptian military officer Ahmad Urabi.

1883–1907   The British send Lord Cromer to Egypt as British Consul. He is the power behind the scenes, effectively running the country.

1888–1906   Muhammad Abduh, a disciple of al-Afghani, active in Egypt, preaches the need to create a revitalized and socially active Islam.

1898   An Anglo-Egyptian army captures Sudan from the Mahdi.

1901   Britain obtains a concession to explore for oil in Iran.

1907   An Anglo-Russian agreement creates spheres of influence in Iran.

1908–1938   Muhammad Iqbal is active in India and puts forth an idealistic notion of an Islamic state which incorporates some Western political concepts.

1911   Italy invades Libya.

1912   Morocco becomes a French protectorate.

1914   World War I begins. Britain lands troops in Iraq and declares Egypt a protectorate.

1915   Henry McMahon, British High Commissioner in Egypt, promises support for Arab independence in exchange for the Hashimite (ruling family in Arabia) revolt against the Turks (who had allied themselves with the Germans).

1916   The Sykes-Picot Agreement divides much of the postwar Middle East between Britain and France. The agreement contradicts British promises of independence made to the Arabs.

1917   Britain issues the Balfour Declaration calling Palestine a Jewish National Home. This declaration conflicts with British promises of independence made to the Arabs.

1920   The San Remo Agreement gives "mandates" to Britain in Iraq and Palestine, and to France in Syria. This agreement institutionalizes their imperial control in these lands.

1921   Reza Khan seizes power in Iran. Britain names the Hashimite Prince Faisel King of Iraq, and his brother Abdullah Amir of Transjordan.

1923–1924   Mustafa Kemal, now in control of a secularized Turkish state, abolishes the old Ottoman institutions of Sultan and Caliph. These offices, associated with the Arab and Ottoman Empires, had great symbolic importance in the minds of those who believed that only an Islamic government could legitimately rule Muslim peoples.

1924   Ibn Saud completes the conquest of Arabia from the Hashimite family and begins the process of consolidation, which will lead to the formation of Saudi Arabia.

1925–1941   Reza Khan reigns as first Pahlavi Shah in Iran. The Shah adopts policies of westernization and modernization.

1928   Hasan al-Banna founds the Society of the Muslim Brothers.

1929   Widespread Arab rioting in Palestine is partly precipatated by conflicts at the Wailing Wall in Jerusalem (a shared Jewish/Muslim sacred religious site).

1932   Iraq is granted pseudo-independence by Britain, which retains military bases and oil rights.

1933   Ibn Saud signs a sixty-year oil agreement with Standard Oil.

1934   ARAMCO (Arabian American Oil Company) is created.

1936–1937   British troops crush an Arab uprising in Palestine.

1941   British troops crush a nationalist uprising in Iraq. Also, in British-controlled India, Abu'l-A'la Mawdudi founds Jama'at-i Islami (the Islamic party).

1941–1979   These years mark the reign of Mohammad Reza Shah in Iran. He will gradually speed up the pace of economic change and modernization and therefore create the conditions of confrontation that eventually brings about revolution.

1942   Hasan al-Banna creates the "secret apparatus" as a self-defense force within the Society of the Muslim Brothers.

1943   Lebanon becomes independent.

1945   Following World War II, in Iran, Ruhollah Mussaui Khomeini begins
            to be vocal in his opposition to the Shah's government. Elsewhere,
            the Arab League is formed as a loose association of Arab countries.

1948   Israel is created, and the first Arab-Israeli war takes place, resulting
            in hundreds of thousands of Palestinians from the newly created state
            becoming refugees. Members of the Society of the Muslim Brothers
            are among the Arab volunteers who fight in Palestine. Elsewhere, the
            prime minister of Egypt is assassinated by a member of the Society
            of the Muslim Brothers.

1949   Hasan al-Banna is assassinated by agents of the Egyptian govern-
            ment.

1951   Prime Minister Mossadegh of Iran nationalizes the Anglo-Iranian Oil
            Company. Egypt renounces its 1936 treaty with Britain. These moves
            toward real independence will lead to confrontation and eventual
            violence between these Middle Eastern countries and Western pow-
            ers.

1952   Nasser takes over Egypt. At first friendly toward the Society of the
            Muslim Brothers, he never really trusts them. Also in this year, Say-
            yid Qutb joins the Muslim Brothers.

1953   A U.S.-sponsored coup overthrows Mossadegh government in Iran.

1954   After an attempt on his life, Nasser begins repression of the Society
            of the Muslim Brothers. In Algeria a war of independence begins
            against France. Abbasi Madani joins the National Liberation Front
            (FLN), the organization leading the fight for Algerian independence.

1956   Nasser nationalizes the Suez Canal, precipitating an Anglo/French/
            Israeli invasion of Egypt.

1963   The Shah of Iran begins his "White Revolution," which extends the
            vote to women and institutes limited land reform. Both of these
            changes are opposed by militant Shi'ite clergy led by Khomeini.

1964   Khomeini is exiled from Iran. In Egypt, Sayyid Qutb's book, *Sign-
            posts Along the Road,* is published. It describes Egypt and the Mus-
            lim world in a state of "jahiliyya," or ignorance. Elsewhere, Algeria
            finally wins its independence from France.

1966   Sayyid Qutb is executed in Egypt.

1967   Second Arab-Israeli war results in Israeli occupation of the West
            Bank and Gaza Strip. The Israeli victory gives added force to the

Islamic fundamentalist call for political and social reform throughout the Arab world.

1969   Ali Shariati publishes *Islamology*, which criticizes the passive nature of the traditional ulama.

1970   Nasser dies in Egypt. Anwar Sadat takes over and will rule until 1981.

1973   The third Arab-Israel war is fought and results in Egypt's recapture of part of the Sinai Peninsula from Israeli forces.

1974   Musa al-Sadr forms AMAL as part of the Shi'ite militant forces in Lebanon.

1978   Mu'ammar al-Qadhafi takes power in Libya and announces a government based on Quranic law (and government-controlled committees to interpret it). Musa al-Sadr disappears while on a visit to Libya.

1979   The Camp David Accords, brokered by the Carter administration, bring "peace" between Egypt and Israel. The Shah leaves Iran and Khomeini returns. The process of creating an Islamic state begins. The U.S. Embassy is seized in Teheran. Elsewhere, Rashid al-Ghannoushi forms the Islamic Movement in Tunisia; the Grand Mosque in Mecca is seized by an extremist group whose leader claims to be the Mahdi; and violence breaks out between the Muslim Brothers and authorities in Syria. Finally, late in the year, the Soviet Union invades Afghanistan.

1980   The Iran-Iraq war breaks out. Muhammad Baqer as-Sadra is executed in Iraq. The United States begins to subsidize Islamic fundamentalists fighting against the Soviet invasion of Afghanistan (which lasts until February 1989). Over the decade these Islamic militants will receive billions of dollars in aid.

1981   Iran releases the U.S. Embassy hostages taken in 1979. Anwar Sadat is assassinated in Egypt by militant Islamists. The assassination is part of a failed coup attempt aimed at creating an Islamic government in Egypt.

1982   Sunni Muslim fundamentalists seize the city of Hama in Syria. The government responds with an attack on the city that kills a reported 10,000 people. Elsewhere, Hezbollah (Party of God) is founded in Lebanon. Also, Israel launches an invasion of Lebanon that will result in the removal of the Palestine Liberation Organization (PLO) forces from the country.

1983   In Lebanon, a truck bomb attack on the U.S. Marine barracks and French headquarters kills hundreds. In the Sudan, Shariah law is imposed.

1984   Islamists make political gains in elections for the National Assembly in Jordan. In Egypt, rioting by Islamic students at al-Azhar University, the most famous Sunni theological college in the Middle East, leads to its temporary closure.

1985   All Egyptian mosques are placed under government control.

1986   The United States bombs Tripoli, Libya, in retaliation for terrorist attacks carried out by Libyan agents in Europe.

1987   Trouble occurs between Saudi authorities and Iranian pilgrims during the annual pilgrimage to Mecca. This reflects Shi'ite-Sunni religious hostility as well as Iranian-Saudi political rivalry in the Persian Gulf area. Elsewhere, Islamist organizations are active in the Palestinian rebellion (Intifada) against Israeli occupation forces on the West Bank and Gaza Strip.

1989   Algeria legalizes political parties, and Abbasi Madani announces the formation of the Islamic Salvation Front (FIS). In the Sudan, Hasan Turabi becomes the power behind the scenes after a military coup. Elsewhere, Khomeini calls for the death of Salman Rushdie and his publishers because of the allegedly blasphemous nature of the book *The Satanic Verses*. In June Khomeini dies. In Jordan, Islamist candidates win twenty-five out of eighty seats in the new Jordanian parliament. In Taif, Saudi Arabia accords are announced, formally ending the Lebanese civil war. And in Afghanistan war comes to an end as the last Soviet forces withdraw.

1990   Umar Abd al-Rahman moves to the United States. In Algeria, the Islamic Salvation Front wins 55 percent of the votes in local and provincial elections. Elsewhere, Iraq invades Kuwait, which leads to the Persian Gulf war.

1991   The Saudi Arabian ulama call on the monarchy to create a Majlis al-Shura, or consultative assembly, as well as a more equitable distribution of wealth and other Islamically inspired reforms. Also, Saudi Arabian and Iranian officials hold talks on their political and diplomatic differences. Elsewhere, the Algerian Islamic Salvation Front wins the first round of national parliamentary elections.

1992   Sensing the pending national election victory of the Islamic Salvation Front, the Algerian government cancels the scheduled second round of the elections and arrests the leadership of the Front. This action sparks civil war in Algeria. In Lebanon, Israeli troops assassinate

Abbas al-Musawi (leader of the Islamic fundamentalist movement Hezbollah) and his family.

1993   The World Trade Center bombing occurs, for which a group of Muslim residents in the United States are later tried and convicted. Among them is Umar Abd al-Rahman. In Norway, the Oslo Accords are reached between Israel and the PLO. These agreements are largely condemned by Islamic fundamentalist groups. Elsewhere, Islamic extremists begin to target journalists, intellectuals, westernized women, and foreigners in what is an increasingly vicious civil war in Algeria.

1994   Jordan and Israel sign a peace treaty. Most of the Islamist groups in Jordan oppose the treaty.

1995   Government officials from many Arab countries including Egypt, Tunisia, Algeria, and Saudi Arabia, meet to discuss cooperative efforts against Islamic revivalist movements. In Saudi Arabia, King Fahd creates a Majlis al-Shura with sixty members. Elsewhere, Yasir Arafat, now head of the Palestine National Authority ruling small sections of the West Bank and Gaza Strip, starts a crackdown on Palestinian Islamic groups such as Hamas. In France, terrorist bombs start to go off. This violence is allegedly in response to France's support for the military dictatorship in Algeria. In Israel, Prime Minister Yitzhak Rabin is assassinated by a right-wing Jewish opponent of the Israeli-Palestinian peace process.

1996   Afghan Islamic forces take over much of the country and impose Shariah law. In Israel, a right-wing Likud party election victory brings Benjamin Netanyahu to power. Subsequent government decisions to expand Israeli settlements puts the peace process on hold. In Saudi Arabia, a car bomb destroys a U.S. military barracks.

1997   Violence intensifies in Algeria with the massacre of unarmed townspeople and villagers. It is believed that these actions are carried out by the Armed Islamic Group. In Egypt, extremist Islamic elements continue to sporadically attack foreign tourists. The government cracks down on westernized Egyptian youth groups, accusing them of "satanism" because of their style of dress, taste in music, and sexual behavior. In Israel, a decision to expand settlements in Arab East Jerusalem leads to violence. In March a Jordanian soldier kills seven visiting Israeli schoolgirls. Suicide bomb attacks hit Jerusalem markets in July and September. In late September the Israeli government releases from prison an ailing Shaykh Ahmad Yasin, a founding member of Hamas. In Turkey, Necmettin Erbakan, the country's first Islamist Prime Minister, is forced to resign because of pressure from the secular-minded Turkish armed forces. In Iran, Muhammad Khatami, a relative liberal candidate for President, achieves a landslide victory.

1998   In February of 1998 Iranian president Muhammad Khatami comes to New York City to address the United Nations. During his visit he gives several interviews which are interpreted as openings to the West. Turkey's Constitutional Court bars the fundamentalist leader Necmettin Erbakan from political activity, marking a setback for Islamic parties seeking to pursue legal avenues to political participation. In Palestine there is extensive rioting in Hebron following the murders of three Arab workers by the Israeli army; also, the Hamas leader Muhieddin Sharif is murdered by unidentified assailants. In Algeria, Islamic extremists kill the popular Berber singer Lounes Matoub, who was a critic of both the military government and the FIS. In August, U.S. cruise missiles destroy Afghan training bases for Islamic militants, as well as the Al-Shafi pharmaceutical plant in Sudan. Both are alleged to be linked to the radical Islamic fundamentalist Osama bin Laden. Bin Laden is thought to have been involved in the planning of attacks on U.S. embassies in Kenya and Tanzania earlier in the month. In December, the United States and Great Britain bomb Iraq (Operation Desert Fox), leading to Iraq's decision to refuse further cooperation with the UN weapons inspectors. Also in December, the Netanyahu government falls in Israel.

1999   Ehud Barak wins election in Israel and eventually transfers 6.1 percent of the West Bank to the Palestinian Authority (PA), while also releasing a small number of Palestinian prisoners. "Final Status Talks" begin but soon prove fruitless. In Palestine, some signatories of a petition against the Oslo process and Arafat's leadership are imprisoned and/or assaulted by PA police. In Jordan, King Hussein dies and is succeeded by his son, Abdullah II. The United Nations Security Council votes to suspend sanctions against Libya after two Libyan nationals suspected of involvement in the Lockerbie airline explosion are turned over for trial by Scottish judges. In Iran, there are widespread student protests following violent police raids on student dormitories.

2000   Following a war of attrition by Hezbollah resistance fighters, Israel retreats from southern Lebanon. In celebration of the Israeli withdrawal, the Lebanese government declares May 25 "Lebanese National Independence Day." In Israel, on September 28, Ariel Sharon, accompanied by 1,000 police and soldiers, moves onto Harem al-Sharif in Jerusalem, the third holiest place in the Muslim world. This act sparks a new Intifada. In the ensuing violence Israeli forces kill

315 Palestinians (including 66 children) by mid-October. Thirty-seven Israelis also die. Meanwhile, a new Camp David summit between Israeli Prime Minister Barak and Palestinian officials is hosted by President Clinton. Barak offers the Palestinians approximately 85 percent of the occupied territories, but in a fragmented form that precludes the possibility of a contiguous state. The summit fails. By the end of the year Barak's coalition government falls and new elections are called for 2001. On October 12 in Aden harbor the *USS Cole* is rammed by a small boat loaded with explosives. Osama bin Laden is accused of being behind the attack.

2001   The Palestinian uprising against Israeli occupation and expansion continues. Israel responds with assassinations, destruction of Palestinian homes, economic blockade, and forms of collective punishment. Palestinian Islamic fundamentalists respond to Israeli actions with a new wave of suicide bombings. In February, Ariel Sharon is elected the country's Prime Minister with 60 percent of the vote. In March, in an effort to halt the violence, the Palestinians and several Arab states call for the creation of a UN observer force in the occupied territories. A Security Council resolution to this effect is vetoed by the United States. In May, an international commission led by former Senator George Mitchell calls for a halt to Israeli settlement activity and greater Palestinian control over violent resisters. This is accepted by the PA but rejected by Israel. CIA chief George Tenet attempts to mediate a cease fire in June. His efforts produce only a brief cessation of the violence. By September, 678 Palestinians and 170 Israelis have been killed. Also in September the United States and Israel pull out of the UN World Conference on Racism due to documented criticism of Israeli treatment of the Palestinians. Later in the year the Israeli assassination of the head of the Popular Front for the Liberation of Palestine (PFLP) results in the revenge assassination of the right-wing Israeli minister, Rehavam Ze'evi. In Iraq, the United States and Great Britain continue periodic air strikes which reach the suburbs of Baghdad in February. In Iran, Muhammad Khatami is reelected President with 77 percent of the vote. However, continued conservative control of the judiciary and police limit the reforms he can put into place. On September 11 Islamist extremists hijack four airplanes in the United States. They succeed in crashing two of them into the World Trade Center towers in New York, one into the Pentagon, and one in a Pennsylvania field. Approximately 3,000 people are killed. This leads to an American declaration of "war against terrorism." There is a subsequent American attack on Afghanistan where Osama bin Laden, accused mastermind of the September 11 attacks, resides under the protection of the Taliban

government. Bin Laden, who eludes capture, issues several video-
taped messages calling on Muslims to wage war against the United
States.

2002   President George W. Bush continues the American "war on terror-
          ism." In February he describes an "Axis of Evil" which, he says,
          includes Iraq and Iran. International backing of U.S. military action
          in Afghanistan wanes as the President threatens to expand the war
          into Iraq. In Palestine the intifada continues. One consequence of the
          on-going struggle is a decline in the popularity of Yasir Arafat and
          his Palestinian Authority. The popularity of the Islamic fundamen-
          talist organization Hamas, however, appears to rise. In Israel, the
          inability of the Sharon government to end the war of resistance
          waged by the Palestinians begins to erode his popularity. Despite this
          fact, in March, Sharon launches a series of bloody incursions into
          Palestinian towns and refugee camps. Also in March the government
          of Saudi Arabia proposes full recognition of Israel and normalization
          of relations on all levels if Israel will withdraw to the 1967 borders.
          Israel rejects the proposal. The United States sends Vice President
          Cheney to the Middle East to seek support for action against Iraq,
          and special envoy Anthony Zinni to Israel and Palestine to attempt
          to broker a cease fire. In Afghanistan, action against surviving rem-
          nants of al-Qaeda and Taliban forces continues.

ISLAMIC
FUNDAMENTALISM
EXPLAINED

I

Historical Narrative

The outlook of Islamic fundamentalism is shaped by a deep reverence for history, especially the history of the Muslim people, which is divided into two phases. The first phase is interpreted by Islamic fundamentalists as a positive, exemplary period with models of behavior and organization to be studied and applied in the present. It encompasses the biography of Muhammad and the early Caliphs (or successors to Muhammad as leaders of the Muslim community), the creation of the first Islamic state, the expansion of Islam out of Arabia, and the spread of great empires that brought Muslim culture and civilization to its height. This exemplary time was followed by a second phase, which was one of decline. It saw military defeat, loss of territory, corruption, and the coming of Western colonialism. Islamic fundamentalists attribute this phase of Muslim history to an abandonment of religious faith and piety. They see a lesson to be learned: that only a revitalization of Islamic ways can restore the fortunes of the Muslim people.

For Islamic fundamentalists, then, history holds the key to understanding not only the past, but the present and future as well. If we are to understand who Islamic fundamentalists are, and why they think and behave as they do, we must know something of the history that motivates them. Therefore, this first chapter will give a brief outline of the two phases of Muslim history. The reader is invited to refer back to this history often as a basis for understanding the contemporary phenomenon of Islamic fundamentalism.[1]

THE RISE OF MUSLIM CIVILIZATION

Islam is more than a set of religious beliefs and practices. It is also a holistic civilizational force that encompasses the believer within a tradition that has profoundly significant historical roots. This tradition, in turn, forms an ideal that gives the pious Muslim a model for the good life that he or she is religiously required to realize. Not only the individual, but also the Muslim community (or ummah) as a whole is expected to strive to realize this ideal. Thus, the good life and the good society cannot be found through the uncritical acceptance of all things modern or the simple imitation of a Western lifestyle. Rather they are to be found in an under-standing and adaptation, within a contemporary context, of the traditional values and worldview of a past time and place—specifically, the time of the founder of Islam, the prophet Muhammad, and the supposedly uncor-rupted society he established. This orientation explains the constant ref-erencing of this past time in the writings and public pronouncements of Islamic fundamentalists.

In the year 570 the prophet Muhammad was born in Mecca, an impor-tant trading center in western Arabia. As an adult, he worked as the man-ager of a caravan outfitting business owned by his wife Khadijah. Although the monotheistic notions of the Christian and Jewish faiths were known in Arabia, the society of the Arabians was still a polytheistic one. It was also a tribal-based society led by clans whose wealth was derived, in the case of Mecca, from trade and other business enterprises. This produced a materialistic environment that left Muhammad spiritually un-fulfilled. His search for spiritual meaning would lead him to his religious calling at about the age of forty. It is not particularly unusual for reli-giously minded people living in very acquisitive cultures to feel alienated. They often find solace in a religious community. But Muhammad had no religious community because he felt estranged from the pagan beliefs of those around him. He attempted to compensate for this by periodic stays at a nearby cave, where he would spend time in meditation and spiritual introspection.

According to tradition, it was during one of these meditative sessions, about the year 610 C.E. (or Common Era), that Muhammad was visited by the angel Gabriel, who told him he had been called upon by God (or

Allah) to convert the Arabs to monotheism. At first, Muhammad was greatly frightened by this experience and unsure of its veracity. But with the support of his wife and a few other family members, such as his young cousin Ali, as well as the periodic return of Gabriel, he became convinced of his calling as prophet and began to preach to the Meccans. The messages given to Muhammad by his angelic intermediary would collectively come to embody the Muslim holy book, the Quran. Quran in Arabic is a word that comes from the verb "to recite." Thus, to Muslims the Quran is considered the literal words of God, and part of Muhammad's job was to make known, or "to recite," those words.

The Meccans did not readily accept Muhammad's preaching, which criticized the values and practices of the wealthy merchant clans as corrupt and unjust. Muhammad insisted that Mecca's leaders needed to subordinate their authority and will to the prophet of God, and to restructure their trading practices and personal behavior according to the principles being divinely transmitted to them through Muhammad. Thus, his preaching seemed to run against the prosperity of the city and against ancient practices not easily abandoned. An adversarial situation grew up between Muhammad and his fellow citizens that would last twenty years.

By 622 Muhammad was no longer safe in Mecca. He and his followers, numbering no more than one hundred, were forced to flee to the northern Arabian oasis town of Medina. Muhammad's preaching had become known to the citizens of Medina and had won their interest and respect. They had, therefore, invited him to come and serve as the city's governor and judge. This move is known in Muslim history as the Hijrah (or emigration) and is counted as the year one in the Muslim calendar.

During his twelve years as prophet in Mecca, Muhammad was cast in the role of a rebel. He stood against traditional authority in his native city and called for a revolution in both morals and politics. Throughout the subsequent history of Islam, even to the present day, this model of Muhammad the rebel has lent legitimacy and respectability to other Islamic reformers working toward a more just and pious society. Indeed, many contemporary Islamic fundamentalist activists see themselves in this light.

With Muhammad's move to Medina, his status changed from that of a rebel against authority to that of a governor and source of authority. He ruled from 622 to 632, the year of his death. In those ten years Muhammad institutionalized Islam not only as a set of religious rituals and beliefs, but also as a set of societal norms of behavior and outlook with the force of law. It must be kept in mind that while Muhammad's movement was a religious one, this was an age that made no distinction between religion and politics. All the political powers of the time were identified with, and enforced, a state religion. The concept of separation of church and state was unknown and unthinkable in Muhammad's day. This point of view has been inherited by present-day Islamic fundamentalists. For them, the precedent set by Muhammad at Medina, a polity run on the basis of religiously sanctified laws and values, serves as the ideal toward which the present-day Islamic activist must strive.

During Muhammad's days at Medina, the norms and parameters of Muslim socioreligious practice were set. All Muslims were designated as members of a common community, the ummah, replacing the fractionalized tribal networks from which they had come. As we will see, this sense of all Muslims belonging to one community explains, in part, the dislike today's Islamic fundamentalists feel for the Western concept of nationalism. The prescriptions put forth in the Quran, as well as the norms established by Muhammad's sayings and personal behavior (Muhammad's Sunna), became the basis for Muslim belief, behavior, and law. Over the centuries, this belief and practice melded with the cultures and traditions of peoples converted to Islam to produce a series of culturally differing societies bound by one religious faith with its common historical reference point of Muhammad's life and times.

With the help of the citizens of Medina, Muhammad and his followers put together an army that fought the Meccans. Muhammad turned out to be a skilled military commander whose victories were taken as proof of God's favor. Soon Muhammad and his growing number of followers were able to subdue the better part of Arabia, including Mecca. By the time of the prophet's death in 632, Islam was firmly established.

After Muhammad's death there followed a period when the expanding Muslim community was ruled by Caliphs (or successors). The first four of these, whose rule extends to 661, are known as the "rightly guided" Caliphs in the Sunni tradition. Sunni is a term used to designate the majority "orthodox" Muslim community. Sunnis adhere to what they believe is the true Sunna, or customary practice of Muhammad and his companions, including acceptance of the rule of the "rightly guided" Caliphs as historically legitimate.

The institutionalization of Islam continued under these initial rulers. The Quran, which began as an oral document, was formalized in an official, written version. Muhammad's sayings, actions, approvals, and those of his close companions that he endorsed, began to be recorded. Collectively referred to as Muhammad's Sunna, each saying, action, or approval is individually known as a hadith (a documented statement). The Sunna, and its hadith, along with the Quran, became the basis of Muslim holy law or Shariah. Over time, a class of professional religious experts, the ulama (or ones who pursue knowledge), evolved to interpret and apply the law and also serve as teachers, clerics, and general religious functionaries.

During this early period, relations were also formalized between the Muslim community and the other prophetically based, monotheistic religions, particularly Judaism and Christianity. Muhammad had seen Islam as following in the footsteps of Judaism and Christianity and being corrective of the "errors" they had supposedly made in interpreting and practicing God's commandments. For instance, both the Jews' belief in their status as a chosen people and the Christian belief in the trinity and Jesus's divinity are described as incorrect in the Quran. Yet, because God had decided to communicate with these groups and send sacred books to them through previous prophets, Muhammad saw these religions as worthy of respect. Thus, the "peoples of the book" attained a special "protected" status in Muslim lands.

The period of the first four Caliphs was also a time when the tensions created by competition for leadership of the ummah, and the distribution of wealth that came from unchecked Islamic conquests beyond Arabia, fueled divisions within the young Muslim community. These differences soon took on religious significance. One of the more important of these differences was the power struggle between the supporters of the third Caliph, Uthman ibn 'Affan, along with the Umayyad clan to which he belonged, and Muhammad's cousin Ali ibn Abi Talib, who briefly served as the fourth and the last of the "rightly guided" Caliphs. The followers of Ali believed that he was the only legitimate successor of Muhammad and, because of his close relationship with the prophet, had received from him special esoteric insight into God's word. Ali's special claim and knowledge were then passed on to his successors through his son Husayn.

The followers of Ali became known as Shi'ites, from the term Shi'at Ali, or the Party of Ali. In their eyes, the first three Caliphs, and subsequent rulers accepted by the Sunni majority, were really illegitimate usurpers. Shi'ites remain an overall minority within the Muslim world, although they do form the majority of Muslims in present-day Iran, Iraq, and a few other places. Over time, some ritual differences and interpretations of hadith have grown up between Sunnis and Shi'ites. Shi'ites also have developed a strong sense of the need to struggle against injustice, in part because of periodic discrimination they suffered at the hands of the Sunni majority.

The Shi'ites lost the power struggle with the heirs of Uthman, who established the Umayyad dynasty. This dynasty ruled an expanding Muslim domain until the year 750, when it was replaced by another dynasty, that of the Abbasids (named for Muhammad's uncle, Abbas). The Abbasids would reign effectively into the tenth century and nominally into the thirteenth. During the rule of these two dynasties (750–1258), Islam spread widely, and what had begun as the religiously inspired conquest of Arabia grew into a culturally eclectic empire of world import and power. Eventually, Muslim control extended from Spain and Morocco in the west to India in the east.

As the Arabs came out of Arabia, they came into contact with the different and often more advanced cultures of the peoples they conquered. By the time of the Abbasid Empire, the Arabs in the conquered territories began to lose their exclusive Arabian identity and merge with the native populations. This assimilation process saw the Abbasid leadership encourage and facilitate the creation of a new hybrid culture that brought together elements of Arab, Latin, Greek, Persian, and Jewish societies. Emphasis was put on the study of ancient texts of the Greco-Roman world (such as that of Aristotle and Plato) and the various sciences. Medicine, astronomy, architecture, and mathematics flourished. Poetry, history, travel literature, and religious studies also reached great heights. There can be little doubt that this eclectic culture of Islam represented one of the greatest civilizations of the time. It was far more cultivated and tolerant of different ideas and worldviews than Europe, which was then going through its "Dark Ages."

In their conquests, the Arabs showed courage, high strategic and tactical skill, and great motivation. The Arab Muslims who poured out of Arabia in this period did so not only for the wealth and power that conquest brought, but also out of the religious conviction that they were called upon by God to expand the land of Islam (dar al-Islam). This call to expansion was inherited by those who succeeded the Arabs as rulers of successive Muslim empires, particularly the Ottoman Turks. These early Muslims viewed expansion as a religious duty based on the belief that they, guided by the word of God, were capable of ruling more justly than anyone else.

This combination of religious mission, military success, and cultural advancement imbued Muslim consciousness with a sense of glorious achievement. Contemporary Islamic fundamentalists share this sense of greatness and use it as one of their terms of reference in judging what Muslims are capable of achieving (though today they seek no foreign conquests). And indeed, the richness and advanced state of Islamic culture throughout the Middle Ages and early modern period was sufficient to guarantee the assimilation of those outside forces that occasionally managed to intrude upon the Islamic lands at times of military weakness.

Eventually, Islamic expansion exceeded the ability of the administrators of the day to maintain unity. The Abbasid Empire fractionalized, allowing invasion by such forces as the Latin Crusaders (eleventh–thirteenth centuries), the Seljuk Turks (eleventh century), and the Mongol Hordes (thirteenth century). But each in turn was absorbed by the Islamic culture of the land they had invaded. There followed a series of Islamic states ruled by non-Arab Muslim dynasties. The longest lasting and greatest of these was the Ottoman Empire (1299–1922).

The Ottoman Empire began as a petty state in northwestern Anatolia, ruled by a family of Muslim Turks. It eventually spread throughout the Balkans, the Middle East, and North Africa. Although the empire was vast, the Muslim religion spread at this time even further into China and Southeast Asia. Up until the seventeenth century the Ottoman Empire had no equal culturally, politically, or militarily. But that would change in the seventeenth century when the Christian states of Europe began to form. By this time the West had emerged from the "Dark Ages" and experienced the Renaissance. Culturally and technologically, the Christian states of Europe advanced rapidly. They soon produced a materialistic culture eventually made overwhelmingly powerful by the industrial revolution of the eighteenth and nineteenth centuries. This emerging European force confronted an Islamic civilization that had considered itself superior to the Christian West in every way for hundreds of years. The confrontation proved the greatest and most traumatic challenge ever faced by Islamic civilization. And it is one that continues to this day.

THE DECLINE OF MUSLIM POWER

That the Muslims were not prepared for the European challenge has much to do with the earlier, repeated intrusions suffered by the Islamic world. While peoples like the Seljuk Turks and Mongols were eventually absorbed into the Islamic religion and culture, their invasions did inevitably result in major displacements of populations, loss of life, and destruction of important centers of Muslim civilization (such as the Mongol sack of Baghdad in 1258). This in turn had a long-lasting negative effect on the intellectual flexibility and adaptability hitherto shown by Islamic thought and culture. Openness to new ideas and influences lessened as the class of Muslim religious leaders, or ulama, responded to the threats of invasion by increasingly emphasizing Islamic ritual and orthodox interpretation of law and doctrine. Where once the use of individual reason (or ijtihad) to determine what was acceptable practice within the Muslim religion was allowed and widespread, now the conservative ulama reserved such judgments for themselves. They became increasingly suspicious and hostile to innovation, especially that inspired by the West, and this attitude reduced the ability of Islamic civilization as a whole to adapt to change. Thus, the ability to sustain an eclectic mix of influences (the original foundation of Islamic culture) was seriously undermined.

In 1683 the Ottoman Empire launched its last significant offensive against the Christian West. The city of Vienna was besieged, but the attack failed. Soon thereafter the balance of power shifted decisively in favor of the Europeans. Their technology, military organization, and general state efficiency now surpassed that of the Muslim world. In 1699 the Ottomans were forced to cede Hungary to the Austrian Empire. In the following century, the Russians expanded southward until they displaced the Ottomans from the lands north of the Black Sea. By the end of the eighteenth century, the retreat of the Ottoman Empire in the Balkans and southwest Asian steppe lands was being complemented by the beginning of Western imperial intrusion into North Africa and the Middle East. Napoleon invaded Egypt in 1798. In the nineteenth century this imperial process would accelerate until most of North Africa was divided between European powers and the foreign trade and public debt administration of what was left of the Ottoman Empire was in Western hands.

How did the Muslim political elite, intelligentsia, and religious leaders respond to this traumatic reversal of power relations? The classical responses were divided into two kinds. On the one hand, the political leadership and a good portion of the intellectual class insisted that Muslims must imitate those aspects of the West that appeared to be the basis for European power. Many in this camp, whom we can call the Westernizers, eventually came to advocate the progressive secularization of Muslim society—that is, separating the religion of Islam from politics, education, and legal systems. This was a radical proposal for a civilization that saw its religion as a guide to all aspects of life. In addition, the Western concept of secular nationalism (nation-states) was popularized as an alternative to the decaying Ottoman Empire. These Westernizers proved politically strong and durable and, along with the European colonial powers themselves, were most responsible for the social and political shape of the Muslim world following World War II.

On the other hand, others, particularly the religiously attuned elements of the intelligentsia, did not believe that it was necessary to replace Islamic ways with Western ones. Rather, this group, whom we can call the Islamic Modernists, believed that one could borrow from the West various models of political, legal, and educational organization and make them work in ways that reflected and reaffirmed Muslim goals. In other words, they proposed to borrow Western organizational structure while imbuing it with Islamic values. The Islamic Modernists also hoped that their approach would revive a process of free inquiry and controlled cultural interplay that they believed characterized Muslim civilization at its greatest height.

But the Westernizers prevailed. Over time the cultural and economic impact of Western colonial power, allied with indigenous pro-Western elites who pushed for policies of secularization, led the Muslim world through a series of reform movements that Europeanized aspects of its culture, and created middle and upper classes with Western tastes in dress, entertainment, education, and general outlook. Politically, the demise of the Ottoman Empire following World War I resulted in the creation of the secular nation-states we now see throughout the Middle East and North Africa. The concept of nationalism and the nation-state is a primary example of a Western notion that directly contradicts and challenges Islamic tradition. It stands in stark contrast to the transregional definition of the Muslim collective (or ummah) and emphasizes the welfare and interests of a particular ethnic or geographical subgroup (that is, a group with a national identity) over that of the ummah as a whole.

If this process of secularization and westernization had brought the restored power and prosperity its promoters promised, the fate of the Muslim world in the twentieth century might have been a better one. However, it failed to do so. Nor did it bring democracy, human rights, or a more equitable distribution of resources. Instead, the Westernizers' program resulted in dictatorial and oppressive secular governments, and wealth for only a relatively small elite. Worse, it did this while eroding Islamic culture and tradition.

The late-nineteenth-century Islamic Modernists would have been horrified at this result. They did not want the westernization of Islamic culture; rather, they advocated Islamization of selective Western institutional models such as parliaments, educational structures, and court systems. This was to occur only after a reexamination of Islamic practices and the drawing of inspiration from the ways of Muhammad and his successors who, the Modernists believed, set examples of flexible and progressive leadership. Unfortunately, the Modernists were opposed both by the political elites and conservative ulama of their day. The ulama resisted the ideas of the Islamic Modernists because they believed they would lead to dangerous innovations in Islamic practice, and also undercut their authoritative position as interpreters of Islamic law and custom. The proponents of Islamic Modernism were in no position successfully to overcome this dual opposition. They were a group of concerned intellectuals who wrote for and preached to the relatively small educated strata of their society. Ultimately, they proved unable to communicate with the uneducated and semi-literate masses who made up the bulk of the population.

ISLAMIC FUNDAMENTALISM

The failure of both the Westernizers and Islamic Modernists to resolve the problems of the Muslim world opened the door to Islamic fundamentalism. Throughout the period of Western imperial intrusion, the majority of people in the Muslim world had watched as non-Muslim influences eroded their religion, culture, values, and polity. Nor did the changes wrought by imperialism and secularization compensate for this trauma by significantly improving the population's economic status. Thus the basis for anti-Western Islamic fundamentalist mass movements, motivated not only by religion, but also by cultural and economic issues, increasingly grew.

The process of realizing Islamic fundamentalist mass movements began in the first half of the twentieth century. Their many supporters shared then, and continue today to share, a set of common assumptions:

1. The Muslim world is in a state of disorder brought on by centuries of political and moral decay. This decay began when, both in the public and private realm, the values and dictates of the Muslim religion were not respected or practiced diligently.

2. This decay made possible Western intrusion which, for all intents and purposes, infected the Muslim world with an alien set of immoral, secularist values and behaviors based on the defining concepts of materialism and (in terms of politics) nationalism. These alien ways were an inherent part of the various Western-inspired governmental and cultural experiments that proliferated in the colonial and postcolonial periods. They included nationalist, pan-Arabist, socialist, and military governmental experiments, as well as the secularizing of law codes, courts, and schools, an opening up to Western goods and advertising, and the adoption of Western dress and ideas of gender equality. The resulting environment fractionalized the Islamic community through the creation of both imperially imposed national boundaries and a westernized upper class alienated from its own Muslim cultural roots. Indeed, from the standpoint of the Islamic fundamentalists, a new period of ignorance (jahiliyya) had dawned—a time akin to the pre-Islamic period of Arabian paganism when the community was ignorant of God and His commandments.

3. In order to combat this perceived decay and infection, the Muslim world must be re-Islamized. This entails the reassertion of classical Islamic ways, particularly the reintroduction of Shariah, or Muslim law, while purging most aspects of Western cultural and political influence. For most Islamic fundamentalists, this does not mean the renouncing of all things modern, or the cutting off of their culture from all contact with the non-Muslim world. For instance, under the rule of an Islamic state, the cities of Iran still use electrical power, modern

appliances, and transportation, and the Iranian armies are equipped with modern weapons. Those modern institutions of a Western nature that are found necessary to the running of society, such as a modern banking system, are maintained but consciously restructured to conform with Islamic norms. The re-Islamization process does, however, have a major impact on the life of the westernized upper class of Muslim countries, as well as other elements of society such as those women favoring Western gender equality.

4. The only way to re-Islamize society is to repoliticize Islam itself. As fundamentalist reasoning goes, Islam began as a religion that preached the rejection of false gods and corrupt practices. The West and Westernizers now represent precisely these evils. Unfortunately, over the centuries, the Sunni ulama became apolitical (this was not as true of the Shi'ite ulama as the behavior of Iran's Ayatollah Khomeini shows), going along with whatever regime held power, and quite often were on the government payroll through official subsidization of mosques, schools, and other religiously affiliated institutions. This situation made the Sunni ulama as a group incapable of leading effective opposition to the westernization and corruption of the Muslim world. Thus, many of the Islamic reform movements were begun and are now led by pious laymen who insist that this passivism be abandoned. They argue that governments must be pressured to reform themselves along Islamic lines or, if they do not, they will be taken over by the forces of Islamic fundamentalism. This, in turn, will inevitably lead to the solving of the problems of corruption and spiritual vacuousness that now seem to pervade society. Islam, representative of a total worldview, is the path to justice and socioeconomic equity. In this regard, Islamic fundamentalists look to Muhammad's example as governor and judge at Medina.

The various movements now active in most Muslim countries work on these assumptions. They thus constitute a direct challenge to (and in some cases have managed to take over) the sitting secular governments of their nation-states. Many of these movements began as fraternal orders, self-help groups, or community action committees that then evolved into political parties with deep populist roots. Their activities include providing health care, education, and basic needs to the poor. In many places they have filled the vacuum left by secular governments that are unable to provide adequate municipal services such as garbage collection and public safety. These services often have made the Islamic fundamentalists genuinely popular and helped them successfully compete on a political level in those countries that have allowed free elections. It should be emphasized, however, that with hundreds of millions of pious Muslims in the world, not all of them are militant Islamic fundamentalists. Nor are all Muslims of one mind when it comes to politics and political activism.

Nonetheless, the grassroots organizing work of Islamic political movements has captured the imagination of a growing number of the pious and
the alienated.

The first significant political victory for Islamic fundamentalism came
in 1979 when the Shah of Iran was forced to flee and his government was
overthrown by the Islamic forces of the Ayatollah (the title given to a
leading Shi'ite religious and legal authority) Khomeini. The Iranian Revolution reflected the tension that historically has evolved between Islamic
activists and the West. For decades, the Shah of Iran had allied himself
with the foreign policies of Great Britain and the United States and used
Western advisers at many levels of his government and military. The Iranian upper class had become increasingly westernized, and Western culture pervaded much of Iranian urban life. Thus, for many pious Iranian
Muslims, their government, as well as aspects of their culture, came to
represent many of the ills they had long lamented.

The success of the Iranian movement provided a great impetus to similar
movements throughout the Muslim world. Sometimes these movements
chose nondemocratic paths, as, for example, in 1989 when a military dictatorship was imposed in Sudan. Soon thereafter the new Sudanese regime
implemented Shariah law under the guidance of a fundamentalist movement known as the National Islamic Front. This movement, led by the
Front's leader Hasan al-Turabi, was supported by a portion of Sudan's
Muslims but not the considerable non-Muslim population in the south of
the country. The result was a civil war.

The example of Sudan suggests two problems inherent in the Islamic
fundamentalist phenomenon. One is that these movements, based on religious tenets and supposed divinely ordained values, do not readily tolerate opposition. This has engendered a debate in the West as to whether
or not Islamic fundamentalism is compatible with democracy. The second
related problem is the precarious political and cultural position non-
Muslim populations sometimes occupy when Islamist movements become
active or achieve power. Despite the fact that Islam has a tradition of
tolerance toward non-Muslim minorities, Sudanese Christians, Egyptian
Coptic Christians, and the Bah'i and Zoroastrian populations of Iran are
all groups whose situation has deteriorated as a consequence of an Islamic
resurgence.

Where democratic systems function, Islamic fundamentalist movements
often seek to exert influence or attain power through the electoral process.
This was the case in Algeria. In 1989 the National Liberation Front (FLN),
which had governed the country as a one-party state since independence
was won from France in 1962, promulgated a new constitution legalizing

other parties. National legislative elections were set for 1991. Among the parties to field candidates was the Islamic Salvation Front (FIS), which was founded by Abbasi Madani and had its roots in populist organizations begun in the 1960s. In the 1991 elections the FIS won a large proportion of the national assembly seats in the first round of voting. The FLN came in third. The FIS would surely have done as well in the second and final round, and thereby won control of the government, if the Algerian army had not stepped in, canceled the second round of voting, and thus prevented the Islamists from achieving power. If the FIS had taken over, Algerian society would have been restructured along traditional Islamic lines. Shariah law would have replaced civil law, Islamic dress codes would have been introduced, and Islamic moral standards would have defined gender relations as well as effectively censored entertainment and the arts.

Secular forces, as well as those who would have suffered politically and economically, stood against these prospects and backed the military intervention. However, the FIS and other Algerians who resented the disruption of the democratic process refused to accept the result. Civil war soon erupted. The relatively moderate leadership of the FIS was arrested by the military authorities who now controlled the state, creating a leadership vacuum within the party. This was, at least in part, filled by more violently minded fundamentalists. The military regime and the Islamists were soon engaged in a expanding cycle of violence that was increasingly characterized by the use of terror. As in Sudan, innocent civilians suffered the most.

The secular forces within the Muslim world are not the only ones to look upon the rise of Islamic fundamentalism with alarm. The Western powers—Europe (including Russia) and the United States—also have reacted to political Islam with fear and suspicion. On the one hand, some of the Western powers believe that, if the various Islamic fundamentalist movements come to power, they might well work against Western strategic and economic interests. This point of view gained credence from the sometimes violent rhetoric of Islamic activists who rail against Western culture and interests. Also, in the competition for power within the Muslim world, violence has sometimes flared, with Westerners among the targets. This has been the case in Iran, Egypt, and Algeria. In Saudi Arabia this competition has spilled over violently so as to affect the West. The result was the devastating September 11 attacks on the World Trade Center and Pentagon. These were perpetrated by Al-Qaeda, a renegade Islamic Fundamentalist movement that stands against both the United States and the royal Saudi government. This event has made even more dangerous the two-way historical factor that magnifies Western-Islamist mistrust. If Islamic fundamentalist hostility toward the West is in good part a function of the heritage of Western imperialism, Western dislike and fear of Islamic fundamentalism (now so heightened that this multifaceted movement is seen as synonymous with "terrorism") is also rooted in a long history of religiously based Christian hostility toward the Muslim world.

Despite these many problems, the West and some religiously minded Muslim states have established and maintained peaceful relations. The West's relationship with Saudi Arabia is a case in point. Saudi Arabia is an Islamic fundamentalist state that actively promotes the causes of political and cultural Islamization throughout the Muslim world. Nonetheless, its association with the West has been and continues to be peaceful and stable. That is why renegade Islamic Fundamentalists such as Osama bin Laden view the royal Saudi government with suspicion and hostility. Beyond the Muslim world, the West also has established stable diplomatic and economic relations with countries of very different outlooks and values, even after years of suspicion and sometimes violent hostility. China is a recent example. Thus, in the long run, even if in particular cases periods of hostility break out, it is still possible to envision political accommodation between the West and those Muslim countries that pursue a fundamentalist path.

Whether or not the West approves of Islamic fundamentalism, it will have to adapt to the reality of it. Islamic fundamentalism is a meaningful political, cultural, and religious phenomenon. The leaders of these movements, as well as the mass of their supporters, believe that politicized Islam flows from Muslim history, is divinely sanctioned, and holds out great promise for the restoration of Muslim pride, prosperity, and power. Whether it can truly fulfill these expectations is still an open question. That the movement, in its many varied manifestations in the different states with large Muslim populations, will seek to do so for the indefinite future is certain. Its deep historical roots and populist appeal, combined with the real and persistent economic, political, and cultural problems faced by the Muslim world, mean that Islamic fundamentalism will be a powerful force on the world stage for a long time to come.

NOTE

1. There is much debate as to whether the term fundamentalism can appropriately be used to describe the religiopolitical movements that are now so widespread in the Muslim world. This is because the term was originally used to describe a Christian outlook—specifically the outlook of Protestants who believe

in a literal reading of the Bible. Thus, today many scholars who study Islam and modern Islamic movements do not like this term. Nonetheless, most of them use it for lack of any really better word to describe the nature of present-day Islamic revivalism. In this book we will use the term fundamentalism and do so for two reasons: First, the expression Islamic fundamentalism has come into wide usage in the West as well as in the Muslim world, where it is rendered in Arabic as al-Usuliyyah al-Islamiyyah. Here the word usuli can be translated as fundamentalist. In fact, it is so generally accepted that it is now the main descriptive expression recognized by all interested parties to describe the Islamic revivalist movements. Second, the term Islamic fundamentalism is sufficiently accurate to describe Muslims who see themselves as adhering to the ultimate fundamentals or foundations of their religion, and also to a literalist interpretation of the Muslim holy book, the Quran.

2

The Society of the Muslim Brothers

The conditions that gave rise to Islamic fundamentalism were most pronounced in the Muslim lands that, in the nineteenth century, came under direct Western imperial control. In those places, Western and Islamic culture directly clashed, and the Muslim sense of vulnerability was most acute. A good example of this can be found in Egypt, the most populous nation in the Middle East, where people had long seen themselves as the cultural and religious leaders of the Muslim world. It is in Egypt that we find al-Azhar University, the oldest and most famous Islamic institution of higher learning. Coming under British occupation in 1882, Egypt gave rise to the Islamic Modernists in the late nineteenth century. In the early twentieth century it produced the Society of the Muslim Brothers—the first modern politically, culturally, and socially oriented Islamic fundamentalist organization. The Society is still in existence today and stands as an inspiration for Islamic activists throughout the Muslim world.

In the first half of the twentieth century, Egypt suffered from many of the problems that beset the Muslim world. The country remained subject to British imperial control. From behind the scenes, a British High Commissioner set the parameters of official action for Egypt's constitutional monarchy. With imperial control came a quickening of an on-going west-ernization of major institutions. Civil law, for example, increasingly displaced Shariah or Muslim religious law, and secular education competed with the religiously oriented mosque schools. Trade had long been directed toward Europe, and a wealthy indigenous upper class had grown up with Western tastes and values. This alien point of view spread, as all things European were touted as modern, progressive, and superior.

For the majority of the people, however—the rural villagers, the urban slum dwellers, the bazaar shopkeepers, the educated yet unemployed or underemployed—Egyptian society and culture were seen as under attack. Not only did a foreign occupier manipulate the government, but also the country's traditional way of life and its customs, morals, and prevailing religion suffered erosion. It was a volatile situation bound to breed resistance.

Into this environment Hasan al-Banna was born in 1906 in the town of Mahmudiyya, 90 miles northwest of Cairo. Hasan was the oldest of five children. His father, a teacher at the local mosque school, passed on to his eldest son his piety and love of learning. Hasan chose the teaching profession and at the age of sixteen entered the teacher training school at Dar al-Ulum in Cairo. He attended to his studies diligently and was active in the many religious clubs and societies affiliated with the institution.

It stood to reason that a youth of pious outlook would be sensitive to the clash of cultures taking place in his country. Hasan al-Banna's many club memberships also suggest someone given to social activism. During his five years at Dar al-Ulum, his opinions took shape and matured as he struggled to understand the decline of Egypt's Islamic way of life. In a senior class essay he wrote, "I believe that my people, because of the political stages through which they have passed, the social influences which have passed through them, and under the impact of western civilization . . . have departed from the goals of their faith."[1]

After graduation in 1927, al-Banna took a position as a teacher in a primary school in the city of Isma'iliyya, in the Suez Canal Zone of eastern Egypt. The British considered the Suez Canal an important enough strategic asset to warrant more direct control than the rest of Egypt. Working within this atmosphere, al-Banna, increasingly aware of the eroding social and religious values he so treasured, rejected the passive posture of the Egyptian ulama of his day and instead, in March 1928, organized the Society of the Muslim Brothers. This action was motivated by his conviction that Muslims were called upon to be socially, economically, and politically aware and active in ways prescribed by Islam. Although the organization had only six members at its founding, it would grow quickly.

The new organization faced many challenges, some of which were suggested by al-Banna's critique of Egyptian society. It was, he believed, in need of thoroughgoing reform. British colonialism, of course, had to be fought against and eventually eliminated. But the corruption of Egyptian institutions by British rule compounded the problem of organizing political resistance. For instance, the major political parties (such as the dominant Wafd party) within the parliamentary political structure encouraged by the British had, in al-Banna's view, been captured by a Western worldview. He associated this worldview with the qualities of radical individualism, gender equality, class conflict, materialism, and atheism. While many of these Egyptian political parties stood for independence, their secular and Western orientation did not allow them to address the country's cultural alienation or socioeconomic woes. Their platforms had little or no Islamic content. Thus, argued al-Banna, Egypt possessed a pseudo-democracy that was only leading the country away from its Islamic traditions and duties of piety, altruism, community fellowship, strong family orientation, domestic roles for women, and social justice. Similarly, Egypt's Western law codes had "no relation to its citizens and does not spring from their hearts." They thus had "perverted the nation's thought, mind and logic."[2]

Egyptian capitalism, as it had evolved under the influence of Western-dominated trade, served only to exploit the land and the peasants. It entailed no acknowledgment of the Muslim belief that wealth comes from God and requires the well-to-do to have a sense of obligation to serve the community. All in all, Egypt was being transformed into a Western country infected with the many social problems one found in Europe. For al-Banna, it meant "slow annihilation and profound and complete corruption."[3]

What sort of future did al-Banna and his young organization offer in the place of this dismal present? As with all Islamic fundamentalists, the Muslim Brothers drew inspiration from the past. As the Brothers interpreted it, the initial period of Muslim rule—the time of Muhammad's rule at Medina followed by the first four Caliphs—set forth the outlines of ideal government. In that period the Caliph was elected by the community, which therefore represented the source of the ruler's authority. Those people elected were pious men well versed in Islamic law. Tax monies were devoted to community needs, and a sense of religious brotherhood prevailed. That the Muslims had fallen from this state of governmental grace was due to the mistakes and sins committed by the Umayyad dynasty and other successor regimes of the first four "rightly guided" Caliphs. After them, the Caliphate was transformed into an hereditary kingship, faction-alism replaced Muslim solidarity, and greed and materialism prevailed. Eventually, these conditions so weakened the Islamic community as to allow foreign invasion to occur. The latest manifestation of this decline was modern Western colonialism.

If the decay and disintegration of the Muslim world were to be reversed, the original virtues, that is, the example set by the earliest Muslims, had somehow to be reinterpreted in light of twentieth-century realities. Hasan al-Banna and his followers did not espouse a return to the lifestyle of the seventh and eighth centuries. Rather, they sought to create a community governed by age-old Islamic ideals, which they thought were inherent in Muslim religious law and practice and also thoroughly compatible with the technical and scientific advances of their day. Thus they sought an Islamic order at once old and new. This goal did not originate with al-Banna. The late nineteenth-century Islamic Modernist intellectuals to whom al-Banna looked for inspiration had preached something similar. They, however, were not able to go beyond intellectual exhortation. Al-Banna would successfully communicate his ideals to the common citizen.

Central to al-Banna's vision of an Islamic order was the reinstitution of Muslim religious law and the concept of rule by consultation (shura). He often quoted the motto, "the Quran is our constitution." As long as the community was governed by these general principles, the particular form of government adopted was secondary. Outright dictatorship, however, was ruled out by al-Banna's interpretation of the nature of the early Muslim polity as being one where the ruler was elected, and by the Quranic injunction that rule was to involve consultation. From these principles, the Muslim Brothers saw the root of authority resting with the community of Muslim believers as a whole. A consultative body of learned and pious men, chosen by the community, would lead both the people and the ruler down the "straight path" and thus produce an environment conducive to a good Muslim life. Neither al-Banna nor the other thinkers produced by the Society of the Muslim Brothers went much beyond these general principles. Yet, in terms of the ideal, most Muslims do not believe, as many Westerners think they do, that Islamic fundamentalist political thought leads only to some form of tyranny.

Hasan al-Banna would seek to convince the Egyptian people that this ideal Islamic order was possible. He did so by establishing a pattern of operation that proved so successful that the organization he founded grew with great rapidity. Energetically preaching in the mosques and coffee houses, he sought to win the support of "opinion makers" (the ulama, the shaykhs of the Sufi religious orders, the heads of leading families and clans, leaders of the various social and religious clubs, teachers, and government functionaries). With their financial support, he would organize community self-help projects such as the building of mosques, clinics, recreation halls, and small community businesses. All of this was organized around the message that improvement and contentment could come by pursuing goals based on altruistic Islamic values: charity, cooperation, generosity, the social responsibility that came with wealth. The message plus the achievement of specific community-based projects tied theory to practice.

By the time World War II broke out in 1939, the Society of the Muslim Brothers was one of the most active and popular organizations in Egypt. Its membership crossed all class and occupational lines, encompassing laborers, peasants, artisans, merchants, educators, students, and civil servants. It ran its own press, youth groups, hospitals, and schools. It even ran athletic training and physical fitness groups.

As the Society grew, it took on an organizational form that could be called "benevolent autocracy." This format did not quite match the consultative and elective ideal the Society held for an Islamic state, but it did reflect the cultural norm in Egypt and much of the Arab Muslim world. That is, in its organization, the Society of the Muslim Brothers reflected the hierarchical arrangements that characterized family, economic, social, and political life in its culture. Al-Banna headed the brotherhood with the title "General Guide." All members took an oath of loyalty in which they swore to "have complete confidence" in the organization's "leadership and to obey absolutely under all circumstances."[4] The day-to-day operation of the brotherhood was managed by a General Consultative Council of twelve to fifteen members out of which a Secretary General was elected. He was the chief operations officer, but both he and the Consultative Council were responsible to the General Guide. The organization also had a Consultative Assembly that met annually to review the Society's status, and periodic mass meetings of members also were held. The ultimate power, however, rested with the General Guide.

Many administrative subdivisions evolved over time. A section devoted to the "propagation of the Message" ran missionary programs, trained speakers for public meetings, and oversaw publications and the general education of members. Other sections of the organization dealt specifically with peasants, laborers, students, and the professions. Each section shaped the message and activities of the brotherhood to the needs of its particular assigned constituency.

At the base of this organizational structure were local chapters or branches, each of which had its own "council of administration." The branches broke down into "families" of five to ten members. Each member was encouraged to see himself connected to each other "family" member in a way that expressed the living out of Muslim values. They were to be mutually responsible for each other in good times and bad, spend time together, and support each other in avoiding such Islamically defined evils as gambling, drinking, usury, and adultery. More positively, they were to encourage each other in the establishment and maintenance of an Islamized home life (cultivation of individual virtue, devotion to wife and children, and restriction of womenfolk to domestic roles). Every "family" was to maintain a "cooperative treasury" contributed to by each member.

One other expression of the Muslim Brothers was the youth group called the Rovers. Based on the model of a scout troop, the Rovers reflected al-Banna's belief that a healthy body was as legitimately a Muslim end as were a healthy mind and spirit. And, indeed, exercise and involvement in sports were encouraged for all Muslim brothers. The Rovers involved themselves in hiking, camping, and various public service projects in the areas of education and health. They also served as a force for the maintenance of order at the Society's mass meetings. Al-Banna had assigned the development of the Rovers to a retired army officer, Mahmud Labib, whose leadership gave the group's training a martial flavor. This was sometimes reflected in periodic clashes between the Rovers and youth groups from secular Egyptian political parties and organizations.

As has been suggested, al-Banna's dedication of the Society to the service of the community in the name of age-old Muslim values proved very successful. It will also be remembered that al-Banna saw Egypt's problems as stemming in large part from a compromised and corrupted political environment that could only be redeemed through an "Islamic order." Thus we have a very large organization with a growing and dedicated membership ultimately seeking the re-Islamization of Egyptian society. The political implications of this stand were undeniable. The Society of the Muslim Brothers could not help but eventually be drawn into politics.

The political cause over which the brotherhood most easily mobilized was anti-imperialism. Muslim brothers were called out repeatedly to demonstrate against the British role in Egypt. In the same vein, they actively supported the Palestinian cause against Zionist settlement. With the outbreak of World War II, the Society advocated a status of nonbelligerency for Egypt. This stance brought the organization into direct conflict with the pro-British government of the day and led to the first serious action against the Society by the Egyptian state. In 1941 al-Banna and other leaders of the Muslim Brothers were temporarily arrested and the Society's publications banned.

During these years of friction between the Brothers and the government, al-Banna developed contacts with a number of young, discontented army officers. This group, known as the "Free Officers," included men such as Gamal Abd al-Nasser and Anwar al-Sadat. Both later became leaders of the Egyptian state. The Free Officers eventually overthrew the Egyptian monarchy in July 1952. The Muslim Brothers generally supported the Free Officers, but ultimately their ends were not identical. The Muslim-guided state the Brothers sought was not the same as the basically secular vision of men like Nasser.

It was also in this time of troubles that al-Banna took another fateful step. In late 1942 or early 1943, he created a section of the brotherhood called the "secret apparatus." It was a clandestine group within the organization designed to defend the Society from both the British and the government. But the secret apparatus also developed an aggressive, offensive capability of an extralegal nature, often expressed through hit-and-run attacks on British personnel and Egyptian police. The identity of those brothers belonging to the secret apparatus was unknown to the Society's general membership, and its leaders reported directly to al-Banna. In theory, he controlled the group and its activities. However, control was never complete, and herein lay a fatal flaw for the future.

The end of World War II did not bring peace between the Muslim Brothers and the government. The economy turned downward, and unemployment rose sharply. A great number of peasants left their villages and migrated to the cities in search of work. The Brothers' response was to expand their schools to offer technical training that would increase the employability of these often unskilled migrants. The Brothers also began more small businesses and increased the number of their medical clinics. While the Society of the Muslim Brothers reached out to the unemployed and the poor, the government seemed indifferent to their sufferings, leaving many Egyptians alienated from the ruling elite. Continuous labor strife as well as on-going antigovernment and anti-British demonstrations marked the postwar period.

Finally, in December 1948, the Egyptian government, fearing that the Muslim Brothers were plotting an imminent uprising, issued orders dissolving the Society (a decree that would remain in effect until December 1951). Much of the Brothers' leadership was again arrested. Although al-Banna was allowed to remain free, he was placed under "strict surveillance." What the Egyptian government failed to realize was that by taking this action it had cut the chain of command between al-Banna and the secret apparatus. As closely watched as he was, he could no longer receive information or issue orders. This meant that there was now a religiously motivated, well-trained group of brothers, whose identity remained hidden, ready to do violence against a government that had declared its intention of suppressing the Society. The one man who could restrain them was beyond communication. On December 28, 1948, one of these secret apparatus operatives assassinated the Egyptian Prime Minister Mahmud Nuqrashi. Al-Banna had nothing to do with the attack and immediately repudiated it, but the government held him ultimately responsible. On February 12, 1949, in an act of revenge, government agents assassinated Hasan al-Banna.

In this sequence of events we see a pattern that has persisted to the present day. Islamic fundamentalist organizations are usually founded by men of relatively moderate outlook, at least in terms of the use of violent tactics. Responding to genuine feelings of alienation and economic injustice, their organizations grow rapidly. Their agenda often draws them into the political arena. If, as is most often the case, the state in which they are operating has no genuine democratic procedures, or seeks to manipulate those procedures to exclude the fundamentalists, confrontation follows. At this point, the relatively moderate leadership is arrested, exiled, or, as with al-Banna, killed. A power vacuum within the fundamentalist ranks results, and new leaders emerge, some of whom are more likely than their predecessors to turn to violence. Alternatively, the original Islamic fundamentalist organization will splinter, with some of the offshoots turning to violent tactics.

Something of this sort happened in Egypt. The assassination of their founding leader did not destroy the Society of the Muslim Brothers. Remaining technically illegal, the Society rapidly regrouped and informally carried on as before, if at a somewhat lower profile. Al-Banna's murder did, however, open a rift in the Society's ranks. On one side were those who advocated the use of violence in fighting against the government and for an Islamic order. The members of the secret apparatus were among this group. On the other side were those who were more comfortable pursuing the re-Islamization of Egypt through the nonviolent cultural and economic activities that had brought the organization such broad support. This latter emphasis was supported by the Society's new General Guide, Hasan Isma'il al-Hudaybi.

Hudaybi, who had served as a judge for over twenty-five years, was essentially a pacifist who disapproved of the membership's participation in violent confrontations. He immediately sought the dissolution of the secret apparatus. But the task proved beyond him. His message of non-confrontation confused many of the rank-and-file members and alienated those who saw it as their own, and the organization's, duty to struggle against injustice and imperialism by any means. The oath to obey the leadership seemed never to be fully followed after al-Banna's death.

On July 23, 1952, troops under the command of the Free Officers occupied Cairo in a successful coup against the government. They set up a Revolutionary Command Council (RCC) to run the state. Soon thereafter, the monarchy was eliminated. The vast majority of Muslim Brothers supported the coup. The pacifist Hudaybi, however, acquiesced in military rule only reluctantly and cautiously.

It was not long before the unresolved question of the Society's relationship to government and state policy once more surfaced. Any government would have wanted to keep a close eye on an organization as large and influential as the Muslim Brothers. This was especially the case with the RCC since the Brothers advocated a reform of the state along Islamic lines that contradicted the secular and socialist developmental model favored by the Free Officers.[5] In truth, al-Banna had always taken the position that the Muslim Brothers should not seek political power until the Egyptian people were sufficiently re-Islamized to accept an Islamic order. As for Hudaybi, he was certainly not a personality to lead the Society to power. Nonetheless, the authoritarian RCC, itself a product of conspiracy, viewed all critics as potential political rivals.

At first, the RCC's attitude toward the Muslim Brothers was positive. When, soon after the coup, the RCC banned all political parties, the Muslim Brothers were deemed nonpolitical and exempted. Al-Banna's assassination was investigated, and those involved were brought to trial. But over time the RCC, being a military government unsure of its popular base, feared the possibility of opposition from the Brothers. There followed a series of disagreements over RCC policies. Hudaybi objected to the new government's land reform program, its plan to create a one-party state, and its basically secular vision of Egypt's future. The RCC in turn grew particularly suspicious that cells of the secret apparatus might exist within the army and the police force.

Abdel Nasser, now the RCC's leading member, began to conspire to remove Hudaybi as General Guide of the Society. When this failed, the RCC, following in the footsteps of the Egyptian government of 1948, decided to dissolve the brotherhood. The decree came on January 13, 1954. The leadership was again temporarily imprisoned, while the government simultaneously announced that the Society's numerous schools, hospitals, clinics, and businesses would continue to operate under different names. In essence, the Muslim Brothers were forced once more to slip into an informal mode of existence and operation. Once again the chain of command was broken. Hudaybi, however, never had the degree of control that al-Banna exercised. The secret apparatus had defied his orders to disband and had gone underground. Before the January 1954 decree, they had remained quiet, at least in relation to the RCC, but the government's action again focused the wrath of these most militant of Muslim Brothers, and again there was no organizational structure to control them.

The Society's estrangement from the RCC intensified when Nasser signed a new Anglo-Egyptian treaty in July 1954. Great Britain's indirect rule of most of Egypt had ended after World War II, leaving its forces concentrated in the Suez Canal Zone. While the new treaty provided for the evacuation of all British troops from the Zone within twenty months, the British retained a seven-year right of reentry in case of an attack on any Arab League state or Turkey. The inclusion of Turkey was due to its common border with the Soviet Union, and this seemed to create conditions by which Egypt could be drawn into the Cold War on the side of the West. Thus many Muslim Brothers and other Egyptians saw the treaty as a betrayal of Egypt's neutrality.

The signing of the treaty, along with the RCC's order dissolving the brotherhood, led to an attempted assassination of Nasser during a political rally in Alexandria on October 24, 1954. A member of the secret apparatus fired nine shots at Nasser from the crowd, missing with each shot. The assassination attempt provided Nasser with a perfect excuse to attempt once and for all to crush the Muslim Brothers. Thousands were arrested. The Society's headquarters was destroyed by mob action, and six accused conspirators were hanged before the year was out. In the RCC's propaganda against the Brothers, the Society's leaders were labeled "merchants of religion" seeking the establishment of a "primitive, barbaric religious state."[6] The RCC's actions largely succeeded in breaking up the Society as an effective public organization and drove the remnants of the brotherhood underground.

The Society of Muslim Brothers did not fully resume activities until after Nasser's death in 1970. At that point, the organization quickly rebuilt itself, while remaining politically cautious. While still standing for the re-Islamization of Egypt, the Society's approach favored the socio-economic activities that had always represented its strongest appeal to the people. State repression and long years of imprisonment had chastened the older men who now led the brotherhood. The secret apparatus had finally been expunged in Nasser's purge.

The low-key approach adopted by the Muslim Brothers from the 1970s onward left the field of violent options open to other, more militant Islamic organizations. The Iranian Revolution of 1979 gave such groups great encouragement, while Egypt's peace with Israel (stemming from the Camp David Accords of 1979), its increasingly close economic and political ties with the West in the post-Nasser era, and the country's on-going disparity between rich and poor—all gave militant Islamic fundamentalists fertile ground for activism. One such group, the Organization for Holy War (Jamaat al-Jihad), managed to assassinate Nasser's successor, Anwar al-Sadat, on October 6, 1981.

The Society of Muslim Brothers founded by Hasan al-Banna has served as a general prototype for many of the Islamic fundamentalist movements of recent times. The organization's great popularity speaks to the depth of Islamic feeling among the masses of people for whom secular government has meant cultural alienation. If these governments had been able to respond successfully to the economic needs of their citizens, Western-style secularism might have fared better. But the truth is that the legacy of colonialism has not met the needs of the majority of Muslims, and so a search for more indigenous, culturally authentic solutions to problems has come naturally and perhaps inevitably.

The Society of Muslim Brothers set precedents for future Islamic fundamentalists with both their peaceful civic-based organizing and the resort to political violence. However, one difference marks the Society's history and the style of some of its successors. The Society of Muslim Brothers never explicitly sought to seize power. No doubt al-Banna foresaw a day when this might happen, but he wanted the people of Egypt prepared beforehand. To that end, he sought to model the future Islamic order on the behavior and service of the Society itself. But such conquest by role modeling could not stand up to the secular forces arrayed against the brotherhood. Other Islamic movements, while learning much from al-Banna's experience, have approached the problem of political power differently. The most famous and politically successful of these can be found in Iran.

NOTES

1. Quoted in R. Mitchell, *The Society of the Muslim Brothers* (Oxford: Oxford University Press, 1993), p. 6.

2. Ibid., p. 223.

3. Ibid., p. 227.

4. Ibid., p. 165.

5. The RCC supported an economic approach known as "Arab Socialism." It advocated the nationalization of large industries and public utilities, as well as a limit on how much land an individual could own. Advocates of Arab Socialism believed it would eliminate foreign control of resources and weaken the economic power of native elites allied with the West. Through state planning, Arab Socialism was supposed to increase production and achieve a more equitable distribution

of wealth. Those who supported this approach were careful to differentiate it from communism, which they rejected as an atheistic ideology. The Society of the Muslim Brothers disapproved of the nationalization called for by Arab Socialism and opposed the power such a move would give a state that, under the RCC, was still secular.

    6. Mitchell, p. 153.

3

Revolutionary Islamic Fundamentalism in Power: The Case of Iran

The Society of Muslim Brothers, founded in Egypt by Hasan al-Banna (see Chapter 2), was the first organized modern effort to re-Islamize a Muslim country. But al-Banna did not anticipate taking political power until the Egyptian people were reindoctrinated with what he held to be true Muslim values. Not all Islamic fundamentalists are this patient. Many believe that re-Islamization will be possible only when Islamic activists have state power at their disposal. The most successful example of this approach is found in the Shi'ite Muslim country of Iran. This case is of particular importance to the United States because the anti-Western sentiment that accompanied the rise of the Iranian Islamic revolt focused on American influence in the country.

THE NINETEENTH CENTURY

To understand the causes of Iran's Islamic fundamentalist revolution in 1979, it is necessary to go back at least to the nineteenth century. At that time, the West's interest in Persia (as Iran was then called) centered on its resources and resulted in extensive imperialist interference in the country's affairs. Russian encroachments from the north and British penetration from the south and west changed the economic and political balance of forces in Persia.

At this time Persia was ruled by monarchs. The prevailing dynasty, the Qajars, belonged to a strong tribe of the same name, in a land of many tribal groups divided along geographic, familial, and ethnic lines. Many of these tribes were mutually hostile, and the Qajars were never able to unite the country. In the end, this disunity, along with the lack of modern weaponry and military organization, meant that Persia could not resist Western military power. Facing Western imperial designs, the Qajars acquiesced in the Western effort to dominate Persia economically. Indeed, they sought to profit from it by selling off lucrative concessions to Western investors.

This process of Western penetration had adverse effects on the traditional economy of Persia. Persian merchants lost control of the import-export trade and domestic crafts, particularly in textiles, because they could not compete with cheap imported goods that were charged little or no duties. The bazaar merchants and crafts people (who constituted the backbone of the traditional economy) experienced much hardship and social dislocation. As a consequence, these "bazaaries" soon became a self-aware class (sometimes referred to as the traditional middle class) trying to resist Western economic encroachment that was also increasingly identified with the policies of the monarchy. In this effort, they found an ally in the country's religious establishment, the Shi'ite ulama (referred to as Mullahs), who felt threatened by the spread of Western culture, values, and ideas that came along with increasing foreign economic influence. These two groups, the bazaaries and the ulama, formed a long-lasting alliance which, in the end, helped realize an Islamic state in Iran.

Another group strongly affected by Western penetration was the Persian intelligentsia. Drawn to the ideas of liberal government and nationalism, these highly educated and secular-minded Persians sought to borrow what they considered the best and most benign aspects of the Western model. Utilizing Western ideas, they hoped to combat Qajar despotism, along with religious traditionalism and imperialist control. Thus their secularism and selective acceptance of Western ideas set them apart from the more traditionalist forces in the country.

By the early years of the twentieth century, enough of Persian society was alienated from the Qajar monarchy to create a revolutionary situation. For their part, the Shahs (or kings) were by this time morally discredited, financially bankrupt, and governmentally ineffective. This created an anarchistic environment rampant with tribal feuding, lawlessness, and economic stagnation. The situation finally came to a head in 1906.

In that year a series of protests and confrontations, momentarily bringing together traditional/religious and secular/liberal opposition groups, forced the Qajar Shah to create a Majles (or parliament) as well as a written constitution. The Majles, however, soon became an arena within which the traditional/religious and secular/liberal forces competed in such a way as to create a legislative stalemate. This meant that the new institutional forms could not readily produce policies that addressed the country's economic and political problems. Although the 1906 constitution became a model for future political reform, the initial constitutional period lasted only a few years. Besides parliamentary gridlock, the imperialist powers with vested interests in Persia were not about to allow the country to go its own way. By 1911 Russian pressure had forced the dissolution of the Majles.

An anarchistic situation again prevailed throughout the years of World War I. Russia occupied the northern part of Persia until the Bolshevik Revolution turned that country inward for a generation, and the British moved troops into the southern part of Persia. The situation was ripe for the ascendance of a strong-man, and eventually he appeared in the person of Reza Khan, a forty-two-year-old military officer. In 1921, with British backing, he and 3,000 followers took over the capital, Teheran. Whereas Ahmad Shah, the Qajar monarch, had been unable to bring order to Persia, Reza Khan, a decisive man with military force at his disposal, suppressed factional warfare and lawlessness. This alone won him much popular support. He was also able to negotiate the withdrawal of Russian forces from northern Persia in exchange for guarantees that the area would not be used to launch attacks on the new Soviet state. Initially satisfied with the post of minister of war, and then prime minister, Reza Khan deposed the last of the Qajar Shahs in 1925. He proceeded to make himself Shah, creating a new dynasty that took the name Pahlavi (after the ancient language of pre-Islamic Persia).

The choice of the name Pahlavi indicated Reza Shah's basically non-Islamic and secular outlook. Indeed, he attempted to modernize Persia along Western lines in all things except political structure. In this, Persia remained an authoritarian monarchy, and a reconstituted Majles functioned only as a rubber-stamp institution. The new Shah's nontraditionalist outlook also created tension between his dynasty and the country's devout Muslims, led by the ulama. It was a tension that was to last, and grow, into the revolution of 1979.

The one problem that Reza Shah could not successfully control was the imperialist influence in Iran. (The name of the country was changed from Persia to Iran in the 1930s.) In 1941 the British, fearing that Reza Shah was pro-German, forced him to abdicate in favor of his twenty-two-year-old son, Muhammad Reza Shah. The young Shah had neither his father's experience nor his close personal relationship to the army, and so increasingly relied on outside support. Thus, he too appeared to embrace the Western powers. Over time, his main ally became the United States, and, in the eyes of many of his subjects, this alliance seemed very much like the power-behind-the-scenes relationship the British had maintained in Egypt.

EVENTS AFTER WORLD WAR II

After World War II, the United States was interested in Iran not only because it had great oil reserves, but also because of the country's strategic position in the evolving Cold War policy of "containment" directed against the Soviet Union. Iran bordered the Soviet Union in the north, and both the United States and Britain considered it important to prevent the spread of communist influence in the country. The "communist threat" in Iran was thought to be centered in the Tudeh party, Iran's major leftist party and one that received financial support from the Soviet Union.

What the United States and other Western powers failed to realize was that the greatest threat to an Iranian pro-Western stance was not Soviet scheming, but the short-sighted nature of their own policies. Their refusal to allow for Iran's economic needs and sense of national pride, and their backing of increasingly autocratic rule were counterproductive in the long run. The first indications of a conflict between Iranian interests and Western policies came in 1951–1953 over the issue of nationalization of the country's oil industry.

This issue played itself out against a background of Iran's growing nationalist consciousness. This heightened self-awareness was a complex affair and worked at many levels. Among the traditionalists and the religiously minded, it included a reaction to Western culture and values. This was similar to the reaction of people like Hasan al-Banna in Egypt. On the other hand, the Western lifestyle, presented to the Iranians through the various media as well as through the large number of Western advisers and businessmen in the country, attracted much of the upper class. Nonetheless, most Iranians, regardless of cultural preference, agreed on the need for economic policies that would promote national independence.

Then, in 1949 the charismatic nationalist Dr. Muhammad Mossadegh formed the National Front, which sought to return Iran to the democratic principles of the 1906 constitution. It also sought to promote a policy of national economic growth, the revenue for which was to be obtained through the nationalization of Iran's oil industry—an industry largely controlled by the British. By 1951 Mossadegh and his call for nationalization were so popular with Iranians of all views that the Shah was obliged to appoint him Prime Minister.

Iran soon became the first Middle Eastern country to nationalize its oil industry. This move, however, proved a direct challenge to Western interests. In addition, Mossadegh's liberal and independent ways challenged the Shah's authority, and, over time, his tolerance of the leftist Tudeh party proved offensive to the traditionally minded and the ulama. In the end, Mossadegh had alienated as many people as he had pleased.

By 1953 a Western boycott of Iranian oil had undermined the country's economy and set the stage for a U.S.-British orchestrated coup. Mossadegh was deposed in August 1953 and the Shah's authority reestablished. The oil industry was denationalized, with Iran not regaining control of its oil until 1973. The Shah's experience with Mossadegh made him determined to keep at bay any individual or group that might compete with him for power. There would be no more strong prime ministers, and the Majles would be packed with "obedient servants." His power came to rest on a combination of three elements, first of which was the state security apparatus. The most feared aspect of this apparatus was SAVAK, a secret police force that employed the tactics of arbitrary arrest and torture against those deemed enemies of the monarchy. The Shah organized this agency in 1957 with the help of the CIA and Mossad, the Israeli security service. The second source of power was a small indigenous upper class that economically benefited from his policies. Over time, members of this upper class became so westernized as to become alienated from their own culture. Third were foreign capitalists and governments, particularly Americans.

Even as the United States became the staunchest supporter of the Shah, it also periodically, and unwittingly, helped undermine him. Given the democratic nature of American politics, periodic shifts in foreign policy emphasis are inevitable. In the 1960s and 1970s human rights became a concern for the American public, and this concern led to a subtle change in attitude toward the Shah of Iran. The Kennedy administration pushed the Shah to adopt a more liberal approach to governance. Along with a moderation of repression, the American government urged the adoption of a land reform program for the Iranian peasantry to help deter the growth of communist influence.

Urged on by the United States, the Shah proposed what he labeled the "White Revolution." Among other things, it espoused land reform, women's suffrage, the sale of some state-owned enterprises, and a workers' profit-sharing program. From the U.S. government perspective, these programs benefited the Iranian people. It is questionable, however, just how well the Americans offering advice on Iran really understood the dynamics of its culture and economy. Even the Shah, who by now had surrounded himself with "yes men" was out of touch with the popular feelings and forces among the masses. Thus, as we will see, the "White Revolution" proved to be a catalyst that ultimately increased ulama involvement in politics and led to the Shah's downfall.

SHI'ITE ISLAM

The dominant religion of Iran is Shi'ite Islam. (For the origin of the Shi'ites, see Chapter 1). Strong religious belief is prevalent among the traditional middle class as well as among the urban working class and rural peasantry. Shi'ism also forms the basis for the country's cultural and societal norms. These norms are most often defined and articulated by the Shi'ite ulama, the leaders of which hold the title of ayatollah. They run the mosques, the religious schools, charitable organizations, and foundations and have considerable influence among the people at the local level. They had shown their potential for political action, particularly in alliance with the bazaar merchants, in 1906 and again in the Mossadegh years of the 1950s.

The Shi'ite historical understanding of Islam makes its believers particularly sensitive to issues of governmental illegitimacy and abuse of power. This can be traced back to their fervent belief that the prophet Muhammad's cousin and son-in-law Ali and his heirs were the prophet's divinely ordained successors. Yet, their rightful place had been usurped by the Sunni Caliphs of the Umayyad and Abbasid dynasties. They believed that the heirs of Ali, known as Imams, were the only ones who could legitimately rule over the Muslim community. Most Shi'ites believe that the twelfth Imam in the line from Ali, who disappeared as a child in the year 878, was in fact hidden by God. He would return at some point as the Mahdi, or "the rightly guided one" who comes just before the Day of Judgment to restore justice to society. In the meantime, governments were lacking in legitimacy, and the Shi'ite faithful gave only qualified allegiance to them. When such governments misused their power, and particularly when they were perceived to rule in an un-Islamic way, the politically minded Shi'ite ulama would seek to organize resistance. This is what happened in the years leading up to the 1979 revolution.

When it came to the Shah's "White Revolution," two aspects of it in particular aroused the opposition of the ulama. One was the Shah's decision to grant women the right to vote, and the other was the issue of land reform.

Women's role in the public sphere, symbolized here by the issue of suffrage, was and remains an issue continuously debated in the Muslim world. In the 1960s and 1970s, seemingly linked as it was to the infiltration of Western notions of women's liberation, the voting issue formed a rallying point for conservative anti-Western Muslims.

The land reform issue touched an even more sensitive nerve with a wide range of Iranian ulama. Over the years, many Iranians had bequeathed all or part of their landed property to charitable trusts in an effort to fulfill the Muslim religious duty to share the wealth that God had granted to them. These trust holdings were often rental property, and the rents helped support schools, mosques, hospitals, soup kitchens, and the like. They were also the basis for the salaries that paid the ulama who administered these institutions. If the land was to be given over to the renters as part of the Shah's land reform program, the financial basis of the trusts would obviously be jeopardized. Thus, the "White Revolution" became a focus for religious resistance to the Shah.

Protests organized against the Shah's policies in the early 1960s were met with violent repression. This only deepened disenchantment with the government and broadened the range of those willing to express opposition to include secular liberal groups. The most important leader of the resistance was the Ayatollah Ruhollah Mussaui Khomeini.

Khomeini was a theology teacher in the city of Qum when in June 1963 he organized large-scale demonstrations against the government. He identified the Shah's policies with Western, and in particular, American influence in Iranian affairs. He labeled the "White Revolution" a "United States conspiracy against Islam" and charged that the United States was attempting to turn Iran into "a colony." Khomeini's leadership of the protest movement turned him into an increasingly popular figure in Iran—so much so that the Shah's government arrested and subsequently exiled him in November 1965.

Resistance to the "White Revolution" increasingly politicized the ulama, who now allied themselves with the bazaar merchants of the country. Conservative and devout in their Shi'ite Muslim faith, these merchants and craftsmen had long been economically hurt by the penetration of Western goods and competition. Under both Reza Shah and his son Muhammad Reza Shah, Iran had moved from an agricultural/service economy to a commercial/industrial/service one. As the transformation progressed, the Shahs had allowed foreign concerns to enter much of the Iranian market, while lucrative domestic businesses often became monopolized by the Shah's family and those allied to it. By the 1960s the bazaar merchants were suffering from inflation and the lack of concern and corruption of a government unsympathetic to their interests.

The urban poor and working class also supported the growing activism of the ulama. In the 1960s and 1970s a major population move occurred from the countryside to the cities. These migrating rural folk held strong religious commitments, and their religious and social centers became the mosques of their new urban neighborhoods. The influence of the ulama with these people would prove to be strong.

Thus, a broad antigovernment coalition evolved in the 1960s which included not only the ulama, bazaaries, urban workers, and poor, but also liberal secular groups who opposed the Shah's repressive policies and hoped the protests against the government would lead to constitutional reform. The liberal secular groups especially looked back to the 1906 revolution and sought to do away with the Shah's authoritarianism through the reestablishment of constitutional and parliamentary government. However, the secular opposition now had to share the stage with a politically conscious and aggressive Islamic movement led by Khomeini and other ayatollahs. The political vision of the future held by the protesting ulama differed significantly from that of the secular reformist opposition.

KHOMEINI'S WORLDVIEW

The Ayatollah Khomeini saw the world in terms of a number of irreconcilable opposites. There was the division between the Islamic and the non-Islamic world; between the oppressed and the victims of injustice on the one side, and the oppressor and the perpetrator of injustice on the other. Khomeini and his followers saw the struggle against the Shah and his U.S. ally in this context.

Indeed, in Khomeini's mind, the Shah stood as a symbol of non-Islamic contamination by an exploitative alliance of Westerners and upper-class Iranians who together were transforming Iran into a secular, materialistic place—the opposite of what Khomeini thought it could and should be. In the process, he believed the Muslim way of life was being undermined and would ultimately be destroyed. This set the stage for what the Ayatollah saw as a literal struggle of good (Islam) against evil (the Shah and the West) in which the contest for political control of Iran was key to its cultural and religious fate.

Khomeini led a group of Islamic fundamentalists who organized as the Islamic Republican party. Their analysis of Iran's situation in some ways resembled that of Hasan al-Banna in Egypt; in fact, in the 1930s Khomeini had had some contact with the Society of the Muslim Brothers. Certainly, he and his followers had studied the history and philosophy of the Society closely. Khomeini, however, would prove much more aggressive and bolder than had al-Banna. While al-Banna had believed that the Muslim Brothers should seek political power only when the Islamic consciousness of the Egyptian people was sufficiently reestablished, Khomeini adhered to no such qualification. Perhaps this was because, unlike al-Banna, who saw the source of sovereignty residing in the collective Muslim community, Khomeini placed sovereignty with God. The people needed to be guided by a religiously righteous government to do God's will. For Khomeini, the answer was first to overthrow the impious Shah and create a government dominated by the pious ulama. Then one would proceed to "purify" Iran of its "contamination."

It is not surprising that in Khomeini's conception of the new Muslim fundamentalist Iran we find a complete rejection of Western culture and values. The Quran and Shariah were to be the basis for all law. A Muslim dress code was to be enforced, Western entertainment was to be banned. Women's role in society was to be based on Muslim cultural norms. If such a completely Muslim system were to be created and properly administered, injustice and exploitation would be eliminated and as near a perfect sociopolitical order as possible attained.

To this end, Khomeini and his followers would develop a governmental system based on an Islamic constitution, at the core of which was the concept of the rule of the jurisprudent (vilayat-i-faqih, or "guardianship of the supreme religious leader"). As Khomeini explained, this office, which he himself was the first to hold, would function as the most powerful and final arbiter within society. In the fundamentalist government that would soon rule Iran, the jurisprudent would be constitutionally endowed with the power to command the armed forces, declare war and peace, control the "Guardian Council" that would approve or disapprove (on the basis of its Islamic compatibility) all legislation coming from the Majles, and appoint the state prosecutor and the chief of the Supreme Court, as well as other key members of the judiciary. He would also be able to dismiss the elected president of the country.

The jurisprudent would not be accountable to the Majles or the people of Iran, and so no mechanism would exist to prevent abuse of his power. He was to be accountable only to God. Of course, it was assumed that the jurisprudent would be wise enough to make abuse of power an impossibility. The privileged position of the jurisprudent stood at the apex of a system designed to ensure the dominance of the ulama and those who accepted the premise that Iranian society must be thoroughly Muslim in the fundamentalist sense outlined by Khomeini. Candidates for all offices, including the Majles, would be screened according to religious criteria. And government agents were expected to be creative and innovative only within the predetermined boundaries of accepted premises—that is, God had already revealed in the Quran the basic legislation necessary for the good life. This legislation had long been elaborated and interpreted in the Shariah. The main job of the government was to implement that divine legislation. The challenge was a tactical one.

Such an outlook left little room for democratic Western political concepts and practices such as checks and balances in government, individual rights of the citizen, and popular sovereignty. A government that was, for all intents and purposes, divinely inspired did not need to worry about violating basic rights, nor did it need to be monitored or restricted in its exercise of power.

This pyramidal form of government reflected the elitist structure of Shi'ite Islam, with its various levels of clerical rank. It also attested to the Shi'ite belief that the ulama held an understanding of the true nature of God's message in the Quran, while the lay population's grasp did not go beyond an "apparent understanding." That is, in Shi'ite Islam, the ulama knew what God wanted in a more accurate way than the masses. Thus, the ulama must guide society. In religious and cultural terms, the faithful were expected to model their behavior after the example of the ulama. Therefore, it stood to reason for many of the clerics that they should run the government. This was the position taken by Khomeini and his followers.

There was, however, a group of Iranian Shi'ite clerics who did not agree with Khomeini's religiopolitical outlook. This minority faction, led by the Ayatollah Kazem Shariatmadari, was known as the Muslim People's Republican Party, and in some ways its outlook was like that of the earlier Islamic Modernists. This more moderate faction did wish to see Islamic values play a more influential role in Iranian culture and politics, but they did not believe this goal required the ulama to dominate all aspects of political and social life, and they stood against any sort of clerical dictatorship. The supporters of Shariatmadari were not opposed to assimilating aspects of the Western political model, such as representative democracy. As such, they recognized the need to adapt Islamic institutions to a more democratic model, and they argued that to do so required the application of Islamic law and tradition in a flexible fashion.

Shariatmadari's arguments did not move Khomeini, and they soon were dismissed as, in 1977, the protest movement against the Shah became increasingly radicalized. Interestingly, it was the actions of yet another liberal U.S. administration that again helped to create circumstances leading to this renewed unrest in Iran.

Just as President John F. Kennedy had urged land reform on the Shah in the 1960s, so in the late 1970s, President Jimmy Carter again pressured the Shah to rule in a less autocratic fashion. Once more the Shah felt obliged to respond at least superficially to the American pressure. Thus, in 1977, he moved to reduce press censorship, liberalize court proceedings (fewer secret trials before military tribunals), end the use of torture, and allow the Red Cross to visit Iranian prisons. This sudden liberalization of a longstanding repressive system only emboldened the Shah's opposition. Both secular and Islamic groups came to believe that the Shah no longer had the unquestioning support of the United States and thus was no longer invincible. Coincidentally, this process of loosening the repressive bonds came at a time of economic downturn due to falling oil prices. Economic discontent fed renewed political protest.

The renewed protests of 1977 were at first nonviolent and essentially reformist in their demands. The initial aim, pushed by the secular opposition, was to transform the government into a constitutional monarchy. But then, in January 1978, two Tehran newspapers published a government-inspired attack on Khomeini, accusing him of being an "agent of colonialism" and a "traitor of non-Persian descent." A peaceful protest against these accusations by theology students in the city of Qum turned violent when police arrived. Many died, and hundreds were injured in the incident. Far from deterring Khomeini's supporters, the clash with police sparked new protests in other cities. Khomeini, whom the government sought to vilify, was instead turned into a nationwide symbol of resistance.

From this point on, Khomeini, who was still in exile in France, skillfully coordinated the evolution of a united front of opposition groups. He pushed a relentless strategy of direct confrontation with the Shah. In the face of this growing movement, the Shah reacted with uncertainty and indecision. Given that he had created a system of one-man rule where all others were discouraged from acting independently, such indecisiveness would prove fatal. He vacillated between periods of compromise (which tended to demoralize his supporters and security forces) and periods of repression (which alienated the moderates in the opposition who might otherwise have been willing to negotiate with him).[1]

There were many reasons for this indecisiveness. One was that, as a personality, the Shah was not particularly clear sighted and determined. Another was his conviction that, while sheer repression might preserve the throne for his lifetime (he was at this time ill with cancer), it was not likely to save it for his son and heir. And finally, there was the fact that he was getting conflicting advice from the United States government. The U.S. ambassador in Tehran, William Sullivan, and the State Department in general urged the Shah to follow a policy of moderation and compromise toward the opposition (he was getting the same advice from his Queen, Farah). On the other hand, the American National Security Adviser, Zbigniew Brzezinski, was urging the Shah to be tough (as was the Iranian security establishment). Under the circumstances Muhammad Reza Shah vacillated. He preferred a peaceful solution to the troubles but was unwilling to give up any of his autocratic powers. In the end, he was able to satisfy no one.

By late 1978 the continuing protests had escalated into national strikes involving the bazaaries, public employees, oil industry workers, and others. The factories shut down, public services were interrupted, and heating oil became scarce as winter set in. At this point, Khomeini, then orchestrating events from Paris, made it clear that the Shah's regime had to go. There would be no compromise of a constitutional monarchy, for Khomeini had ruled that monarchy was incompatible with Islam. By this time, the leaders of the secular opposition concurred with the demand, though not with the religious reasons Khomeini offered. There was less enthusiasm among them when Khomeini followed up his demand for the Shah's removal with the assertion that what the revolution was to put in his place was "an Islamic Republic." But by this time (November 1978) Khomeini was nearly unstoppable. His unparalleled ability to communicate with the broad masses of Iranians, and his great skill at organization building and revolutionary strategy, had put him at the forefront of events. On December 10 and 11, 1978, massive peaceful demonstrations involving millions of people took place in all the major cities of Iran. These demonstrations declared Khomeini's leadership and called for a new government based on the tenets of Islam. A little over a month later, on January 16, 1979, the Shah left Iran for good.

A few weeks after the Shah's departure, on February 1, 1979, Khomeini returned from exile to Iran. There would follow an interim period of provisional government during which Khomeini and his followers consolidated power through the creation of revolutionary Islamic institutions such as the Komites (vigilante committees that sprang up in neighborhoods, factories, schools, and universities), revolutionary courts, and the Pasdaran (a powerful party militia also called the Revolutionary Guards). Slowly, the secular opposition and the more moderate ulama led by Shariatmadari were pushed aside and neutralized. More forceful opposition to Khomeini, which came from organized groups on the left, was violently suppressed.

In April 1979 a national referendum asking simply "Do you favor an Islamic republic or a monarchy?" was held. According to reported results, 98.2 percent of 15.7 million votes cast were in favor of an Islamic republic. Subsequently, an Assembly of Experts was elected to write a draft constitution. This assembly was dominated by the ulama and members of Khomeini's Islamic Republican Party. The constitution that it created was thoroughly Islamic and contained the unique and powerful post of jurisprudent. There were also provisions for a legislative assembly (or Majles), presidency, and guardian council.

Subsequent events seemed to encourage the evolving autocratic direction of the Islamic government. The American embassy in Tehran was seized by militant Muslim students in late 1979. While this was not done on the orders of Khomeini, he did decide to go along with the action after the fact. The embassy seizure had been triggered by the admittance of the Shah into the United States in October. The Shah was fatally ill with cancer at this time and, after brief stays in Egypt, Morocco, and Mexico he sought permission to enter the United States for medical treatment. This triggered a debate within the Carter administration. The U.S. government had reliable information that admitting the Shah would cause a crisis in Iranian-U.S. relations and very likely lead to some form of retaliation against American citizens and property in Iran. Nonetheless, under great pressure from the Shah's friends in Congress and other influential Americans (particularly Henry Kissinger), the administration granted permission for the Shah to come to the United States. In Iran, this decision was seen as a provocation and the result was the embassy seizure and the holding hostage of its sixty-three resident Americans. This hostage crisis lasted for 444 days.

Before the situation could be resolved, Iraq invaded Iran in September 1980, thereby beginning a long (1980–1988) and destructive war. All of these events intensified the Islamic revolutionaries' sense of religious and national purpose and were used to label all opposition to the new Islamic regime as traitorous. By 1983 all political groups except the Islamic Republican Party and its immediate allies had been destroyed or driven underground.

ISLAMIC FUNDAMENTALISM COMES TO POWER

Revolutionary Shi'ite Islamic fundamentalism is now in power in Iran. At least in this one case, we can see how such a politically empowered Islamic society might look and act. In social and cultural terms, the Islamic Republic of Iran has sought to create a new society wherein the citizens' values, outlook, and behavior are guided by Shariah law. To this end, the Iranians voided all non-Islamic laws created since 1907 and required that all judicial judgments had to flow from the Quran or accepted hadith or Shi'ite-based theological precedents.

Education in Iran has been fundamentally altered. Curricula from grade school to university have been restructured to teach not only the tenets of Islam, but also a version of history that condemns the old monarchy as criminal and pictures the ulama as defenders of justice and all that is right and moral. The teacher corps has been purged of those believed to be untrustworthy or religiously unfit, and there are now religious ideological criteria for admission to the universities.

An outward public morality is enforced. The Islamic Republic established an Office for the Propagation of Virtues and Prevention of Sins, which is empowered to assure that public behavior accords with Islamic moral standards. Not abiding by the Islamic dress code (in the case of women this means wearing a full body length, loose-fitting robe called the chador, and men must wear modest, loose-fitting clothing) when appearing in public or other obvious non-Islamic behavior can result in harassment or arrest by what amounts to roving squads of "morals police." In addition, bars, discos, nightclubs, and the like have been shut down. Western films are banned or censored, modern music is prohibited, and alcohol forbidden.

The change in public morals has focused mainly on women, perhaps because the "liberation" or modernization of women's condition had been a policy of the Shahs. Under the Shahs' regimes, women became better educated and entered the labor force and professions; also, divorce and other laws were modified in their favor, and the veil was banned in public places as early as 1936.

Such "liberal policies" alienated the ulama and devoutly religious who saw modernization as leading to the corruption of women and thus the moral undermining of Islam. Since the process seemed to be linked to the westernization of the country (or what some Iranians like to call gharb-zadegi or "westoxication"), it was also felt to be part of an alien attack on tradition. Women's issues became a primary battleground in the struggle against both the Shah and the West.

When the Islamic Republic was established, policies having to do with women were quickly revised. Compulsory veiling was reinstituted, and women were segregated in public places. They lost the right to participate in certain professions such as the judiciary, and laws concerning divorce and the family were changed to comply with the government's interpretation of Islamic norms. Again, these actions can be seen as much as a defense against the West as an attempt to re-Islamize Iranian women. In the minds of Iran's Islamic reformers, the two issues are closely related.

Nonetheless, having reconstructed what is considered a proper sociocultural context for women, the Islamic Republic allows women a participatory role in society. Women still have relatively wide access to the labor market (in part, thanks to the Iran-Iraq war), including the government bureaucracy. They still vote, and they can run for many offices and sit in the Majles. What is more, women in Iran are increasingly active in lobbying for more rights, with apparently occasional, if limited, success. For instance, the government initially opposed day care for children as a foreign, anti-Islamic concept that threatened a woman's relationship with her children, but now it is accepted and promoted so as to allow women easier access to the workforce. Custody laws also have recently been modified in favor of mothers. In part, this constitutes the regime's recognition that women played an important part in the revolutionary organizations that brought down the Shah. However, the long-term situation for women in Iran remains uncertain.

THE POSTREVOLUTIONARY SITUATION

In June 1989, after guiding the Islamic state for a decade, the Ayatollah Khomeini died. His death led to a shift of forces within the fundamentalist camp that has persisted over time. As with all revolutionary movements, what might look from the outside as a united effort on the inside really is a multifaceted affair. We already have seen that not all of Iran's ulama agreed with Khomeini's goals and policies. Just so, within the Iranian Republican party camp, various factions existed behind a facade of unity. Moshen Milani, a scholar of Iranian politics, has described these factions as "conservatives, crusaders and pragmatists."[2]

The "conservatives" are devout Muslims of wealth: successful merchants, large landowners, and some of the senior ulama. They espouse traditional capitalist economic views and favor continuing, if guarded, relations with the West. When it comes to religion, they insist on a close observance of Shariah law.

Differing from the "conservatives" are the "crusaders." This group is more representative of the middle and lower classes: shopkeepers, laborers, and middle-eschelon ulama. Quasi-socialist in economic orientation, they want emphasis placed on state run business to encourage a fair distribution of wealth. They also argue that the state should maintain control of foreign trade. Their foreign policy is much more assertive than that of the "conservatives" inasmuch as they advocate the exporting of the revolution, particularly throughout the Persian Gulf area.

Standing between the "conservatives" and the "crusaders" are the "pragmatists." An eclectic group, mostly technocrats of middle-class background, they move back and forth between the other two camps according to the issues. Their major concern is with the revival of the Iranian economy, which has suffered much damage from Western boycotts and the Iran-Iraq war. Thus, they support peace and improved relations with the West.

The competition between these factions led to legislative stalemate in the 1980s and no effective government policy in the areas of economics and foreign affairs. The "crusaders" often controlled the Majles and passed legislation in accord with their philosophy, while the Guardian Council, which had to pass on all legislation to assure its compatibility with Islamic norms, was controlled by "conservatives" who regularly vetoed the laws passed by the Majles. Only after Khomeini's death did this stalemate seem to break with the ascendancy of the "pragmatist" faction. Their policies were reflected in the government of the Jurisprudent Ali Khamenei and President Ali Akbar Rafsanjani which took over in 1989. Subsequently, Iran's oil industry was revitalized, state ownership of nonstrategic industry relinquished, and a guarded opening to foreign trade and investment begun.

This "pragmatic" outlook was reaffirmed in the May 23, 1997, presidential elections. Here Muhammad Khatami, a soft-spoken and reform-minded cleric, defeated his more conservative opponents in a landslide victory. Khatami's election as Iran's president reflects a popular desire for a more open climate that takes public opinion into consideration in the formulation of government policy. Many hoped for less concentration on ideological purity (for instance, a possible relaxation of Islamic laws governing press, literary, and other artistic expression) and more attention to economic and social problems. In the year 2000, Khatami's relatively liberal supporters won control of the Majles, the Iranian parliament, and in June 2001, Khatami was relected President with just under 77 percent of the vote. While overwhelmingly popular, Khatami still must contend with a Guardian Council and judiciary firmly in the hands of conservatives. The police and army, the instruments of force and coercion in Iran, also remain in the hands of conservative forces not subject to election under the Iranian constitution. This has limited the impact Khatami has had in terms of reform. Thus, a struggle over the limits of acceptable behavior is ongoing in Iran and we may consider its revolutionary society still in flux. However, even though the relatively moderate policies of the "pragmatists" will help to lessen its fanatical nature, Iran will likely continue to adhere to the basic moral and religious tenets laid down by the revolution.

CONCLUSION

The fundamentalist revolution in Iran stemmed from two roots. First was the deep-seated attachment to Islam, not only as the religion of most of the people, but also as the age-old definer of Iranian culture. There was, however, an historically active secular opposition to the Shah, and indeed it had at times been even more prominent than the ulama. But the secular opposition never could substitute for the inherently Islamic outlook of the majority of Iranians. In the end, the only unifying basis for successful revolution against the monarchy proved to be an Islamic one.

The second root was fear and suspicion of the West. There was a fear that Iran was being reduced to a colonial status that would rob it of its resources and impoverish her people and, worse, steal away the very cultural character of the nation. That fear, too, was defined in Islamic terms. The Shah was identified with this fear because he was seen to be in a corrupt alliance with imperialist forces. Again, the proper response to this situation was debated by the secular and religious opposition, and even among the ulama there were differing reactions. In the end, however, it was the fundamentalist camp that mobilized millions of Iranians around this theme.

As is the case with most victorious revolutionary movements, success in Iran came from masterful organization and strategy, as well as a clear and consistent ideological message that touched the hearts and minds of the majority of citizens. As the revolution proceeded, a radicalization process occurred. Violence intensified as the fundamentalists fought first against the Shah to achieve power and then against various rivals to consolidate power. Much bloodletting often occurs in this sort of factional rivalry. Victory goes to those who can rally the masses and also build the most reliable and mobile political organization to be used in the most effective, timely, and even ruthless fashion. The Ayatollah Khomeini proved a master at all these things. He certainly proved a more adept revolutionary leader than either his secular or religious rivals.

As it manifests itself today, the Islamic fundamentalist state in Iran is ideologically authoritarian. To participate in public life, one must endorse the Shi'ite Islamic principles espoused by the Islamic Republican Party. If one does so, then one enters a political arena in which plenty of debate takes place over policies, personalities, and other particulars. But there can be no public questioning of basic premises. Nor can one be culturally eccentric in public. Outside one's own home, there is no right to dress or act in a way that goes against the official conception of Islamic norms. Morals are a public matter subject to legal regulation to an extent unknown in the secular West.

These two aspects of the Islamic Republic of Iran, ideological and cultural authoritarianism, are best understood only as one group's interpretation of Islam. To be sure, it is a powerful group, dominant in Iran. Nonetheless, another reading of Islam's overall cultural history would focus on a record of widespread borrowing and amalgamation of aspects of other cultures both Eastern and Western. And this can argue for Islam's potential for flexibility and humaneness. Indeed, many of today's Muslims prosper in and share, the cultures of countries that are Christian, Buddhist, Hindu, and secular in nature. Although Khomeini and the other fundamentalists like him have turned a blind eye to these facts, they nevertheless stand as testimony that Islam need not be intolerant or insular.

The authoritarianism expressed in Iran can be seen as a result of Islam transformed into a cultural and political doctrine claiming to possess rigidly interpreted truths. Where one has in power an ideology that makes such a claim, whether it is religious or secular, it will tolerate no resistance. Ideologies that express themselves in this way are inherently authoritarian. Under the circumstances, although Iranian Islamic society may evolve over time, it is unlikely that it will ever become democratic in a Western sense, nor will it be as sensitive to individual rights as are societies not guided by rigid, truth-claiming ideologies.

NOTES

1. See Mohsen M. Milani, *The Making of Iran's Islamic Revolution: From Monarchy to Islamic Republic* (Boulder, Colo.: Westview Press, 1994), 115.
2. Ibid., pp. 198ff.

4

Nonrevolutionary Islamic Fundamentalism in Power: The Case of Saudi Arabia

In Iran, an Islamic state was established as the result of a religiously inspired revolution against a basically secular government. Elsewhere, as in Sudan and Pakistan, Islamic fundamentalists seized control of the state in military coups. Yet another means whereby Islamic forces have gained power is through the intertribal competition that has made up much of the history of Arabia, the very birthplace of Islam. Here, in what today is known as Saudi Arabia, we find the oldest established Islamic state. Saudi Arabia is also the most important Islamic country for the United States, and the West in general, because of its immense oil resources.

HISTORICAL BACKGROUND

Saudi Arabia occupies about four-fifths of the Arabian peninsula, the land from which the Arabs originated. Bounded on the west by the Red Sea and on the east by the Persian (or for some it is better known as the Arabian) Gulf, today it is populated by about 15 million people. All of its permanent population is Muslim, and within its confines lay the two holiest cities of the Muslim world, Mecca and Medina.

Until the twentieth century, the population was mostly desert nomads (or Bedouin) and small village and town folk who lived in a harsh desert environment. The desert and, after the year 800, the Islamic religion largely shaped the people's character. As befits those who were the first to convert to Islam, the Arabians became very devout Muslims. Even today, the Saudi Arabians follow a particularly austere brand of Islam known in the West as Wahhabism. The origins of this sect are intimately bound up with the origins of the Saudi state, producing in Arabia the closest thing to an official brand of Sunni fundamentalism.

The story of Saudi Arabia and its fundamentalist Islamic outlook begins in 1744 when an alliance was struck between a local, politically ambitious Arabian prince, Muhammad ibn Saud of Diriyah (a town in the Najd, a central region of the Arabian interior), and a crusading religious reformer, Muhammad ibn abd al-Wahhab. Al-Wahhab preached a return to the basic, pure elements of Islam as they were thought to have been practiced in the days of the prophet Muhammad. In particular, he sought to strip away all the nonoriginal rituals and practices that had accrued to the faith over its years of expansion. In this effort, al-Wahhab and his followers, known as Wahhabis, saw themselves as "unitarians" (or mowahhidin, the term they use to refer to their brand of Islam)—that is, those who stand for the "unity of God." By this, they mean that there is but one God, and people must direct their worship exclusively to that single deity.

In the eighteenth and nineteenth centuries, this outlook caused the Wahhabis to take violent exception to Sufi and Shi'ite practices.[1] These practices included the visiting and praying at tombs and shrines of Shi'ite martyrs or Sufi saints. For the Wahhabis, this sort of practice violated the strict monotheistic nature of Islam and so constituted heresy. This, in turn, justified a crusade like war in the name of restoring the true faith against those who pursued such practices.

The alliance with ibn Saud put the military force of an ambitious tribal chief at the disposal of an equally ambitious and aggressive religious reformer. The union founded a movement that would eventually conquer a good part of the Arabian peninsula. The Wahhabis occupied Mecca and Medina in 1802 and proceeded to destroy the shrines and tombs of the two holy cities (including the tomb of Muhammad) as well as massacring a good number of the residents as idolators. They also raided northward into Syria and Iraq, destroying the Shi'ite shrines in the holy city of Karbala. This act provides one of the historical roots of a Saudi-Iranian hostility that lasts to this day.

Wahhabi violence sent shock waves through the Muslim world and drew the attention of the Ottoman authorities. At this time, Arabia was at least nominally part of the Ottoman Empire. In a campaign that lasted from 1819 to 1822, Egyptian forces acting in the name of the Ottoman Sultan, and armed with gunpowder weapons, put down the Wahhabi uprising. They leveled Diriyah and drove the Saud clan into exile.

In the early twentieth century one of the heads of the Saud clan, Abd al-Aziz ibn Saud (1879–1953), reasserted the family's claim to power in Arabia. Through the years the Sauds had never ceased to champion the Wahhabi brand of Islam, and so when ibn Saud slowly won back control of much of the peninsula (he reconquered the Najd by 1906 and the Hijaz, or western coastal area, by 1925), Wahhabism reasserted itself with him. By 1932 the territory that now constitutes Saudi Arabia had been consolidated, and a central government, in the form of a monarchy controlled by the Saud clan, imposed order upon the disparate tribes of the region. In the process, Islamic symbolism was skillfully used to create a united community of believers. The Shariah became the basic law of the land. The flag adopted by the new state testifies to the successful combination of religion and politics. It has the Muslim profession of faith written across it along with two crossed swords representing the allied strength of the houses of Saud and Wahhab.

While ibn Saud was a devout Muslim of Wahhabi persuasion, he was also a pragmatic political strategist. In the 1920s and 1930s he understood the real power of the European imperialists and the modern technological forces they controlled. Unlike some Islamic fundamentalists who reject intercourse with the West, ibn Saud came to an understanding with the British and allowed them to mediate frontier treaties between his own regime and those on his borders. Secure from external threat, the Saud family proceeded to suppress all intertribal feuding and banditry and made trade and pilgrimage routes safe. The family also encouraged a slow and careful movement in the direction of utilizing scientific and technological know-how. The Saud clan leaders realized that only by a process of gradual modernization could the monarchy satisfy the future economic needs of the population and secure the wealth that would assure its ability to maintain power.

This process of gradual modernization would prove one of the regime's most difficult challenges. Inventions taken for granted in the West—such as telephones, telegraphs, automobiles, and televisions—aroused considerable fear and resentment among conservative Arabians. They rightfully feared that the modernization of their world would destroy their traditional way of life. So we have in Arabia a classic case of one world, pietistic and devoted to tradition, being melded with another world that is modern and technology based. The Saudi monarchy has been remarkably successful in finessing the resulting tensions, in part by using religious precedent to rationalize selective change.

A good example of the Saudi method can be seen in the development of oil reserves in eastern Saudi Arabia. Oil provided the source of Saudi wealth and prosperity. In 1933 ibn Saud signed a sixty-year concession with the Standard Oil Company to search for oil in Saudi territory. In 1934 the Arabian American Oil Company (ARAMCO) was created. At first its arrangement with the Saudis involved a modest yearly royalty payment, but when the extent of Arabia's oil wealth was realized, the monarchy successfully secured, in the 1940s, a 50–50 profit-sharing arrangement. Today, the Saudis effectively control ARAMCO.

The Saud family quickly took a liking to the Americans who were involved with ARAMCO because, unlike some of the representatives of other Western powers, they appeared only to be concerned with oil and not with the new country's internal affairs. By the end of the 1930s, commercial quantities of oil were discovered in the Kingdom and the Americans moved in to help extract it. The appearance of many Western oil technicians and their alien equipment in Arabia soon brought resistance from traditionalists who accused the King of importing unbelievers into their land and aiding non-Muslims in making a profit from Muslim resources. In 1944 ibn Saud answered the charges before a panel of ulama at the royal court in Riyadh. Standing before them, he declared that, "I am now not the King, but only a Muslim, like you a servant of the Prophet . . . appealing for judgment to the ulama, the judges of the Islamic law which binds us both equally." Ibn Saud then cited Islamic tradition in the form of stories of how the prophet Muhammad himself had employed non-Muslims. "Am I right or wrong? . . . Am I breaking the Shariah law, therefore, when I follow the footsteps of the Prophet, and employ foreign experts to work for me? The Americans at El Kharj, and the other foreigners who operate machines are brought here . . . to increase the material resources . . . placed by Allah beneath our land and intended for our use. In doing so, am I violating any Muslim law?" The ulama who sat in judgment found that ibn Saud was in compliance with the law.[2]

Ibn Saud's willingness to "employ foreign experts" allowed Saudi Arabia to amass immense wealth. And with it the country was transformed from a poor land (by modern standards) to one of great prosperity. Over time, economic development and selective modernization made possible decent housing, education, and health care for nearly all the kingdom's citizens. Standards of living for most Saudis rose quite high, and a general contentment set in. Yet, as noted, the on-going effort to reconcile modernity and tradition did not satisfy everyone. The approach taken by the royal family to modernity and the West has met with persistent criticism from a small number of religious opponents who feel it is evidence of the House of Saud's betrayal of Islam.

THE NATURE OF SAUDI RULE

The Saud family chose to rule Arabia through a monarchical form of government, with the King being informally elected by a council of royal princes. While monarchy is not religiously sanctioned in Islam (and it will be remembered that, in the case of Iran, the Islamic fundamentalists specifically disowned monarchy in their attack on the Shah), there is historical precedent for it. The Abbasid Caliphate in particular was a form of monarchy.

The royal family asserts that theirs is not an "absolute monarchy," for the royal house is as subject to Shariah law as all other citizens. Thus, at least in theory, the royal family must live and rule according to Islamic law. If any Saud family member significantly breaches the law, he will be dismissed from his government post or otherwise punished. Yet this is true only in a qualified way. So much wealth has been amassed by the roughly 4,000 princes of the Saud clan that, human nature being what it is, a certain amount of corruption, immorality, and ostentatious living is an on-going problem. And it is questionable whether a Saudi prince is subject to the same punishments as an ordinary citizen (though periodically examples are made of family members caught breaking the law). Thus, the behavior of the Saud family also provides potential grist for the mill of religious opponents to Saudi rule.

Gross misbehavior that politically threatens the monarchy is always dealt with, however. Witness the case of Saud ibn Abd al-Aziz, son of ibn Saud and king from 1953 to 1964. Overly extravagant in his lifestyle, ibn Abd-al-Aziz doubly angered the royal family by being an incompetent administrator who jeopardized the Kingdom's relationship with ARAMCO. He was deposed by a council of senior princes who were careful to underpin their decision with a religious ruling from the ulama sanctioning the transfer of power to his brother Faisal.

Thus it is that all official actions of the monarchy from the employment of foreigners to the deposing of a king are justified by religion. Indeed, religion pervades every aspect of Saudi life, and the Saudi monarchy has turned Islamic "purity" to good political use. Saudi Arabia has no written constitution, no legislature, and no political parties. The Saud royal clan sees no need for them for, as King Faisal explained in 1963, "What does a man aspire to? He wants 'good.' It is there in the Islamic Shariah. He wants security. It is there also. Man wants freedom. It is there. He wants remedy. It is there. He wants propagation of science. It is there. Everything is there, inscribed in the Islamic Shariah."[3]

If the Shariah allows the royal family an excuse not to have a constitution or legislature, it does tie them to the traditional interpreters of Islamic law, the ulama. Thus, the religious establishment has come to play a large public role in the country and has cast itself as the guardian of the Islamic character of state and society. As heirs of the Wahhabi legacy, it also sees itself in an on-going alliance with the Saudi monarchy. This alliance is reinforced by the ulama's status as well-paid public employees functioning as official advisers to the King, educators, administrators of mosques and other social and welfare agencies, and judges (all personal and criminal law cases are handled by religious courts). The Sauds have paid particular deference to the al-Shaykh family, the descendants of ibn abd al-Wahhab. Members of this family usually hold three or four seats in the Saudi cabinet. As well, the Saud clan has made it a practice to intermarry with the al-Shaykh family, thus creating an ever closer alliance. The differences that do exist between the royal family and the religious establishment come over questions of the type and pace of policies dealing with modernization. Even here, the monarchy is careful to put its arguments and decrees in terms of Islamic precedent. In this way, the King is usually able to convince most of the important ulama to accept his decisions.

Issues of modernization make clear that Shariah law cannot cover all the circumstances of contemporary life. In those areas where additional law and regulation are needed, the King and his council of ministers, after consultation with the ulama, lay these down by royal decree. The King's ability to act in this fashion also derives from Islamic precedent, for it is generally recognized that in cases where the Quran and Shariah law do not cover a situation, the ruler (or the judge in his court) may use such techniques as analogy, individual reasoning, or an appeal to public welfare to create new law. In this way, Saudi commercial law has been modernized to conform with international standards. The nation's labor relations acts, civil service codes, and social insurance laws also have been fashioned by royal decree, as has the bureaucracy, which dates only from the 1950s. For matters that relate to royal decrees or non-Shariah areas of law, there are special Mazalim, or Complaint Courts, presided over by non-ulama judges.

One can contrast this structure with that of Iran. While in both countries an ideologically autocratic mindset does not allow for any challenge to the Islamic basis of the state, and an executive with dictatorial powers rules, Iran has an active parliament to create new law. It is an arena of lively debate, and one in which the government is subject to criticism. No such institution exists in Saudi Arabia, and all new law comes from the King.

One institution that operates in both Saudi Arabia and Iran, and that reflects the hold tradition still has on issues of personal conduct, is the "morals" or "religious" police. In Saudi Arabia this agency, created as early as 1929, is called "The Organization for the Enforcing of Good and the Forbidding of Evil." The "morals" police generally supervise the public behavior of both citizens and visitors. Thus, for example, they assure that people dress modestly when in public, that there is no public consumption of alcohol, that shops close at the times of prayer, and that the public adheres to the Ramadan fast.

As in Iran, the issue of public behavior in Saudi Arabia has largely affected women. And here too we find similarities and differences between the two countries. In both lands, the veil is mandatory for women appearing in public. In Iran, women find it easier to travel alone or in groups than in Saudi Arabia where they must often be accompanied by men. In Saudi Arabia, women are forbidden to drive automobiles. In both countries, there are limited though growing facilities for female education. In the case of Saudi Arabia, this is in large part due to the efforts of Iffat al Thunayan, the wife of the late King Faisal. Finally, in Saudi Arabia, women have no public life. In Iran, while that life is certainly limited when judged by Western standards, women do have the right to vote and can hold elected office. No such rights exist for them in Saudia Arabia.

SAUDI FOREIGN POLICY

Saudi Arabia's Islamic fundamentalism is also evident in its foreign policy. This is so despite its close relationship with the United States, which is largely a function of long-standing economic convenience for both powers rather than a function of ideological compatibility.

The Saud royal house considers itself the natural leader of the Islamic world. They claim such authority in part because they see their Wahhabi sect as the purest expression of Islam, and also because they possess and supervise the holy cities of Mecca and Medina.

Because of the traditionalist, conservative, and purist nature of Wahhabism, as well as its function as the basis of Saudi rule, Saudi Kings have opposed other more secular Arab movements, including the "Arab socialist" government of Gamal Abdel Nasser in Egypt and the secular Arab regimes of Hafez Assad in Syria and Saddam Hussein in Iraq. The fact that the United States also has had its problems with many of these regimes has enhanced the close American relationship with the Saudis, as did the Saudis' dislike for the "atheist" Soviet Union. The fact that the Saudis do not have good relations with the Iranians, due to the ancient Wahhabi–Shi'ite animosity and, more recently, Iran's antimonarchical stand, also endears them to the United States. On the other hand, the Saudis see Israel as their enemy. But with so many other reasons for maintaining good relations, both the United States and Saudi Arabia normally play down this point of disagreement.

Because of Saudi Arabia's economic importance (that is, its oil production), the United States also has turned a blind eye to Saudi activities which, when carried out by a country like Iran, arouse suspicion and criticism. To counter the more secular political and cultural trends in the Muslim world, the Saudis have promoted Islamic fundamentalism. They have created and financially sponsored a large number of pan-Islamist associations, such as the Organization of the Islamic Conference, which seeks to coordinate the activities and efforts of Islamic-oriented governments. The Saudis' objective in all this, as one scholar has put it, is "the Islamization of . . . governments and societies and the support of Muslim organizations such as the Muslim Brotherhood in Egypt."[4] Of course, the Iranians, though otherwise in competition with the Saudis, seek the same end.

INTERNAL DISSENT

As the Iranian fundamentalist regime appeals to Shi'ite history and tradition, so the Kings of the House of Saud use the Wahhabi version of Sunni Islam as a basis for their claim to power. However, as John Esposito has observed, "the appeal to Islam can be a two-edged sword."[5] This is because the claim to be the defender, and indeed almost the personification of contemporary Islam, creates a standard by which one's critics can call one to account.

In the case of Saudi Arabia, there have been several violent expressions of this sort of criticism. One famous incident took place in November 1979 when Islamic militants, one of whom claimed to be the Mahdi (the "rightly guided one," as noted earlier, who would come to prepare the way for the Day of Judgment), seized the Grand Mosque in Mecca. They denounced the Saudi monarchy for "impiety" (for example, corruption and a too materialistic lifestyle) as well as its various modernization schemes, which allegedly undermine the Islamic way of life. The ulama were also denounced for cooperating with the government. More recently, the activities of Osama bin Laden have drawn attention to dissent against the Saudi regime and its alliance with the United States. Bin Laden, born in Saudi Arabia but stripped of his citizenship in 1994, has denounced the Saudi government for allowing American troops (that is non-Muslim soldiers) to remain in the "holy land" of Arabia after the end of the Gulf War. This animosity took deadly form in 1996 with attacks on U.S. troops stationed in the Kingdom. The investigations into these attacks revealed vast cultural and political differences between Saudi and American ways of carrying out policies and procedures. In the United States, these and subsequent events have generated criticism and questions in Congress about the wisdom of keeping troops in that country.

On a less spectacular level, there has been relatively consistent criticism of the "un-Islamic" behavior of parts of the royal family. Luxurious living, corrupt business practices, siphoning off public funds for private use, drinking, and gambling are among the charges critics regularly level against them. The implication of these charges is that a number of Saudi princes are hypocrites, who claim to be good Muslims but do not live as such. As a consequence, there is a more or less permanent, though small, underground opposition of Islamic reformers in Saudi Arabia.

To date, the royal family has been able to handle all of this opposition. The high standards of living of the general population and the personal piety of at least some members of the royal family usually combine to isolate the critics. But the tensions brought by wealth and modern ways, an increasingly unpopular alliance with the United States, and the lack of public participation in the exercise of power, makes the regime vulnerable, particularly in times of crisis. At such times, there usually arises a demand for some modicum of "consultation" (shura) in the form of an advisory council to aid the monarchy in running the government. An example of this occurred after the Persian Gulf war when both nonreligious and religious groups in the country petitioned the King for the creation of such a council. In response, King Fahd, in 1992, issued by royal decree the Law of the Consultative Council, which established an assembly of some sixty appointed members to advise the King on issues the government submitted to it. Membership in the Council is limited to men over the age of thirty who have sworn allegiance to "the faith, the king, and the country." How significant this reform really is remains open to question; it certainly has not removed the issue of whether the monarchy is "Islamic enough" for its critics. Nonetheless, no sign of overwhelming or dangerous levels of opposition in Saudi Arabia has yet arisen, and the monarchy's rule appears secure for the immediate future.

SAUDI ARABIA, IRAN, AND THE UNITED STATES

Both Saudi Arabia and Iran are Muslim fundamentalist states. Both use the Quran and Shariah as their basic law. Both demand public adherence to a code of Islamic behavior and morals. And both seek to encourage the adoption of Islamic fundamentalist models of governance outside their borders. They also both support an array of Muslim social, cultural, and political organizations in other countries that promote the spread of Islam.

On the other hand, there are many differences between Saudi Arabia and Iran. Saudi Arabia is a monarchy without representative institutions. Iran, though ideologically authoritarian and possessing the dictatorial office of jurisprudent, is a republic with a parliament and an electoral process. Saudi Arabia strictly forbids female participation in the public realm, whereas Iran leaves some space for women in this regard.

Given these comparisons, it would seem that, in terms of institutions and their potential for "democratic evolution," the Islamic Republic in Iran has much more to recommend it to the West than does Saudi Arabia. Why then, one might ask, is the United States so much more hostile to Iran than to Saudi Arabia? The answer gives the lie to the charge that it is Iran's Islamic fundamentalism alone that is the basis of hostility. If this were true, there should be equal or greater American animosity toward Saudi Arabia. Instead, there is, in that case, a long history of friendship.

The United States' hostility to Iran and friendship for Saudi Arabia have much more to do with history, foreign policy orientation, and economic interest than with religion. For decades, the United States supported the Shah's monarchy in Iran and continued to do so even after it was clear that it was unpopular, corrupt, and oppressive. When the Shah was overthrown, the fundamentalists who took power identified the United States with the deposed government. The new Iranian government's predictable hostility made difficult any reconciliation between the two powers and fueled continued American animosity. That American politicians and media often attribute all this only to Muslim religious fanaticism is a misleading interpretation that fails to take into account the nature of U.S. support for the Shah.

On the other hand, American relations with Saudi Arabia have been based on a decades-old understanding of mutual economic and security interests. Both countries are vital to each other's economic prosperity, and heavy Saudi investment in Western economies has only increased this fact. The Saudis also have recognized the need for American military support. The Iraqi invasion of Kuwait in 1990 and the American-led coalition that in 1991 defeated the Iraqis and secured the Saudi borders greatly reinforced the growing security relationship of the two nations. Because the

Saudi monarchy has clearly understood the importance of its relationship with the United States, except for the brief oil boycott of the early 1970s, it has done nothing to directly challenge U.S. economic interests. Indeed, Saudi weapons purchases, to the amount of $40 billion over the past 12 years, have helped keep the American arms industry profitable. The United States, in its turn, perceives the Saudi royal house as friendly, stable, and cooperative, and so its Islamic conservatism is most often irrelevant. Indeed, to the extent that it encourages the Saudis to be antirevolutionary, it is deemed an asset.

The case of Saudi Arabia shows that Islamic fundamentalism as a generic expression of Islam is not necessarily at odds with Western, or American, interests. It only comes into play as a point of contention when other political or economic reasons for hostility exist. At that stage, Islamic fundamentalism becomes an ideological factor focusing the attention of those on both sides who believe that there must be an incompatibility of interests between the West and the Muslim world.

NOTES

1. Sufism is a populist brand of Islam that often integrates both orthodox practices and popular beliefs and rituals. The tombs of Sufi holy men and women, particularly those who have founded Sufi orders, are often visited by those seeking cures or the answer to prayers. Shi'ite practice includes the veneration of martyrs such as Ali's son Husayn.

2. Cited in John L. Esposito, *Islam and Politics* (Syracuse, N.Y.: Syracuse University Press, 1991), p. 107.

3. Ibid., p. 105.

4. Ibid., p. 110.

5. Ibid., p. 111.

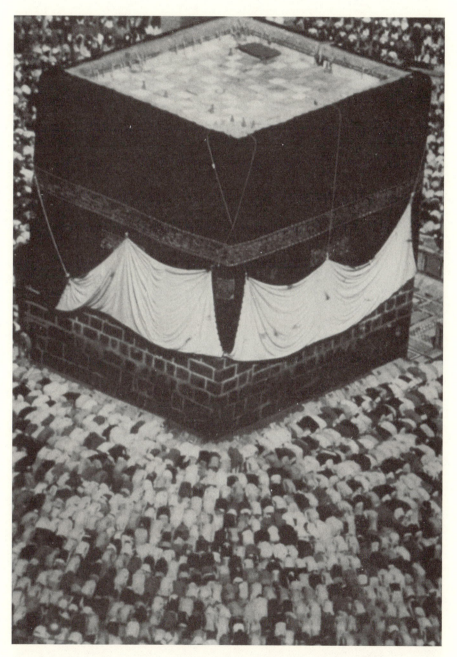

The Kabah at Mecca surrounded by praying worshippers. The Kabah, thought to have been originally erected by Abraham and Ishmael for the worship of Allah or God, now constitutes the holiest site of the Islamic religion. Photo by S.M. Amin. Used by permission of Aramco World.

Western cultural influence in the Muslim world is a major issue for Islamic fundamentalists. Here movie billboards with Western-inspired motifs are found on an Egyptian street. Photo by Jacques Pavlovsky. Used by permission of Sygma Photo News.

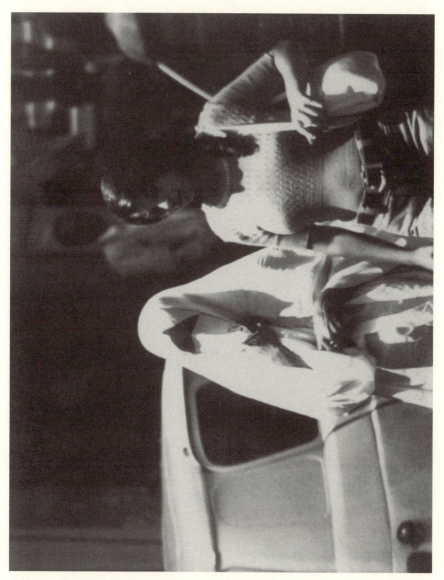

The cultural contrasts of today's Middle East are found in this picture of two Algerian women. Photo by Mokhless al-Hariri. Library of Congress, 1980.

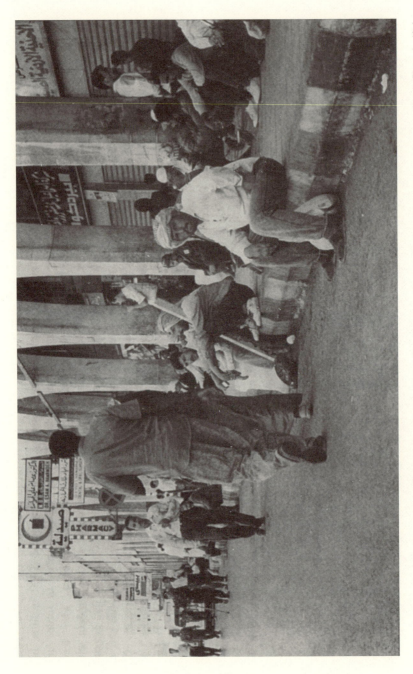

High unemployment makes the fundamentalist call for an Islamic state more popular. Here unemployed Jordanian workers are shown. Photo by Kirk Albrecht.

Muslims who support fundamentalist causes can be found all over the world. Here Iranian students in the United States demonstrate in support of the 1979 Iranian Revolution. Library of Congress, U.S. News and World Report Collection (MST).

Throughout the Middle East, the United States is identified as the supporter and protector of Israel. Therefore, anger over Israeli policies toward the Palestinians also becomes anger at the United States. Here anti-Israel demonstrators burn both Israeli and American flags. ©Reuters NewMedia Inc./CORBIS.

It is not only men who are active supporters of Islamic fundamentalist causes. Here armed women demonstrate their support of Islamic rule in Iran as part of a "Woman's Day" celebration. Photo by Christine Spengler. Used by permission of Sygma Photo News.

On September 11, 2001 Islamic fundamentalist extremists piloted two hijacked airliners into the World Trade Center towers in New York City. As described later in communications from Osama bin Laden, these attacks were in response to American policies in Saudi Arabia, Iraq, and Palestine. ©AFP/CORBIS.

American citizens are not the only ones who suffer the death and destruction that comes from terrorist acts. Israeli citizens have suffered from such acts, but Palestinians have also suffered terrorism at the hands of the Israelis. Here a Palestinian schoolboy sends a message that terrorism is a common enemy. Reuters/Nayef Hashlamoun

FBI TEN MOST WANTED FUGITIVE

MURDER OF U.S. NATIONALS OUTSIDE THE UNITED STATES;
CONSPIRACY TO MURDER U.S. NATIONALS OUTSIDE THE UNITED STATES;
ATTACK ON A FEDERAL FACILITY RESULTING IN DEATH

USAMA BIN LADEN

Date of Photograph Unknown

Aliases: Usama Bin Muhammad Bin Ladin, Shaykh Usama Bin Ladin, the Prince, the Emir, Abu Abdallah, Mujahid Shaykh, Hajj, the Director

DESCRIPTION

Date of Birth:	1957	**Hair:**	Brown
Place of Birth:	Saudi Arabia	**Eyes:**	Brown
Height:	6' 4" to 6' 6"	**Complexion:**	Olive
Weight:	Approximately 160 pounds	**Sex:**	Male
Build:	Thin	**Nationality:**	Saudi Arabian
Occupation:	Unknown		
Remarks:	Bin Laden is the leader of a terrorist organization known as Al-Qaeda, "The Base." He is left-handed and walks with a cane.		

CAUTION

USAMA BIN LADEN IS WANTED IN CONNECTION WITH THE AUGUST 7, 1998, BOMBINGS OF THE UNITED STATES EMBASSIES IN DAR ES SALAAM, TANZANIA, AND NAIROBI, KENYA. THESE ATTACKS KILLED OVER 200 PEOPLE. IN ADDITION, BIN LADEN IS A SUSPECT IN OTHER TERRORIST ATTACKS THROUGHOUT THE WORLD.

IF YOU HAVE ANY INFORMATION CONCERNING THIS PERSON, PLEASE CONTACT YOUR
LOCAL FBI OFFICE OR THE NEAREST U.S. EMBASSY OR CONSULATE.

REWARD

The Rewards For Justice Program, United States Department of State, is offering a reward of up to $25 million for information leading directly to the apprehension or conviction of Usama Bin Laden. An additional $2 million is being offered through a program developed and funded by the Airline Pilots Association and the Air Transport Association.

www.fbi.gov

June 1999
Poster Revised November 2001

Osama bin Laden has now been designated the West's most dangerous terrorist enemy. This status is reflected in the wanted poster issued for bin Laden by the U.S. government.

5

Western Perceptions of Islamic Fundamentalism

HISTORICAL ROOTS

Western perceptions of Islam and the concerns that arise from them are rooted in a long period of Judeo-Christian and Muslim historical interaction. A brief description of that history will help provide answers to some important questions. How have Western nations such as the United States reacted to Islamic fundamentalist movements? What particular concerns have been expressed thereby? Are all Westerners of one mind in their reaction to Islamic fundamentalism?

Relations between the Judeo-Christian world (or what is now popularly termed "the West") and the Islamic world (popularly thought of as part of "the East") have had a long and often confrontational history. From the time of the prophet Muhammad (570–632), the religions of these two civilizations have come into conflict, despite the fact that Muhammad conceived of Islam as heir to the two great monotheistic faiths, Judaism and Christianity. However, he considered Islam not only as an heir, but also as a culmination and fulfillment of those faiths. Thus the Quran did not just stand in the line of the Old and New Testaments, but being God's final revelation, it also adjusted and "corrected" the supposed erroneous interpretations and uses Christians and Jews had made of them. Given that

Christians and Jews refused to accept Muhammad as the final prophet (the "seal of prophecy") and the Quran as God's final revelation, a great rivalry was bound to develop. And, in an age that knew no boundaries between religion, politics, and culture, religious rivalry inevitably led to a political and cultural clash as well.

This rivalry occurred with the earliest contact of the religions. Friction developed between Muhammad and the Jews of Medina in the 620s, when the Jews refused to accept Muhammad's status as prophet. Later, under the second Caliph, Umar (ruled 633–644), all Arabia was declared a Muslim sacred land and Jewish and Christian tribes were expelled. Arab expansion beyond Arabia brought the early Muslims into direct military confrontation with the major Christian power of the day, the Byzantine Empire.

The established Eastern and Western Christian churches of the time also contributed to this confrontational beginning by their uniformly negative view of Islam. Their opposition is not surprising, for the very success of Islam as it spread out of Arabia challenged Christian interests and Christianity's own expansionist missionary program. Thus, despite the relatively benign Muslim treatment of Christians and Jews in conquered lands, and the fact that the Muslims did not force conversions, Westerners viewed Islam as the arch-enemy of the Christian faith. Muhammad was variously pictured as an immoral fraud or the anti-Christ, and was even rumored to be a renegade Christian. Ideological castigation supported military confrontation, and both set the tone for the subsequent centuries of rivalry.

From the ninth into the sixteenth centuries, the Islamic world held the upper hand in this rivalry. Expanding Arab forces conquered the southern tier of the Byzantine Empire, including North Africa. Europe proper was invaded through Spain. Later, Muslim Turkish armies conquered the rest of the Byzantine lands and penetrated eastern Europe through the Balkans. Twice, Muslim armies laid siege to the city of Vienna.

In the West, the original denigration of Islam and Muhammad evolved into a popular view suggesting that all progress and community development ceased wherever Muslims ruled Christians. Nationalism, which in the Western mind became associated with the idea of progress in the late eighteenth and nineteenth centuries, was also denied fellow Christians in Muslim-ruled Greece, Serbia, and other Balkan lands (then part of the Ottoman Empire). Westerners regarded Muslim rule in the Balkans as a barbaric and backward affair—an act of Muslim imperialism over European and Christian peoples.

This view of Muslim rule, as somehow illegitimately extending into what are really Christian lands, was even projected into the heartland of the Middle East. Palestine generally, and the holy city of Jerusalem in particular, both of which had been under Muslim rule since the ninth century, had never ceased to be popularly perceived in the West as Judeo-Christian places. The West gave little thought to the area's historical and religious importance to Muslims. Rival claims to this region were first contested in the era of the Crusades (tenth to thirteenth centuries), when Christian armies invaded the area with murderous violence. The result was to ingrain in the Muslim psyche an image of the West as not only culturally backward (an image long held by this time) but aggressive and barbaric in every other way as well. Thus, the two sides came to hold a deep mutual dislike of each other, laced with bitterness and mistrust. Among some, these feelings persist to this day.

The balance of power between the Christian West and the Muslim East gradually shifted. Muslims were pushed out of Spain in the fifteenth century. The Ottoman Empire was slowly forced to retreat from southeast Europe in the seventeenth and eighteenth centuries. Eventually, Muslim imperialism in Christian Europe gave way to European imperialism in the Muslim Middle East. Nonetheless, the fact that Western views of Islam are rooted in a past where Muslim power was seen as a strategic threat has had its influence on the present outlook. It has affected Western interpretations of the Arab-Israeli wars, the threat of oil embargoes, the Iranian hostage crisis, the media images of rulers such as Saddam Hussein and the Ayatollah Khomeini, and most recently the threat represented by Al-Qaeda. Deeply embedded in the Christian psyche, this age-old feeling of hostility helps to explain the infusion of religious feeling into conflicts that have erupted in the borderlands between the two civilizations (such as in Bosnia), as well as the tendency in the West to think of international terrorism as coming first and foremost from the Middle East.

Many Muslims now reciprocate by drawing their images of the West not only from the Crusades, but also from the more recent period of Western colonial occupation that spanned the nineteenth and first half of the twentieth centuries. It is with this period of Western aggression that most Muslims associate the formation of the state of Israel. To this can be added the resentment felt over postcolonial Western economic and cultural domination, as well as American support for many of the region's authoritarian regimes. Then there are other questionable Western actions such as the devastating Iraqi sanctions that have taken thousands of lives. The negative symbols inherent in the historical consciousness of both the Christian West and Muslim East have intermingled and now reinforce each other. The result is mutual suspicion and conflict, the bloodiest examples of which are the Arab-Israeli wars, the Persian Gulf war, and the September 11, 2001 attacks on the World Trade Center and Pentagon.

SOME MAIN ISSUES

Three main issues—violence (particularly in the form of terrorism), democracy, and women's rights—dominate Western concerns about Islamic fundamentalism. Democracy and women's rights have become important aspects of an expanding Western culture. But today the Islamic religion is also resurgent and expanding. The Islamic resurgence has led to a sense of fear and cultural incompatibility on the part of both Westerners and Muslims. For Islamic fundamentalists, the advocacy of Western forms of governance and lifestyle for the Muslim world seems proof of the West's unwillingness to accept Islamic culture as a legitimate, if different, way of life. Not surprisingly, resistance to the Westernization of Muslim society has sometimes led to violence as in Iran. Some Westerners, in turn, have interpreted this resistance not as an act of cultural self-defense, but rather as an attack on Western civilization. In this chapter we will take up the issues of democracy and women's rights. The following chapter will be devoted to the question of violence and terrorism.

Islam and Democracy

Distorted perception seems to preclude any possibility of finding shared values. For just as some see the Muslim world as perpetually threatening and violent, so they also see it as perpetually repressive and undemocratic. Indeed, a widespread assumption persists in the American mind that Islam is inherently antidemocratic and that Islamic countries are incapable of evolving in a democratic direction. The noted historian Bernard Lewis has observed that

Liberal democracy . . . is in its origins a product of the West—shaped by thousands of years of European history. . . . It remains to be seen whether such a system, transplanted and adopted in another culture, can long survive. . . . No one, least of all the Islamic fundamentalists themselves, will dispute that their creed and political program are not compatible with liberal democracy.[1]

Many Western observers see this to be the case because some militant Islamic leaders and regimes have defined the rights of women, those citizens who do not believe in a religiously based state, as well as ethnic and religious minority groups, in a more restrictive manner than occurs in liberal Western democracies. Religion, like secular ideologies, can be a vehicle for enforcing conformity when taken to the extreme.

However, not all Western experts agree that Islam inevitably leads to repressive politics and social policies. John Esposito and John Voll, both

respected scholars and experts on Islam, have observed that Muslim thinking on the question of democracy is not uniformly negative. They point
out that several aspects of the Islamic tradition lend themselves to the
evolution of democratic institutions:

Several Islamic concepts have a key role in the development of Islamic democracy: consultation (shura), consensus (ijma), and independent interpretive judgment (ijtihad). These terms have not always been identified with democratic
institutions, and even today have a variety of usages. Nonetheless, like reinterpreted concepts such as citizen and parliament in the Western tradition, they have
become crucial concepts for the articulation of Islamic democracy.[2]

There are examples of these concepts growing into potentially viable
democratic institutions. We have seen that a popularly elected parliament
now exists in Iran. Another example that might speak in favor of Esposito
and Voll's position is the tentative steps being taken toward greater citizen
participation in the political affairs of the small Gulf emirate of Qatar. In
Qatar elections have been held for a Municipal Council to advise the
Minister of Municipal Affairs and Agriculture on policies having to do
with food and public hygiene. What is significant about this is that the
election was based on universal suffrage, and women not only voted but
also stood for office. There are also plans for an elected parliament and a
written constitution.

Also in Qatar we find the Arab Middle East's most successful experiment in the exercise of free speech. The satellite TV station Al-Jezeera,
begun in 1997, has attracted millions of viewers across the region and the
world. Its journalists, many of whom once worked for the BBC's Arab
service, are thoroughly professional, and its equipment is state of the art.
Many of the region's dictators, from Egypt's Mubarak to the Saudi monarch, have complained about Al-Jezeera because equal time is given to
critics as well as government representatives. Such complaints are examples of some Arabs' insensitivity to freedom of the press. However, the
U. S. government has acted in a similarly hostile fashion toward the station.
During America's bombing of Afghanistan, Al-Jezeera televised images
of civilian damage and casualties, as well as the periodic speeches of
Osama bin Laden. The fact that it was also televising interviews with
American officials such as Defense Secretary Donald Rumsfeld did not
prevent the U.S. government from filing an official protest about Al-
Jezeera coverage with the Qatar government. In the end, the Americans
bombed and destroyed Al-Jezeera's television facilities in Kabul, Afghanistan.

Such behavior is seen as hypocritical in the Middle East and makes it more difficult for the United States to encourage Islamic countries and movements to nurture young, democratically oriented experiments such as Al-Jezeera. Yet it would seem to be in the interests of Western countries to see freedom of the press and other potentially democratic concepts such as those mentioned by Esposito and Voll as worthy of support. However, in the end, political development in the Middle East will flow from the region's history. Whatever direction government in the Muslim world takes, it will inevitably be influenced by two aspects of the region's history, neither of which will particularly encourage the type of liberalism and pluralism that characterizes Western democracy. One aspect is certain to be the religiously inspired culture of Islam. As Islamic fundamentalism testifies, Muslims can read the Quran in such a way as to see themselves called upon to be politically aware and active. It also can be read creatively in such a way as to empower the average citizen. But even an Islamic government that allows its people to express themselves politically will hardly turn out an exact replica of any of the Western varieties of liberal democracy. This is so if for no other reason than the fact that Western democracy is based on the separation of church and state.

The other aspect of history that is likely to influence government in the Muslim world is the colonialist experience. Much of the Muslim experience with the West has not been one of receiving lessons in democratic rule. Western political intervention within the Muslim world was an exercise in imperialism. The parliaments and assemblies, along with their accompanying electoral laws, that the Western powers introduced into places like Egypt or Syria were seen by the indigenous subject peoples as facades behind which the Europeans exercised ultimate control. Thus, Muslims need not only to restructure the concept of democracy to fit their own traditions, but also to overcome a Western-taught message that says democracy is just a sham—something to be manipulated by a behind-the-scenes source of real, authoritarian power.

Since the end of World War II, the colonialist legacy has strongly influenced political institution building in the Middle East. The combination of that legacy with the patriarchal and autocratic features of Middle Eastern culture has created an environment that favors authoritarianism rather than democracy. Thus, the forms of rule that have dominated the political scene in Muslim lands for the last fifty years have been principally secular, autocratic, and dictatorial. Many of these, in turn, are now actively supported by Western powers such as the United States. Many people of the region have come to see these dictatorships as political as well as economic and social failures. In reaction, some are turning to the Islamic aspect of their history in hopes of finding a more successful formula for government—a government in tune with what they consider a more traditionally authentic way of life. Islamic fundamentalism is an expression of this trend. Therefore, for the indefinite future, whatever new political forms do come to the fore are likely to possess Islamic characteristics.

What sort of characteristics might an observer look for? A basic one relates to the question of sovereignty, or the ultimate source of political power. For most Islamic political thinkers, the source of sovereignty does not emanate from the people, as is the case in a democracy like the United States. Rather, sovereignty lies with God. God's will is expressed through the Quran, and therefore its principles would set the criteria for law and policy. A parliament or congress, whether or not popularly elected, could not legislate away or change these Quranic injunctions. Thus, one can view the Quran as a sort of constitution that is God-given and not open to amendment. As with other constitutions, however, the principles set forth in the Quran might be open to reasonable legislative interpretation by a popularly chosen government. To date, the practice in those Islamic states now operating has been one of clerical review of parliamentary actions to ensure that the government does nothing in violation of religious doctrine. How an Islamic government ultimately interprets the Quran and other primary sources of Islamic law will determine not only the extent of popular political participation, but also its treatment of women and non-Muslims.

The question of whether democracy is applicable to Islamic government (and if so, what form it should take) is now being openly debated in much of the Muslim world. How this debate will influence present and future Muslim governments is still to be seen. Observers of the Muslim political scene are rightly concerned about such issues as whether or not governments run on Muslim precepts will allow for a full range of human rights and freedoms. As the Iranian experience suggests, Islamic democracy is not likely to be as broad based or pluralistic as that found in the United States or Western Europe. More realistically, one can expect at best only a limited form of democracy. As John Esposito observes,

Without a reinterpretation of the classical Islamic legal doctrine regarding non-Muslim minorities . . . an ideologically oriented Islamic state would be at best a limited democracy with a weak pluralistic profile. Its ideological orientation would restrict the participation of non-Muslims in key government positions, and the existence of political parties representing competing ideology or orientation . . . non-Muslims would be second class citizens.[3]

Finally, questions can be raised about the sincerity of Western concerns over Islamic political behavior and its prospects for a democratic future.

Despite their protestations, some in the West may not really wish to see democracy come to the Muslim world. As the case of Algeria suggests, democracy may very well bring with it the establishment of Islamic governments. Western states, including the United States, often have allied themselves with pro-Western autocratic regimes. They have come to rely on these nondemocratic governments for the stability necessary to maintain Western economic interests in the area. To promote democracy might disrupt that status quo because most of the elites who rule through the present autocratic regimes have failed to meet the economic needs of their populations (the only exceptions being in sparsely populated and oil-rich countries such as Saudi Arabia and Kuwait). This failure means the elites are unlikely to prevail in free and fair elections. In an open contest for people's loyalties and interests, Islamic parties critical of the West are increasingly likely to succeed.

Even if prospects for a Western-style democracy improve in any Islamic state, the transition from one culturally and historically conditioned form of government to another is a long-term affair. As late as the nineteenth century, many governments in Europe were authoritarian, and some were still "divine right" monarchies. The transition to democracy in the West took centuries, and if we are to factor in Russia and eastern Europe, it is still shakily in progress. Perhaps we need to take a long-term view on this subject for the Muslim world as well.

The Question of Women's Role in Society

History and culture also helped determine the expression of other rights and values on which Westerners tend to judge Muslim society. One of these is the position and treatment accorded to women within that society. Some Muslim fundamentalists interpret a modern lifestyle for women—that is, their access to the labor market, higher education, and the political arena; their free mingling with men outside the home; and their adoption of non-Islamic dress—as a symptom of the Western corruption of Muslim society. Such fundamentalists assert, for instance, that working women neglect their families, tend to have fewer children, become materialistic, and "take on male characteristics" such as assertiveness and ambition.

Thus, in the drive to regain an "authentic" Muslim society, women's issues have moved to center stage. In some extreme cases this has led to the restriction of women's activities and the harassment of allegedly "westernized" women, especially women who refuse to wear the veil, who choose to dress in Western fashion, and who work or study in mixed-gender environments. Such incidents have occurred, for instance, in Algeria, where Karima Bennoune, an Arab-American lawyer and human rights activist, observed, "The FIS [the Islamic Salvation Front, the leading Islamic political organization in the country] was obsessed with women's behavior, such as working, housekeeping, childrearing, etc., and used so-called failings of women in these contexts as explanations for various social evils."[4] Before the 1992 suppression of the FIS by the Algerian military, those municipalities that had elected Islamic city councils and mayors barred women from public facilities, such as recreation and cultural centers. As the civil war that erupted after the FIS suppression progressed, women who were deemed too Western were, according to Bennoune, "deliberately targeted and assassinated, principally by the two main armed fundamentalist groups."[5] In the case of Afghanistan, the radical regime of the Taliban also greatly restricted women's rights. Women were prevented from receiving public education, could not appear in public unless completely covered in the traditional burka robe, and were prevented from participating in most professions. It should be noted that some of these restrictions, such as the wearing of the burka, preceded the Taliban regime and constituted traditional behavior particularly in the Afghanistan countryside. For the growing urban female population, however, Taliban restrictions meant a major restriction in behavior and rights.

Both Western and moderate Muslim observers have condemned such behavior, which tends to feed the image of Islam as the antithesis of Western civilization. But, as the Iranian experience suggests, the oppression of women has not inevitably accompanied Islamic government. In Iran the initial wave of repressive measures restricting women's rights in the name of "Islamic purity" provoked a societal debate wherein Iranian women, allied with more moderate Shi'ite clerics, successfully argued that, given the important role women played in the overthrow of the Shah, they had the right to participate in the building of the Islamic state and society. In addition, once the requirement of wearing the veil in public was established in Iran, it served as a vehicle of access for women into the public realm. As Nesta Ramazani, a freelance writer who specializes in women's issues in the Middle East noted, the Iranian Islamic government's

attempt to cloak women in an Islamic identity distinct from the "tarnished" Western one . . . has initiated a lively debate on Islam and women's issues. The same leaders who have promoted women's hijab (veiling) have encouraged women in education, work and other social participation. Paradoxically, hijab has become the means to social activism. By wearing the badge of purity, women can move about freely. By wearing the badge of modesty, they may fight for women's rights.[6]

Today in Iran, women stand for and are elected to the nation's parliament as well as a variety of municipal offices. Recognizing the multiple roles women play in the culture, as homemaker, wife, and worker, laws are now in place allowing women to work part time but receive full time wages. Other reforms that favor women have been enacted, but only after intense debate. This struggle reflects a deep divide in Iranian society between those who interpret Sharia law in a very conservative way and those who approach the law more liberally and adaptively.

In this struggle a concern for tradition may very well reflect the mind set of many women. The revival of Islamic values and ways has not been a purely male phenomenon. Yet, while Islamist women reject Western standards and the "commodification" of women's bodies (turning them into a commodity through advertising and entertainment) and reassert the primacy of "family values," many women also call for a reinterpretation of the Quran to purge from society and law restrictive and abusive attitudes toward women. These women point out that such policies as female circumcision, the seclusion of women, the isolation of women from economic activity, and even restrictions on women attending the mosque are not really Islamic in origin. They are cultural add-ons that have come to be identified with Islam over the centuries.[7]

There can be little argument that by Western standards some aspects of culture found in Muslim lands harm women, or that some Islamic fundamentalists have promoted policies in the name of Islam that are anti-women. Western culture has its own problems in this regard. In fact, the principle of gender equality and its related values and behaviors are very recent developments even in the West and certainly have not yet attained acceptance worldwide.

SOME CONCLUSIONS ON WESTERN ATTITUDES

Why do some people in the West find Islamic fundamentalism so objectionable? John Esposito argues that the root cause is philosophical.[8] That is, in modern Western culture the perception is that religion does not belong to the public sphere. This comes from past Western experience with state-affiliated churches that persecuted religious dissenters. Over time, Western societies moved from church-based states to the modern democratic state that practices religious toleration. Today, the Western perspective is that the separation of church and state is not only "normal" but also a requirement for a modern and progressive society. Societies that do not subscribe to such "modern" values and political orientation are often perceived as backward, "irrational," or "extremist."

Yet, in most Muslim lands and for most of Muslim history, there was little or no persecution of non-Muslims—at least not on the scale of that in the Christian West. This was so despite the tensions that grew up between Muslim and Christian states. And, as we have seen in Chapter 1, in Muslim lands the Islamic religion became the most important basis of law and values. Thus, the "normal" case for the believing Muslim is no separation of church and state. What is abnormal for the modern Judeo-Christian world is normal for Islamic culture, and vice versa.

With little exposure to the Muslim world in the regular educational curriculum, and little reporting on Islamic affairs except during times of crisis, much of America views Islamic fundamentalism without historical context or cultural insight. The tendency of the media to sensationalize violent events exacerbates this situation. Also, government policymakers and academics regarded as experts, many of whom have little first-hand familiarity with Islamic fundamentalism, most often focus on the actions and statements of religious extremists. All of this makes it more likely that the general public will mistake the anti-Western spokesman for all Muslims in an Islamic world of 1 billion people.

Such an outlook is maintained at the cost of ignoring a much broader, and growing, populist phenomenon. The revival of Islamic values and lifestyle among all classes of Muslims living in every Muslim country from Morocco to Indonesia constitutes a pervasive and deep-rooted movement that is now, as Esposito observes, "part of the mainstream of Muslim life and society."[9] In those countries where they are allowed to operate legally, Islamic fundamentalist organizations run a vast array of enterprises ranging from hospitals to banks to handicraft businesses. They tutor students, collect trash, run youth centers and health clinics, and much more. Western critics who dismiss all this activity and the Islamists who undertake them as "nonrepresentative" or "radical" miss the significance and appeal of Islamic fundamentalism.

NOTES

1. Bernard Lewis, "Islam Has Weak Democratic Traditions," in Paul A. Winters, ed., *Islam: Opposing Viewpoints* (San Diego, Calif.: Greenhaven Press, 1995), p. 103. For similiar views, see the comments of Patrick Clawson, Joshual Muravchik, Barry Rubin, and Robert B. Satloff, all American commentators and researchers on the Middle East, in *Middle East Quarterly* 1 (September 1994), 12–17.

2. John Voll and John Esposito, "Islam's Democratic Essence," in *Middle East Quarterly* 1 (September 1994), 7.

3. John Esposito, *The Islamic Threat: Myth or Reality?* (New York: Oxford University Press, 1992), p. 189.

4. Karima Bennoune, "Islamic Fundamentalism Represses Women," in Winters, ed., *Islam*, p. 67.

5. Ibid., p. 65.

6. Nesta Ramazani, "Islamic Government Need Not Repress Women," in Winters, ed., *Islam*, p. 76.

7. A very good representation of this position can be found in the video Women and *Islam*, which is part of the "Islamic Conversations" series listed in the Bibliography.

8. Esposito, *The Islamic Threat*, p. 198 ff.

9. Ibid., p. 212.

6

The Issues of Violence and Terrorism

Long before the attacks on the World Trade Center and Pentagon, most Americans saw the Moslem and Arab world as violent and hostile. Research done on American mass media presentations of the Middle East, Arabs, and Muslims by noted scholars has demonstrated a consistent tendency among Americans to portray the peoples of the region as primitive and aggressive. As Jack Shaheen, a scholar noted for his studies of Arab images, has put it in reference to television, the media "tends to perpetuate four basic myths about Arabs: they are all fabulously wealthy; they are barbaric and uncultured; they are sex maniacs with a penchant for white slavery; and they revel in acts of terrorism."[1]

Reinforcing these television images are print media sources such as newspapers, magazines, and journals that focus attention on the alleged violent nature of Islam and its practitioners. The historian Edward Said has observed that such sources (as part of overall media coverage) lead Americans "to view the Islamic world . . . reductively, coercively, oppositionally . . . [presenting] Islam as a resurgent atavism, which suggests not only the threat of a return to the Middle Ages but the destruction of what is regularly referred to as the democratic order in the Western world."[2]

As a result of these negative stereotypes, some Americans have adopted a theory of conspiratorial violence—the belief that there exists a "world-wide Islamic terrorist infrastructure" that is responsible for such disparate acts of violence as the World Trade Center bombings in 1993 and 2001, various airplane hijackings, attacks on U.S. military installations in Lebanon in 1983 and Saudi Arabia in 1997, and the like.[3]

There are several reasons why Americans have come to view Middle Easterners in general and Muslims in particular in these negative ways. One important reason is the prevailing ignorance of Middle Eastern culture and history, as well as the Islamic religion. These subjects either are not taught in American schools or are often presented in a biased fashion. Michael Suleiman, a political scientist who has studied American high school textbook presentations of Arabs and Muslims, has concluded that they present them as "backward, primitive, uncivilized people who . . . appeared warlike, powerful, barbaric and cruel."[4] In addition, while the number of Middle Easterners and Muslims in the United States is growing, they still constitute a small minority. Thus, most Americans do not have the direct contact with these groups that might help overcome negative images.

Other observers have speculated that the collapse of communism in eastern Europe has helped focus American attention on the anti-Western activities of Islamic fundamentalist organizations. As this theory goes, for those Americans who want or need enemies, the post of chief ideological rival became vacant with the demise of the Soviet Union in 1990. Therefore, the tensions and frictions that had long existed between the West and Muslim lands, except in the case of the Arab-Israeli conflict, had been overshadowed by the American fixation on the Soviets, could now claim attention. The alleged desire of the communists to conquer the world was readily replaced by the fearful notion of "worldwide" Islamic jihad.[5] As David Ignatius, a long-time commentator on U.S. foreign policy, has put it,

The Cold War has barely ended, but already the search seems to be on for a new global, universal enemy around which the United States can orient its foreign policy. . . . Topping the global list has been our all-too-reliable nemesis: fundamentalist Islam. Islam seems in many ways to fit the bill, enemy-wise: It's big; it's scary; it's anti-Western; it feeds on poverty and discontent; it spreads across vast swaths of the globe that can be colored green on the television maps in the same way that communist countries used to be colored red.[6]

Finally, another reason Americans have come to view Muslims as violent and "evil" stems from an ignorance of their country's foreign policy in the Middle East. Most Americans, including many politicians, assume that the United States pursues policies that promote democracy in the region. This is often not the case. The United States has long supported, both diplomatically and militarily, authoritarian and repressive governments such as those in Egypt, Iraq (before the invasion of Kuwait), Jordan, Saudi Arabia and the Gulf area, Iran prior to the Islamic revolution, and elsewhere.

In 1953 the CIA was directly involved in the overthrow of the popular and constitutionally appointed Iranian Prime Minister Muhammad Mossadegh. In 1957 the United States was involved in an unsuccessful attempt to overthrow the Syrian government. In 1958 President Dwight D. Eisenhower sent U.S. Marines to Beirut in order to support a minority government considered friendly to America. In 1983 President Ronald Reagan intervened in the Lebanese civil war on the side of minority Christian parties. The results of this last adventure were disastrous and included the death of hundreds of U.S. Marines and some diplomats, and an increase in kidnappings and terrorism directed at Americans.

Often, the United States has switched sides in the Middle East, attacking today those we armed and trained yesterday. For example, prior to Iraq's invasion of Kuwait, the American government materially aided the dictatorship of Saddam Hussein because of its animosity toward Iran. Then, following the Gulf War, the United States pressured the United Nations to impose draconian sanctions on Iraq that contributed to the deaths of many Iraqi citizens, particularly children.[7] We thus generally weakened the same population we hoped would overturn the Iraqi government. During the Afghan war against the Soviet Union, America helped arm, train, and supply Muslim fundamentalist fighters, including Osama bin Laden and his followers. Later, during the war in Afghanistan, the United States allied with Pakistan despite the fact that this country had armed and supported the Taliban regime. While each of these alliances seemed expedient at the time, in the long term they hurt U.S. interests and certainly contradicted the ideals America was supposed to represent.

Finally, the United States has long armed and diplomatically protected (largely through the use of its veto in the UN Security Council) the State of Israel. This support has facilitated Israeli behavior in the Palestinian occupied territories that is often considered oppressive, expansionist, and in the opinion of many scholars and legal experts, in violation of international law.

The peoples of the Middle East, Muslim and otherwise, are well aware of these U.S. policies and actions even if Americans are not. This history has convinced some Islamic fundamentalist groups that the United States is an active ally of those governments they believe are responsible for the region's ills and thus is an enemy. Therefore, when they take up arms against these regimes it is but a small step to seeing the United States and its representatives as legitimate targets.

The American people's ignorance of both Middle East history and their own government's actions in the region means that they are unaware of what might motivate some Middle Easterners to become so angry that they might take up terrorism. Thus the attacks of September 11, 2001, seemed to many Americans to come without a discernable cause. The ubiquitous question following that event was "Why do they hate us?" President George W. Bush's answer to that question was, variably, the attackers and their sponsors "hate liberty," or "they are jealous of our freedoms," or they are just "evil-doers." These assertions seem dangerously naïve. The former mayor of New York City, Rudolph Giuliani, in his speech to the United Nations on October 2, 2001, asserted that the motivations of the attackers were irrelevant. He explained that "those who practice terrorism—murdering or victimizing innocent civilians—lose any right to have their cause understood by decent people and lawful nations." Yet seeking to understand motives and the historical context of actions is not the same as justifying those actions. And, such an understanding is necessary to any effective, long-term response.

If the United States is to change attitudes in the Middle East and therefore minimize the possibility of future terrorist attacks coming from that region, Americans must come to an understanding of both sides of the present divide. If the United States is to insist on civilized behavior, the end of actions that harm innocent people and the promotion of human rights and freedoms such as democracy, then it best be sure that it too follows the rules it insists others follow.

ISLAMIC FUNDAMENTALIST GROUPS AND VIOLENCE

Several Islamic fundamentalist organizations have resorted to violent tactics. However, it must be kept in mind that the vast majority of Muslims do not support extremist violence.

Afghanistan, the Taliban, and Al-Qaeda

The Soviet invasion of Afghanistan in December 1979 triggered a resistance war that not only involved indigenous Afghans, but also volunteer fighters from around the Muslim world. Most of these volunteers, called mujahedin (warriors of God), were devout young men fighting not just for the independence of Afghanistan from a secular foreign power, but for the victory of a puritan version of Islamic government. The United States too was interested in resisting Soviet expansion. The Reagan administration directed the CIA to work with the Pakistanis and Saudis to train, arm, and fund the resistance fighters in Afghanistan (including Osama bin Laden) despite their fundamentalist orientation. The U.S. aim, according to Zbigniew Brezinski, President Jimmy Carter's national security advisor, was to turn Afghanistan into the Soviet Union's Vietnam. After pouring into that country millions of dollars and 65,000 tons of American weapons, the United States succeeded.

One million Afghans died in the struggle against the Soviet Union, and one-third of the population was displaced into refugee camps. A large number of male war orphans ended up in religiously oriented orphanages in Pakistan. Some of these institutions, and the schools associated with them, became the training ground for future Taliban fighters (the word "taliban" comes from the root term talib or student). In other words, the American-supported war against the Soviets in Afghanistan helped create the conditions for the rise and eventual coming to power of the Taliban regime.

Another group established during the war was Al-Qaeda (meaning the base, or the firm base). Funded by the wealthy Saudi, Osama bin Laden, and based in Pakistan, its original purpose was to lend logistical support to the resistance fighters in Afghanistan. However, in 1986 bin Laden set up bases in Afghanistan and directly joined in the anti-Soviet fighting. He and his followers did so with the help of training from both Pakistan and the United States. As the war with the Soviet Union wound down, Afghanistan fell into civil war and much of the country was ruled by violent war lords. Bin Laden was able to operate freely in this environment and continued to hold his mujahedin together as a fighting force. Eventually this group, Al-Qaeda, expanded its operations into the Middle East, still fighting for a "purer form of Islam."

Initially, Al-Qaeda's major targets were the governments of Saudi Arabia and Egypt. Both were seen as corrupt and overly influenced by the United States. However, Osama bin Laden turned his anger on the United States in particular after a joint Saudi-American decision to maintain U.S. military bases in Arabia even after the Gulf War ended. Keeping American (non-Muslim) forces in the sacred land of Arabia was considered by bin Laden to be an act of heresy. The result was escalating attacks on U.S. targets by Al-Qaeda. These included the 1993 truck bombing of the World

Trade Center, a deadly attack on a U.S. military residence in Saudi Arabia in 1996, the bombings of American embassies in Africa in 1998, the attack on the U.S. naval ship *Cole* in Aden, Yemen, in 2000, and the devastating attacks on the World Trade Center and Pentagon in 2001.

Meanwhile, in Afghanistan, the Taliban had been formed from the thousands of students orphaned by the war. Now armed and trained, they were able slowly to put an end to the civil war by taking over most of the country. However, the restoration of law and order came at a high price, particularly in terms of women's rights. The Taliban's radical brand of Islam was to shock both the West and much of the Muslim world as well.

The Taliban's leader, Mullah Omar, developed a friendship with Osama bin Laden and soon Al-Qaeda came under the protection of the Taliban government. From this "firm base" bin Laden was able to issue statements condemning the United States and lay his plans to battle against Western presence in the Middle East. By the time of the 2001 attacks, Al-Qaeda and the Taliban were hardly distinguishable in the minds of American officials. As a result, the U.S. "war on terrorism" focused first and foremost on Afghanistan.

Even before the events of September 2001, the United States had attacked bin Laden. Under President Clinton there had been missile attacks on Al-Qaeda camps in Afghanistan. Later, when the Taliban refused to hand over Osama bin Laden to the United States as the suspected instigator of the 2001 World Trade Center attack, President Bush organized a united front against the Taliban. For this he needed Pakistan to cut off the aid it had consistently supplied the regime. The United States succeeded in separating the Pakistanis from the Taliban, and in October 2001 began an attack that would quickly destroy the Afghan regime and scatter most of the surviving Al-Qaeda leadership and fighters to other regions.

Although military success appeared to be swift, a real victory against terrorism would continue to elude the United States. Only a few voices have asked how the cycle of violence, retribution, and more violence might be halted. The policies of the Taliban, and the tactics of Al-Qaeda, both represent the behavior of a tiny minority of Muslims. However, as long as there exists widespread support in the Middle East for resistance to U.S. policies and the regimes associated with those policies, some will find terrorism an acceptable tactic. The only way to undermine terrorist groups is to address the problems from which they take their strength. In this endeavor the United States has to ask itself if there are policy changes that can be made that will better serve the national interest. Can the United States achieve its ends without becoming identified with oppressive regimes?

Lebanon and Hezbollah

In Lebanon the best-known Islamic fundamentalist group is the Shi'ite organization known as Hezbollah (Party of God). Hezbollah was formed in the early 1980s in reaction to events in Lebanon, such as civil war and an Israeli invasion that had traumatized the nation. Lebanon had long been dominated by Christian and Sunni Muslim communities, and the Shi'ite Muslims represented a poor and discriminated sector of society. However, Lebanese Shi'ites gained inspiration and encouragement from the Iranian Revolution of 1979, and members of Hezbollah soon used Iran as a model for what they wished to see in Lebanon. They originally considered themselves a revolutionary party with the following agenda:

1. The overthrow of the Lebanese state and its replacement with an Islamic Republic along the lines of Iran.
2. The waging of jihad, or holy war, against the enemies of Islam and Lebanon. These included Lebanese Christian and Sunni groups, Israel, France, and the United States.
3. The acceptance of martyrdom and self-sacrifice to attain these goals.

The strong influence of Iran and the organization's anti-Western stance can be seen in its early manifesto, which read in part as follows,

We, the sons of Hezbollah's nation, whose vanguard God has given victory in Iran . . . abide by the orders of a single wise and just command currently embodied in the Supreme Ayatollah Khumaini. . . . We have opted for religion, freedom and dignity over humiliation and constant submission to America and its allies and Zionism. . . . We have risen to liberate our country, to drive the imperialists and invaders out of it and to take fate in our hands.

One of the founding members of Hezbollah was the Lebanese Shi'ite leader Abbas al-Musawi, a former school teacher. Musawi had become dissatisfied with the more moderate policies of the dominant Shi'ite militia organization in Lebanon known as AMAL (Arabic for "hope"). Objecting to AMAL's acceptance of a Lebanese secular state that gave considerable power to the Christian minority, Musawi went to the city of Baalbek in the Bekaa Valley of eastern Lebanon. There he established a new militant organization committed to the formation of an Iranian-style Islamic republic. This new group would become Hezbollah. Musawi had come to Baalbek because it was a center of Iranian-inspired activity in Lebanon and the headquarters of 1,500 Iranian revolutionary guards who, in 1982, had volunteered to fight in Lebanon against the Israeli invasion. The Iranians provided weapons and training to Hezbollah.

Hezbollah grew rapidly into a series of chapters and militias organized around mosques in Beirut, the Bekaa Valley, and southern Lebanon. Leadership became vested in young Shi'ite clerics who saw fundamentalist Islam as an alternative to the secular political systems of the capitalist West and communist East. Thus, the organization did not begin as a centralized political party but rather was a coming together of like-minded people attracted by Musawi's militancy. They shared a common analysis of Lebanon's problems and held similar ideas of what were the proper solutions to those problems. Hezbollah became more structured over time. A Supreme Consultative Council made up of clerics and militia leaders was formed, and regional committees were set up. Influential clerics emerged as "spiritual guides" to the organization. For instance, there was Shaykh Muhammad Husayn Fadlallah, a Shi'ite religious scholar and activist who wrote *Islam and the Logic of Force*. In this work, he argued for the use of force in the struggle against social, political, and economic injustice. However, Hezbollah never became truly centralized. To this day, its structure remains a relatively loose one, and individual Hezbollah chapters often operate independent of each other. This is why attempts (most often made by the Israelis) to destroy the organization by assassinating its leaders (Musawi was killed in 1992) have proved ineffective.

Hezbollah leaders have maintained close connections with Iran. In the 1980s the Iranian embassy in Damascus, Syria, coordinated the distribution of money and supplies to Hezbollah. Such aid amounted to some $10 million a month. Hezbollah used this income for two types of activities. One type was the creation of a network of social welfare programs for the poverty-ridden Lebanese Shi'ite community. This network included schools and educational scholarships (Hezbollah was reported to have subsidized the education of nearly 40,000 students), hospitals and clinics, food cooperatives, and low-income housing projects. The other type of activity was the waging of war against those whom the organization saw as enemies of Islam and responsible for oppression and injustice in Lebanon. This not only included many of the country's Christian and Sunni groups and Israel, but also Westerners.

Thus, in the 1980s and early 1990s, Hezbollah "martyrs" carried on "holy war" against Americans and other Westerners in Lebanon. The organization was involved in the 1985 hijacking of TWA flight 847 at Beirut, as well as the kidnapping of Americans such as the journalist Terry Anderson (who was the last American hostage to be released in Lebanon in December of 1991) and Colonel William Higgins. Higgins, who was assigned to the UN peacekeeping force in Lebanon, was accused of being a CIA spy by Hezbollah, and was executed while in captivity in 1989. Hezbollah was also responsible for a large number of car and truck bombings that killed many foreigners as well as Lebanese. The most infamous of these was the October 1983 suicide truck bombing of the U.S. Marine barracks on the outskirts of Beirut. Two hundred and fifty Marines were killed in this attack. Similar actions were mounted against the U.S. embassy and French facilities in Beirut.

With the end of the civil war in Lebanon in the early 1990s, Hezbollah's violence diminished and its political radicalism modified somewhat. Kidnappings and bombings ceased. And while the organization still espouses the eventual creation of an Islamic state in Lebanon, it no longer calls for the violent overthrow of the government. Hezbollah now participates in the democratic process by fielding candidates in local and national elections. Several members of Hezbollah sit in the Lebanese parliament. However, Hezbollah still maintains its armed militia, which operates widely throughout southern Lebanon. There the organization's dedication to "jihad" proved effective when Israeli occupation forces finally withdrew from southern Lebanon in 1999.

Following the U.S. declaration of a "war on terror," President George W. Bush issued an executive order freezing whatever financial assets Hezbollah had in the United States. In this way the Bush administration put Hezbollah in the same category as the Taliban and Al-Qaeda. An objective view of the situation might indicate that this is a mistake. In the Middle East Hezbollah is almost universally seen as a resistance organization that has successfully challenged Israeli aggression that itself used terror tactics. The Lebanese government has stood by the organization, whose fighters are considered heroes by the citizenry, and has refused to cooperate with U.S. efforts to damage Hezbollah. In the Middle East these efforts on the part of the Americans are seen as a sign of U.S. arrogance and proof of Israeli influence on the American government.

Despite adapting to changing circumstances within Lebanon, the common vision of a society run according to the principles of Islamic fundamentalist belief still motivates Hezbollah. The Iranian model continues to be revered by its members. And when the organization deems it necessary, Hezbollah is still capable and willing to act in a violent manner.

The Occupied Territories and Hamas

Another well-known Islamic fundamentalist organization whose violent activities have made news in the West is Hamas. Hamas is the Arabic acronym for the Islamic Resistance Movement. Hamas grew out of the first Palestinian Intifada, or popular uprising, which lasted roughly from 1987 to 1991. The Intifada, in turn, was a direct result of the military occupation of the West Bank and Gaza Strip (collectively known as the "occupied territories") and colonial settlement policy maintained by Israel since 1967.

Hamas was first organized in December of 1987 in the Gaza Strip by religiously minded residents who were active members of the Palestinian branch of the Society of the Muslim Brothers. An important early organizer of Hamas was Sheikh Ahmad Yasin, the founder of the Islamic Center in the Gaza Strip. There were others as well, mostly professional men such as doctors, pharmacists, and teachers. These men were disillusioned with the Palestine Liberation Organization (PLO), which represented a number of secular political movements that had long led the Palestinian resistance to Israel. In their judgment, the PLO had failed in its efforts to free Palestine from Israeli rule and to inspire the Palestinians to create a new and more wholesome community. Their deep Muslim faith led them to the conclusion that only a new movement based on Islamic fundamentalist principles and seeking the establishment of an Islamic republic in Palestine could do the job. Their message became a very popular one, particularly among Palestinian youth as well as the general membership of the Muslim Brothers. Thus, Hamas grew quickly and established branches in Jerusalem and the towns and cities of the West Bank.

Hamas, like Hezbollah, developed a decentralized organizational structure and leadership. In this case, decentralized leadership proved to be a virtual necessity because of continued harassment and arrests by Israeli occupation forces. (Yasin was arrested in 1989 and sentenced to fifteen years in prison.) Over time, many of Hamas's leaders were forced into exile and now reside in Jordan, Iran, Sudan, and other Muslim countries. In terms of broad policy, today the organization is run by a Consultative Council whose members can be found both within and without the occupied territories.

Hamas's first actions involved the organizing of and participation in anti-Israeli demonstrations that successfully fused Palestinian nationalist and Islamic fundamentalist themes. Hamas claims to represent not only patriotism and resistance, but also moral uprightness, religious vision, and, ultimately, community salvation. Its announced immediate goal was to force Israeli withdrawal from the occupied territories and replace it with an Islamic government. Tapping into the very large general membership of the Muslim Brothers, Hamas was able to numerically enhance the Intifada's demonstrations and strikes, as well as sustain them in the face of the sometimes brutal Israeli use of force.

As the first Intifada continued, Hamas's response took a more violent character than the stone-throwing that most often characterized the on-going demonstrations. A special Hamas branch named Kata'ib 'Izz-al-Din al-Qassam (Regiments of Izz-al-Din al-Qassam) was formed and author-ized to use firearms against selected Israeli targets, as well as Palestinians collaborating with occupation authorities. Such violent tactics have been maintained beyond the end of the Intifada (1991) in response to continued Israeli occupation and such policies as the expansion of Jewish settlements in Jerusalem and the West Bank. Sometimes Hamas's violence takes the form of terrorist actions such as suicide bombings and shootings. In 1996 and 1997 such attacks targeted Israeli commuter buses, cafes, and shop-ping centers both in the occupied territories and Israel proper. To these more spectacular, headline-making events can be added dozens of other annual actions that include drive-by shootings, knife attacks, and fire bombings that have killed or wounded hundreds of Israeli soldiers and civilians.

The Intifada did not end Israeli occupation of the West Bank and Gaza Strip, nor did the Oslo Peace Accords (announced in 1993) achieve this end, except in a very small percentage of the occupied territories. Thus, the influence and popularity of Hamas among Palestinians has continued. Working under the motto, "God is the goal, the Prophet is the model, the Quran is the constitution, the jihad is the path, and death on God's path is our most sublime aspiration," the organization has expanded its activ-ities. Like Hezbollah, it now provides social services, which it funds through contributions from Muslims and other sympathizers worldwide. Some subsidies from Iran are also said to reach Hamas. Such activities, along with its established militancy and reputation for being free of cor-ruption, have made Hamas the major political opposition to Yasir Arafat's Palestine National Authority.

Despite the efforts of both the Israelis and the Palestine National Au-thority to curtail Hamas's influence and activities, there is little reason to believe the organization can be completely suppressed without an end to the Israeli occupation of the West Bank and Gaza Strip. After the Oslo Accords were signed (1993) and the Palestine National Authority was allowed to operate in small designated parts of these territories, there was much hope among the Palestine population. This optimism was reflected by a significant drop in the support given to the violent activities of groups such as Hamas. However, as the "peace process" has languished and Israeli settlement activity expanded, disillusionment has returned and support for Hamas has increased.

A second Intifada against Israeli occupation began in the fall of 2000. Triggered by Ariel Sharon's provocative intrusion into the Al-Aqsa (Temple Mount) mosque in Jerusalem, the open resistance of the Palestinians was met with brutal repression on the part of Israeli occupation forces. In the first year of this Intifada some 700 Palestinians were killed and close to 16,000 were injured. Israeli tactics such as the assassination of Palestinian leaders, the shooting of children, the destruction of Palestinian homes, draconian curfews, destruction of agricultural land, and the expansion of colonial settlements in violation of international law have, regrettably, given new support to the more violent elements within such groups as Hamas. In response to Israeli repression an increasing number of suicide bombings have taken place aimed not only at Israeli soldiers and armed settlers, but also at civilian targets.

The cycle of violence calls out for resolution based on international law and firm commitment to human rights. Repeated UN resolutions seeking to resolve, or at least ameliorate, the crisis (the latest coming in December 2001 calling for the introduction of UN observers into the occupied territories) have repeatedly been vetoed by the United States. Likewise, efforts to achieve ceasefires or revive the moribund "peace process" have been regularly derailed by violent actions perpetrated by both sides.

Combined American and Israeli pressure on the Palestinian Authority (PA) to rein in Hamas and similar groups has been largely ineffective. The cause for this may be that the Israeli violence itself has largely undermined the authority of the PA in a manner that at once weakens its ability to act effectively (for example, the targeting of PA policemen and facilities) while boosting Hamas's motivation to act against Israel.

The position taken by the United States, which supports UN-condemned behavior on the part of Israel while assigning most of the blame for this Middle East crisis to the Palestinians, is basically a political position reflecting the strength of America's pro-Israeli domestic lobby and historic ties to Israel. In this case, politics play a more important role than an understanding of the objective, historically contextualized reality of the Palestinian–Israeli struggle.

No end to this struggle is in sight. Israeli occupation and the resulting Palestinian resistance, including the violence of Hamas, likely will go on until the Palestinians are granted a viable state of their own.

Algeria and the Armed Islamic Group

Algeria is another country in the Muslim world that has witnessed violent activities by Islamic fundamentalist organizations. This violence is largely a function of the Algerian civil war, the origins of which are explained in Chapter 1 of this book. This war continues to this day (2002) and has bred an increasingly vicious spiral of violence perpetuated by both the secular-minded, military-dominated government and at least half a dozen small Islamic extremist groups. These groups appear to operate in an independent fashion, and their number reflects the fractionalization of the Islamic movement in Algeria over the last five years.

The most notorious of the violent Algerian Islamic organizations is the Armed Islamic Group (AIG). Little is known of its internal organization or size. Some of its members are disaffected Algerian Islamists who were cut adrift from the Islamic Salvation Front when this mainstream Muslim group was suppressed by the government in 1991. Others are Algerians who had fought as volunteers in the Afghan war against the former Soviet Union. All of its participants feel that Algeria has lost its Muslim identity and fallen into a condition of corruption and economic depression that only an Islamic government can repair. In terms of leadership, the name most often associated with the direction of AIG activities is Muhammad Said. Said was a former member of a group of Muslim intellectuals who, in the 1970s and 1980s, preached Islamic reform at the country's schools and college campuses. As persuasion gave way to confrontation, Said turned increasingly to violent tactics.

The AIG attacks an array of targets: government forces and officials, foreigners (all of whom have been warned to leave Algeria by the AIG), women and girls who do not wear Islamic dress, and intellectuals and particularly journalists who do not follow an Islamic line, and even entertainers who are seen as a threat to Islamic culture. Indeed, just about anyone who is not avowedly pro-Islamic, or who is suspected of supporting the government, is subject to attack. Some of the more notorious AIG actions have included the killing of foreign oil field workers and foreign clergy such as French missionary priests, the hijacking of a French airliner, the massacre of whole Algerian families suspected of collaboration with the government, and in 1995, the bombing of the Paris subway because France is seen as an ally of the Algerian government.

In 1996 the Algerian government sponsored changes to the country's constitution that banned political parties based on, among other things, religion. But pro-Islamic parties simply changed their names or boycotted future elections which were now seen as less than fair and open. An attempt at a truce between Islamic armed groups and the army was made in 1998 but did not hold. In 1999, however, the Islamic Salvation Army, the military wing of the Islamic Salvation Front (FIS) declared an end to its war and the government responded with an amnesty and release of

2000 prisoners. Other Islamic armed groups such as the GIA continue to fight.

Thus terrorist incidents and military confrontations have gone on. In 2001, over 66 terrorist acts were reported in the first three months of that year. Deaths, many of them civilian, still run into the thousands each year. The military controlled government has yet to find a formula for achieving either peace or victory and, as a result, Algerian civil society continues to be brutalized.

Egypt and Extremist Violence

Finally, Egypt now finds itself subject to increasing Islamic violence. A number of revolutionary Islamic fundamentalist groups have been active in Egypt for the past thirty years. Many of these groups were formed in reaction to Egypt's devastating defeat in the 1967 Arab-Israeli war. To many Muslims that war seemed to demonstrate the bankruptcy of most of the secular regimes in the Arab world. Some of the more prominent of the Egyptian radical fundamentalist organizations are the Islamic Liberation Organization (al-Tahrir al-Islami), the Holy War Society (Jamaat al-Jihad), the Islamic Group (Gam'a Islamiya), and Excommunication and Emigration (Takfir wal-Hijra).

The philosophy of these groups centers on the belief that holy war, or jihad, is a religious obligation of all true Muslims. They condemn the more traditional notion that jihad really means a personal pursuit of righteousness. This, they say, distorts the true, revolutionary meaning of Islam. The Egyptian radical Islamic fundamentalist interpretation of jihad was described in a tract written by Muhammad al-Farag entitled *The Neglected Obligation* (1982). In it, he asserted that jihad was really "the sixth pillar of Islam," but had been purposely downplayed by the ulama and thus forgotten by most Muslims. All true Muslims are called upon to wage jihad against two enemies: One is nonbelievers, and particularly Westerners, whose influence the Muslim radicals see as responsible for such maladies as Egypt's political corruption, social injustice, and the decline of religion. The other enemy is the Egyptian government itself, together with all those who, either through active support or knowing compromise, support it.

This conception of jihad has set Egypt's militant Islamic groups at odds with the country's more moderate established ulama, whom the radicals denounce as financially dependent and therefore subservient tools of the secular-minded government. For the radical fundamentalists a government that does not strictly uphold Islamic law is no government at all. This means that the several regimes that have ruled Egypt in the recent past, particularly those of Nasser, Sadat, and Mubarak, are to be seen as illegitimate. From the Islamic militant's point of view, they have helped transform Egypt into an "atheist state" and therefore must be fought against by any and all means.

While the various Egyptian radical fundamentalist groups coordinate their activities through an umbrella consultative council, they operate independently and under different leadership. Some groups, like Excommunication and Emigration (Takfir wal-Hijra), are highly centralized and disciplined. Takfir is led by Shukri Mustafa, a college graduate in agricultural science, who runs the organization as its Amir (ruler or prince). Mustafa has instructed his group to live righteous lives in a communal fashion, as he believes was the case with the prophet Muhammad and his followers. Takfir's aim is to establish a model community separate from corrupt Egyptian society. The concept of martyrdom also plays an important role in Takfir wal-Hijra. All members are expected to be ready to sacrifice their lives for the cause of creating a revolutionary Islamic state. On the other hand, the Islamic Liberation Organization, founded by Salih Siriya, a man who holds a doctorate in science education, is reported to be a more democratically structured group in which an executive council makes decisions after consultation with the membership.

Most of the members of these radical organizations are educated men of lower middle- or middle-class backgrounds. Many are college graduates and have pursued professional careers, but few have been professionally trained in religion. Only a minority of them have peasant or lower-class origins. Many, however, do come from villages and small towns and, upon emigrating to the cities of Egypt, underwent a form of culture shock that caused profound disillusionment. In the cities such as Cairo and Alexandria they found poverty, severe housing shortages, and high unemployment side by side with ostentatious wealth and the pursuit of Western lifestyles, and they saw the traditional Islamic values, with which they were most comfortable, undergoing rapid erosion. Scandalized and alienated by what they found, confused and disheartened by the outcome of the 1967 Arab-Israeli war, and dissatisfied with the relatively moderate response of the older Islamic organizations like the Society of the Muslim Brothers, they formed new, more aggressive, and radical organizations.

The result has been a steady campaign of violence against the Egyptian government and others deemed enemies of true Islam. The Egyptian militants' most spectacular act was the October 6, 1981, assassination of Anwar Sadat, attributed to the Holy War Society (Jamaat-al-Jihad). Earlier, in 1974, the Islamic Liberation Organization attempted to spark the overthrow of the government through the seizure of Cairo's Technical Military

Academy. In 1977 Takfir wal-Hijra kidnapped and executed Husayn al-Dhahabi, the former Egyptian Minister of Religious Endowments, because he had strongly criticized the behavior of the Islamic militants. In recent years Egypt's Islamic fundamentalist extremists have turned their attention toward the country's intelligentsia. Journalists, educators, and writers who do not follow an Islamic line have been targeted. In 1994 Egypt's eighty-two-year-old Nobel Prize–winning author Naguib Mahfouz was attacked by a knife-wielding Islamic extremist. Earlier, in 1992, the writer and politician Faraq Foda was shot to death because he advocated the development of Egypt as a secular society. In 1993 Islamic militants brought suit against Abu Zayd, a professor of Arabic who argued that the Quran should be interpreted as a product of seventh-century Arabian social and political conditions. The Islamists took this interpretation as an attack on the Quran's "eternal" message and labeled Zayd a heretic. Among other things, the suit sought to force him to divorce his wife on the basis that a heretic could not remain married to a Muslim woman. When an Egyptian court actually upheld this argument, Abu Zayd and his wife fled into exile in Europe.

Non-Muslims, such as Egypt's Coptic Christian community, have also been harassed and, in sporadic fashion, attacks have been made on Western tourists visiting Egypt. In the case of attacks on tourists, the group thought to be most responsible is the Islamic Group (Gam'a Islamiya). This is the organization that considers Shaikh Omar Abd al-Rahman (now in jail in New York after being implicated in the World Trade Center bombing) to be its "spiritual guide." What this means is that Rahman has issued religious opinions rationalizing the Islamic Group's actions. In 1994 this organization began a bombing campaign against Western banks in Egypt. Eight tourists were injured when the group attacked trains in upper Egypt, and in August 1994 a Spanish national was killed when Gam'a Islamiya attacked a tourist bus. This action was seen as a warning against foreign participation in an upcoming UN-sponsored Conference on Population and Development. The conference was held in September of 1994 under heavy security and went on without incident.

Over the past few years the government of Hosni Mubarak has made every effort to suppress radical Islamic violence in Egypt. At the same time the government has allowed Islamic-based legislation having to do with cultural and personal matters. This constitutes a carrot-and-stick approach to the Islamists that has been relatively successful. Egypt is now relatively quiet. However, the essentially repressive nature of Egyptian political life and continuing economic woes, as well as a widespread identification of the Mubarak regime as an ally of the United States, means that radical Islamic violence can break out at any time.

Americans are rightly concerned about acts of violence and terrorism perpetrated by these and other groups. Such concern is also felt by the vast majority of Middle Easterners and Muslims, both fundamentalist and nonfundamentalist, who daily must face the threat of such actions. Violence and terrorism, of course, are not unique to the Muslim world. However, the notoriety given Middle Eastern countries that regularly turn up on the U.S. State Department's list of nations "sponsoring terrorism" implies that such tactics are predominantly a Muslim affair. Muslims see this as a form of double standard and note similar types of violence committed by Christian and Jewish groups and non-Muslim countries. Both sides tend to end up pointing fingers at each other and accentuating each other's aggressive actions. Thus, today, some Americans and Middle Easterners (including some Islamic fundamentalists) have come to share similar views of each other as violent enemies. The hostile aspects of their mutual history dominate perceptions and postures of and toward one another. For those who see the relationship this way, violence is a self-fulfilling prophecy.

NOTES

1. Jack G. Shaheen, *The TV Arab* (Bowling Green, Ohio: Bowling Green University Popular Press, 1984), p. 4.

2. Edward Said, *Covering Islam: How the Media and the Experts Determine How We See the Rest of the World* (New York: Pantheon Books, 1981), p. 51. For a listing of sample books and articles describing Islamic fundamentalism from a Western point of view, see Ahmend Bin Yousef and Ahmad AbulJobain, eds., *The Politics of Islamic Resurgence Through Western Eyes* (North Springfield, Va.: United Association for Studies and Research, 1992).

3. This view has been expressed by Steve Emerson, a journalist who has written for the *San Diego Union Tribune* and the *Washington Post*. See his essay, "Political Islam Promotes Terrorism," in Paul A. Winters, ed., *Islam: Opposing Viewpoints* (San Diego, Calif.: Greenhaven Press, 1995), p. 161. Somewhat similar opinions have also been expressed by author and researcher Daniel Pipes, who edits the journal *Middle East Quarterly* (see his piece on political Islam entitled "Same Difference" in the *National Review* of November 7, 1994); and Amos Perlmutter, professor of political science at American University in Washington, D.C., and editor of the *Journal of Strategic Studies* (see his piece entitled "Islamic Threat Is Clear and Present" in *Insight on the News*, February 15, 1993).

4. Michael Suleiman, *The Arabs in the Mind of America* (Brattleboro, Vt.: Amana Books, 1988), p. 2.

5. Most cultures have a minority of people who see the world in terms of conspiracies that threaten their country and their way of life. The United States

Conclusion

Any study of Islamic fundamentalism brings to the fore a number of issues and questions. A primary issue is history and how it is read. The history that plays a major role in shaping the outlook and goals of Islamic fundamentalists is both an ordinary one describing human activity and one that has a special biblical-like component that centers around God's instructions to humankind, and the Muslim community's reaction to this divine message. This message contains God's instructions on how the individual and his community are to live a good and pious life.

In the Islamic fundamentalist interpretation of this history, the Judeo-Christian West has played a role of antagonist to the protagonist part enacted by the Muslim community. Particularly in the recent past, the West is seen as an imperialist and aggressive enemy that represents not only a military threat, but also a source of cultural contamination. Since the end of the seventeenth century, the Muslim world has not fared well in this conflict. The Islamic world has been in decline, prompting Muslims to search for reasons why this should be so. Islamic fundamentalists have come to the conclusion that it is because Muslims have abandoned or forgotten the divine aspect of their history—God's instructions to live a good and pious life—that they have suffered such a fate. "God has not forsaken Muslims," they often say, "rather Muslims have forsaken God." To create once more a great Islamic civilization, Muslims must return to the "straight path," outlined by God in the Quran, elaborated in the Shariah law, and historically modeled by the life of the prophet Muhammad and his companions.

When we take up examples of how Islamic fundamentalists have attempted to return Muslim society to the "straight path," other issues and questions arise. What is the best way to accomplish this task? Hasan al-Banna was the first modern Islamic fundamentalist to address this question in an organizational way. He believed that the Muslim people—specifically, those of his native Egypt—must first be re-Islamized before a successful Islamic state could be established. To this end, he sought to build an organization that would provide a role model for the piety, compassion, and community spirit he felt was the true message of Islam. To a great extent, this approach worked, and the Society of the Muslim Brothers that he founded grew rapidly. But success only heightened the expectations and desires of his followers for an Islamic state, while creating corresponding suspicion and fear on the part of Egypt's secular rulers. In the ensuing clash, al-Banna was killed and the brotherhood repressed.

This brings up the question of violence. Islamic fundamentalist organizations seek to re-Islamize societies that are already politically and economically ruled by powerful secular elites with vested interests. These elites are often allied to Western powers and are willing to defend their position with violence. On the other hand, Islamic fundamentalists are increasingly willing either to initiate violence in their own pursuit of change, or to respond to state violence in kind. In recent years, Western allies of oppressive Middle Eastern regimes have also been considered legitimate targets. The result is often a cycle of violence and terror in which innocent civilians suffer and die.

The lesson many Islamic fundamentalists drew from the fate of Hasan al-Banna and the Society of Muslim Brothers was that state power must first be achieved before the process of re-Islamization can succeed. This was the approach unsuccessfully taken by Islamic fundamentalists participating in national elections in Algeria in 1991, but successfully pursued through confrontation and revolution in Iran in 1979. In Iran the attitudes and goals of Islamic fundamentalism were further shaped by the Shi'ite nature of Iranian Islam. Shi'ites place a particular emphasis on martyrdom and the struggle against injustice. This emphasis added to the revolutionary ardor of the Iranian Islamic fundamentalists.

The success of the Iranian movement raised issues of governance and social organization. What was a revolutionary Islamic state to look like?

Within the modern context, it was not sufficient simply to try to replicate eighth-century Medina. Because the Iranians had struggled against the monarchy of the Shah, they rejected kingship and instead established a republic. And because the organizational nature of Shi'ite Islam is hierarchical, the governmental structure Iran's Islamic fundamentalists created was also hierarchical, with a Pope-like executive office called the jurisprudent.

The Islamic Republic of Iran provides a picture of what might be expected of future Islamic states. While a republic, with an electoral process and a parliament, it is not a democracy in the Western sense. Opposition to the Islamic nature of state and society is not permitted. For instance, no political party advocating the separation of church and state is allowed to function. Morality and gender relations are regulated by the state according to Islamic norms, and a Western lifestyle is not possible in Iran. Culture is what the government says it should be. Other examples of present-day experiments in Islamic rule are also very different from Western democracy. We have examined the case of Saudi Arabia and have seen that, in many ways, it is even less politically and culturally progressive than Iran. The Sudan and Afghanistan are essentially military regimes with Islamic pretensions, and, until recently, the same could be said of Pakistan.

It may be that an Islamic state cannot be democratic in the Western sense. Any ideology (Islamic or otherwise) that claims a monopoly of truth, and sees its content as divinely posited, is unlikely to tolerate political opposition. In addition, today's Islamic fundamentalists are reacting against a long period of Western imperialism and continuing Western cultural encroachment. These experiences do not encourage sympathy for Western politics or values, and most Islamic fundamentalists believe that any Islamic state will have to attempt to restrict Western influences and ways as a prerequisite to the re-Islamizing of society.

On the other hand, an important part of Islamic history and tradition was open, eclectic, and experimental. Indeed, the magnificent culture created by Muslim civilization at its height (ninth to twelfth centuries) was achieved by borrowing and synthesizing the best of Greek, Roman, Persian, Jewish, Christian, and even Hindu learning. Today, as the biographies offered in this volume suggest, this potential for eclectism is reflected in the wide range of opinions held by Islamic fundamentalists on the issues of politics and economics. All of them, however, claim to ground those opinions in their reading of the Quran, Shariah law, and the life of Muhammad. All opinions must attempt to justify themselves through these canonical sources.

Islamic fundamentalism is growing in popularity throughout the Muslim world, and more countries will likely have Islamic fundamentalist governments in the future. The campaign for Islamic fundamentalist political power and cultural revival is often accompanied by much anti-Western rhetoric and violence directed against targets in the West. The reaction in the West has been a counter-chorus that condemns Islamic fundamentalism and proclaims the absolute incompatibility of the Western and Muslim worlds. Much of this hostility echoes a past rivalry between the Judeo-Christian and Muslim worlds that was marked by crusades, imperialist aggression, and religious conflict. Maintaining such an antagonistic posture is self-destructive on the part of the West. It aligns the Western powers with increasingly unpopular and corrupt dictatorships. This, in turn, invites the kind of violence Americans witnessed on September 11, 2001.

The fact that the religious, political, and cultural outlooks of secular Westerners and Islamic fundamentalists are very different does not have to result in the "clash of civilizations" that has been predicted by some of the more extreme Western observers. Liberal democracy and secular culture are relatively recent phenomena in the history of societies and certainly not the only model for political or cultural organization. And, in recent years, the Western democracies have shown themselves able to overcome periods of bitter enmity with countries like China, Japan, and Russia, so as to establish peaceful political and economic relations. Saudi Arabia is a case where it has been demonstrated that a conservative Islamic state can find common ground for good and stable relations with the West. There may well be future periods of tension between the democratic, secular West and some Islamic fundamentalist movements and states, but, given the convergence of economic and strategic interests, in the long run the two different societies might just as likely find ways to accommodate each other.

Biographies: The Personalities Behind Islamic Fundamentalism

Below are brief biographies of leading Islamic fundamentalists. Literally thousands of influential Islamic activist leaders live throughout today's Muslim world, and those included here are only a representative sample. It is important to note that there are significant differences among them. The popular Western belief that Islamic fundamentalists are all of one mind is true only in the narrowest sense. Whereas all of them do seek to bring about societal renewal through the revival of Muslim values and traditions, how one interprets those values and traditions, or how one goes about their revival, are matters of much debate. Similarly, to what degree they accept or reject Western ideas and institutions is also under debate. Noting the differences as well as the similarities will provide a more accurate, "real-life" sense of the range of Islamic activism.

Sayyid Jamal al-Din 'al-Afghani (1838/1839–1897)

An inspirational and innovative early Islamic modernist and anti-imperialist, Afghani was born in Iran and received a Shi'ite education that included study in the Shi'ite religious centers of Iran and Iraq. Because of the Sunni world's on-going hostility to Shi'ite Islam, Afghani and his disciples sought to hide his Iranian origins, and he adopted an Afghan alias.

Afghani spent his life traveling widely, including visits to the Western countries of England, France, and Russia. His longest stays, however, were in Egypt and India. His arrival in India coincided with the famous Indian Mutiny against British rule (1857). His experiences in India gave Afghani a lifelong dislike of imperialism in general and British rule in particular. He became convinced that British rule in Muslim lands sought the erosion of Islam and its replacement with Christianity.

In the face of Western encroachment, then reaching its peak in the late nineteenth century, Afghani sought to use Islam as a vehicle to promote international Muslim solidarity against imperialism. To this end, he began a reinterpretation of Islamic beliefs and values, seeking to draw from them a basis for the modernization of Muslim life. A more modern, rationalist Muslim life would more readily inculcate science and other up-to-date aspects of thought that would in turn allow the Muslim world to strengthen itself against the West.

Afghani, therefore, rejected the uncritical traditionalism espoused by many of the ulama. Yet his anti-imperialism also caused him to reject any slavish imitation of the West. He sought a middle ground—a modernized, yet essentially Muslim social and cultural revival.

Afghani was also politically active. While in Egypt (1871–1879), he openly opposed the government of Khedive (the title then given to the Egyptian head of state) as well as growing British influence and intrusion within the country. This activity set a precedent for future Islamic political activism, but also eventually led to his expulsion from Egypt in 1879.

Afghani was probably not a strong believer in orthodox Islam. He made a distinction between what he saw as a rationalistic religious worldview fit for an intellectual elite and the more traditional, storybook religion of the masses. This elitism ultimately limited the influence he and his disciples had with the general Muslim population.

Nonetheless, Afghani's boldness, perseverence, and charisma, combined with his intellectual and analytical brilliance, caused him to become a major early leader of a movement that advocated transforming Islam from a staid religious faith based on traditionalism and passivity into a religiopolitical ideology. As such, Islam would ultimately become a movement for social and political reform, as well as a basis for international solidarity against foreign cultural intrusion.

Hasan al-Banna (1906–1949)

Hasan al-Banna, founder of Egypt's Society of the Muslim Brothers, was born in the Egyptian delta town of Mahmudiya in October 1906. His father was both a religious scholar and a tradesman who repaired watches. As a youth, al-Banna went to lay schools but also joined a series of religious societies, the most important of which was the Hasafiya Sufi order. His early upbringing oriented him toward an active interest in and concern for the community's welfare, which he saw in Muslim religious terms.

In 1923 al-Banna left home for Cairo where he entered Dar al-Ulum, Egypt's teacher training college. He believed that teachers were in the best position to influence the future course of society. While in Cairo he personally witnessed the process of transformation Egypt was undergoing as Western influences permeated the local culture and affected the lifestyles of the country's middle and upper classes. Banna became convinced that Egypt was drifting toward a materialistic, secular, and immoral state such as that which existed in the West.

After graduation from Dar al-Ulum, al-Banna was assigned as an instructor in Arabic at the primary school in Ismailiya, the town along the Suez Canal which was also the site of the Suez Canal Company's headquarters. Here he experienced at first hand the racism and foreign dominance that went with British imperialism. It was under these conditions that al-Banna, in 1928, founded the Society of the Muslim Brothers.

Al-Banna believed that the root cause of Egypt's (and generally the Muslim world's) problems was its deviation from a true Islamic community. Therefore, the goal of his Society was to bring Egypt's Muslim population back to a true understanding and practice of Islam. This meant going back to a lifestyle based on the Quran and Sunna, as well as assuring a government that ruled on the basis of Muslim values and norms. Egypt had fallen away from this true path centuries before due to selfish and corrupt rulers and passive ulama. This decline had in turn so weakened society in general that it was not able to resist Western imperialism or cultural contamination.

Al-Banna was not an original thinker in philosophical or religious terms. He clearly built on the precedents of men like al-Afghani and Abduh. But these earlier thinkers did not have the skill or opportunity to turn their ideas into practice by building a grassroots organization. It is here that al-Banna's talent and genius lay. A charismatic leader, exceptional public speaker, and a man with a genuine interest in and compassion for the average citizen, al-Banna was able to put together an effective, hierarchally ordered national organization dedicated to the Islamic revival of Egypt. He infused the Society of the Muslim Brothers with his own enthusiasm. It was an accomplishment that serves as a model for Islamic revivalist movements to this day.

Under al-Banna's leadership, the Society of the Muslim Brothers grew to be one of Egypt's largest organizations. It is uncertain whether al-Banna ever had any definite plans to take over the Egyptian state. His hopes probably lay with conversion rather than conquest. He always asserted that an Islamic government had to await the thorough re-Islamization of the Egyptian masses. He did, however, allow for the Society to defend itself with force through the creation of a "special apparatus" unit that sometimes acted independently and violently. Confrontation with the secular-minded Egyptian government was probably inevitable, and, on February 12, 1949, Hasan al-Banna was assassinated by members of the Egyptian secret police.

Sayyid Muhammad Husayn Fadlallah (b. 1935)

Sayyid Muhammad Husayn Fadlallah, a principal spokesman for the Lebanese fundamentalist organization Hezbollah, was born in Najaf, Iraq on November 16, 1935. His father had migrated to Najaf from the village of Aynata in southern Lebanon in order to pursue religious studies. Fadlallah grew up in Najaf, which is a city of Shi'ite religious schools and holy shrines. Here he received a thoroughly Shi'ite Muslim education. He proved to be precocious and gifted—an accomplished poet and charismatic speaker. According to one historian who has studied his life, Fadlallah possesses "immense powers of persuasion."

In 1966 the repression exercised by the secular-minded Iraqi regime against the country's ulama forced Fadlallah out of Iraq and back to Lebanon. He settled first in the mixed Shi'ite-Palestinian shantytown of Nabaa, which was part of east Beirut. There he became the community's teacher and preacher. He developed a strong bond with the poor and oppressed of the area, setting up clinics, youth clubs, and Islamic schools. In the sermons he delivered at his mosque, he spoke of the need for an Islamic government as the best means of solving Lebanon's social and economic problems. He also denounced the imperialist economic and cultural policies he believed the West pursued in the Muslim world, as well as the existence of the state of Israel. He perceived Israel as "an instrument of the West."

In the mid-1970s, at the beginning of the Lebanese civil war, Fadlallah wrote a book entitled Islam and the Logic of Force. In this work he said that the Shi'ites must arm themselves not only in self-defense against other aggressive Lebanese sectarian groups, but also so as to participate in a broader war against imperialism and Israel. He predicted that Lebanon would be a "flashpoint" in a worldwide struggle between Islam and the West. Muslims had to prepare for this struggle by gaining absolute faith in their cause. This faith would banish the fear of confronting militarily superior foes and give them the strength to make necessary sacrifices. On the other hand, he espoused careful and realistic planning. "Legitimate and effective violence," he noted, "could only proceed from belief welded to sober calculation."

The civil war forced Fadlallah out of Nabaa in 1975, and after taking refuge in south Lebanon he was again forced to flee in 1976 because of Israeli attacks. He finally resettled in the southern Beirut neighborhood of Bir al-Abd. Here he slowly rebuilt his congregation and social service network.

The 1979 Iranian Revolution gave Fadlallah and most of his fellow Shi'ite clerics great encouragement. The notion of an Islamic government was no longer a dream. Fadlallah cooperated with the Iranian representatives in Lebanon, but initially he opposed the creation of militant organization Hezbollah because he feared it would split the Shi'ite community. Most Shi'ites already gave their allegiance to a more moderate group called AMAL. Instead Fadlallah wanted to transform AMAL into an Islamic fundamentalist organization. However, Hezbollah was established with Iranian aid and soon was involved not only in the civil war, but, by the early 1980s, also in fighting the Israelis and other foreign forces in Lebanon. Fadlallah supported Hezbollah in these efforts and used his great powers of persuasion to justify such actions as the October 1983 truck bomb attacks on the U.S. Marine and French military barracks in Beirut. He explained that such suicide attacks were justified when they were part of a jihad recognized by legitimate Muslim authorities. He also observed that since the Shi'ites did not have the modern war machines of the West and Israel, they were forced to use other means. They did not have to play by the rules set by their enemies.

On the other hand, Fadlallah regretted the need for violence against civilians. He opposed the 1985 Hezbollah hijacking of a TWA airliner at Beirut and generally disapproved of hostage taking. However, his opposition to such tactics was kept within Hezbollah circles. Publicly, he supported the organization and tried to explain the reasons for its behavior. Through this role of justifier, along with his public anti-American and anti-Israel stance, he became identified as one of the Hezbollah leaders responsible for terrorism. In the 1980s there were repeated attempts on his life reportedly organized by both Israeli and American agents. Fadlallah survived them all, giving his supporters the impression that he was divinely protected.

With the end of the Lebanese civil war in 1989, Fadlallah's realism helped move Hezbollah to accept the country's re-created democratic government and to participate in elections. While still dedicated to the eventual creation of an Islamic state, he argued that the Lebanese situation was very different from that of Iran, and so Muslims must learn to use the ballot box to "spread Islam and revive it." At the same time he continued to strongly oppose the Israeli presence in south Lebanon and support military action against it.

While identified with the violent tactics of Hezbollah, Fadlallah is one of the organization's more adaptable and compromising leaders. As he put it, "I learned to be pragmatic and not to drown in illusions." Such an attitude has allowed him to combine religiously derived principles and tactical realism. As a result, his following and influence have remained great.

Rashid al-Ghannoushi (b. 1941)

Rashid al-Ghannoushi, Tunisia's leading Islamic fundamentalist reformer, was born into a peasant family in southern Tunisia in 1941. He received a classical religious education and then a college education in philosophy at the University of Damascus. He also studied in France. Upon returning to Tunisia, he began a career as a teacher. In the 1970s he became part of a collective of young intellectuals who lectured and preached from an Islamic perspective on the country's cultural, moral, and religious shortcomings and needs. At the outset the group was not political. Rather, it concentrated on expanding Islamic education and moral awareness, and its audience came basically from the country's poor youth.

Tunisia was (and is) ruled as an authoritarian one-party state, the policies of which have increased the gap between rich and poor. The government's unjust actions politicized Ghannoushi and his fellows. In 1979 he formed the Islamic Association (later known as the Islamic Tendency Movement or MTI), which focused on the political, social, and economic plight of the Tunisian people. Appealing to a growing class of unemployed and underemployed workers, the new organization sought a "humanitarian restructuring" of the economy based on Islamic values, as well as popular participation in the political process. It rejected violence as a means of change and carried on peaceful propaganda and demonstrations. The Tunisian government's response was to arrest Ghannoushi and many of his compatriots in 1981.

Ghannoushi remained in prison until 1984. Even when released, however, he was forbidden to speak in public, teach, publish or travel abroad.

Ghannoushi proceeded to clandestinely rebuild the MTI and expanded its influence to include middle-class professionals. As a consequence, he was rearrested in 1987 only to be released the following year, after a new strong-man, Ben Ali, took over the government. Ben Ali initially promised greater political freedom. To accommodate the new regime, Ghannoushi changed the name of his movement to Hizb al-Nahda, or the Renaissance Movement, and redefined its goals in a way that avoided direct reference to Islam. Nonetheless, when the 1989 elections in Tunisia were held, the government refused Ghannoushi's party the right to stand for election. Frustrated and angry at the government's actions, members of the al-Nahda ran as independents and won 15 percent of the overall vote. They took up to 30 percent in some cities. Thus, without officially running, Ghannoushi's party emerged as the strongest opposition group in Tunisia. The government of Ben Ali reverted to form and began a massive crack-down on al-Nahda. Ghannoushi, knowing that his rearrest was just a matter of time, went into exile in Britain in May 1989. He remains there as a vocal critic of the Tunisian dictatorship.

Rashid al-Ghannoushi is a prolific intellectual (he has written fifteen books and hundreds of scholarly articles and lectures) as well as a man of political action. But most of all, he is an excellent example of a relatively moderate Islamic activist who has consistently resisted any recourse to violence. In addition, he does not condemn the West out of hand; rather, he seeks to integrate Islamically compatible Western intellectual and political concepts into the Tunisian milieu. For instance, he accepts a largely Western definition of democracy, including popular elections leading to the possibility of periodic changes in government. He promotes the notion of human rights for Muslims and non-Muslims alike and supports the rights of women to be active in the community. Thus, Ghannoushi stands as an Islamic leader whose values and outlook are compatible with a progressive and modernist perspective.

Hojjatoleslam Mohammad Khatami (b. 1943)

Mohammad Khatami was born in 1943 in the town of Ardakan which is located in Iran's central province of Yazd. He was born into a religious family and his father was a respected Ayatollah in the region.

Upon completion of his lower-grade schooling, Khatami attended the universities of Isfahan and Tehran, and then went to the theological seminary in the city of Qom. During his time as a university student Khatami became an opponent of the Shah's regime, and was involved in organizing rallies and debates. He spent the years immediately leading up to the 1979 revolution in Germany as the head of the Hamburg Islamic Center. There he helped turn the Center into a campaign post against the Shah and in support of the Ayatollah Khomeini.

After the revolution Khatami stood for election to the first Majles or Iranian parliament (1980), winning a seat from his hometown of Ardakan. His administrative abilities were soon recognized, and in 1982 he was appointed Minister of Culture and Islamic Guidance. It was at this point that his more open and liberal attitudes toward what was and was not permissible first brought him into conflict with conservatives. Khatami's philosophy is that Sharia or Muslim law must be interpreted in light of modern conditions. Its adaptability is what makes it relevant to changing times. To insist on a strict reading of the law is to breed unnecessary opposition to the Islamic revolution in Iran. During the war with Iraq Khatami served as head of the Office of War Propaganda. In the 1990s he served variably as cultural adviser to President Rafshanjani, and as head of Iran's National Library.

Khatami came forward as a relatively unknown candidate for the presidency in 1997. Soon, however, his personalized style of campaigning, and comparatively liberal views won him the support of a majority of Iranians. He won that election with 70 percent of the vote. In 2001 he won reelection with 78 percent of the vote. Nonetheless, his ability to use the office of the President to liberalize the Iranian state has been very limited. His power is much less than that of the country's more conservative supreme religious leader who controls the state's instruments of force: the army, police, and revolutionary guards. As a result, a continuing struggle exists between the elected, more reform-minded, forces and the powerful conservative and entrenched sections of the government that do not answer in any democratic way to the Iranian people.

Ayatollah Sayyid Ruhollah Mussaui Khomeini (1902–1989)

Ruhollah Mussaui Khomeini, leader of the 1979 Iranian Revolution, was born in the small village of Khomein in central Iran on September 24, 1902. The Khomeini at the end of his name simply designates his village origin. He was born into a family that traced its lineage back to the prophet Muhammad through the line of the seventh Shi'ite Imam, Musa al-Kazem. The youngest of six children, he first attended a government school as well as a maktab, or religious school for children. In the maktab, Khomeini was taught a Shi'ite version of history that emphasized the historical wrongs done to the Shi'ite community within the context of an on-going struggle between good and evil. All his studies past the elementary school level were of a religious nature. Intelligent, disciplined, and hard working, in the early 1930s Khomeini became a recognized mujtahid, or learned interpreter of Islamic law. It was also at about this time that he married and would eventually father five children.

Khomeini's studies and interests covered a wide range of religious subjects. He was interested not only in Islamic law and philosophy, but also in mysticism. He believed in an inner search for contact with God and an inner exploration of the true nature of reality. This striving carried over into a belief in the perfectibility of man and his institutions and the obligation of the enlightened leader to push the Muslim community in the direction of greater moral and social perfection. In his struggle with the Shah of Iran, he would turn this belief from theory into practice.

Khomeini's early professional life was characterized by frustration over the corrupt and secular-oriented rule of the Pahlavi Shahs as well as the apparent decay and passivity of the clerical establishment in the face of state repression. He remained in the background, however, out of deference to senior clerics and his own teachers. Meanwhile, in the course of his developing career as a teacher at various religious schools, he built up a considerable student following. Many of his students would later assume influential religious positions throughout Iran and the Shi'ite world generally.

Khomeini began to be more vocal in his opposition to the government after World War II. The new and young Muhammad Reza Shah had just taken the throne, and Khomeini's seniority within the religious establishment was growing. It was at this time that he began to articulate the notion that "government can only be legitimate when it accepts the rule of God and the rule of God means the implementation of the Shariah." In the early 1960s the Shah pushed ahead with secular reforms that included women's suffrage and a land reform bill that would have cut into clerical income. An escalating confrontation began between the government and the Shi'ite clerics in which Khomeini emerged as the militant leader. Following violent protests in the holy city of Qum, Khomeini was arrested and finally, in 1964, he was exiled. In exile he spent time in Turkey, Iraq, and then Paris.

Khomeini would demonstrate a high degree of political shrewdness and manipulative talent as he built and maintained a powerful religiously oriented revolutionary movement. As he did so, he refined his notion of the Islamic state, at the core of which would be the institution of the jurisprudent, or Vilayat-i-Faqih. Following the overthrow of the Shah in 1978, Khomeini would eventually attain this unique position and through it rule Iran. As ruler of Iran from 1978 to his death on June 3, 1989, Khomeini strove to create an institutionally stable Islamic state. In doing so, he found that he had to make compromises with his ideal of perfection. These compromises came only grudgingly, as is reflected in Iran's rather poor human rights record at this time. In the realization of the Islamic state, God took a vengeful form. Nonetheless, Ruhollah Khomeini was the first man in modern times to successfully realize the establishment of a revolutionary Islamic state. That he sought the well-being of the masses of Iranian people, particularly the poor, is generally accepted by most of those who study this period of Iranian history. And there can be no doubt that his legacy goes far beyond Iran, for his success continues to inspire Islamic fundamentalists throughout the Muslim world.

Osama bin Laden (b. 1957)

Osama bin Laden was born in 1957 into the wealthy bin Laden clan of Saudi Arabia. His father, Awad bin Laden, started as a poor laborer but ended up owner of the largest construction company in the country. The bin Ladens have been close to the royal Saudi family for decades.

Osama was his father's seventh son. Awad died when the boy was only thirteen. Osama was educated in Jedda and eventually received a college degree in public administration. He was also raised as a religious Muslim. He has almost no experience outside of the Muslim world and little understanding of Western secular culture.

As a student Osama was disciplined and hard working, but did not stand out. He appeared to be nonconfrontational in nature. When the Grand Mosque in Mecca was taken over by Islamic radicals in 1980, he opposed the action. Nonetheless, the religious orientation of the family, as well as its high social position, brought him into contact with numerous Islamic fundamentalist leaders and scholars. These contacts no doubt deepened his faith and caused him to accept the need for activism.

Soon after the Soviet invasion of Afghanistan, bin Laden started to raise money to support the resistance. By 1984 he had established a "guest house" in Peshawar, Pakistan, to house Arab and other fighters bound for the Afghani front. It soon turned into something of a logistical center involved in training, religious support, and the funneling of men and equipment into Afghanistan.

By 1986 bin Laden was using his immense wealth to establish his own camps within Afghanistan. He had his own command structure, recruited men with military experience from Syria, Egypt, and elsewhere, and thus created his own private army. The entire apparatus became known as Al-Qaeda, or the firm base. Between 1986 and 1989 bin Laden saw considerable combat. He was involved in at least five major battles and hundreds of smaller operations. With the Soviets in retreat, bin Laden had reason to believe that his efforts had helped defeat one of the world's two great superpowers.

When bin Laden returned to visit Saudi Arabia in 1989, the government banned him from leaving the country. The reason for this was the Saudi fear that bin Laden would now spread his military operations to other Muslim lands, attacking those regimes perceived as corrupt and inimical to Islam. He was also giving talks throughout the kingdom warning of Iraqi plans to invade Kuwait and Saudi Arabia. This embarrassed the Saudi government which, at the time, was on good terms with Saddam Hussein.

When the Iraqis did invade Kuwait in 1990, bin Laden submitted a detailed plan to the Saudi king for the defense of the state. As part of this plan he offered to mobilize the Arab fighters he had commanded in Afghanistan to confront the Iraqis in Kuwait. His reasoning was that if these fighters could defeat the Soviets they could certainly take on Saddam's forces. Instead of accepting his offer, the Saudi government accepted American military assistance. The Americans had a lot at stake in the Gulf and so were anxious to stop the Iraqis. They were not going to leave the security of their oil interests in the hands of bin Laden's fighters. Bin Laden reacted with disapproval, and he expressed this publicly as well as to many of the kingdom's religious scholars and Muslim activists. The Saudi government then limited his movements to the city of Jeddah. In 1991 he was finally able to slip out of Saudi Arabia. He went first to Pakistan and then into Afghanistan where he sought to mediate between the factions then fighting a civil war for control of the country. The Saudis made several attempts to kidnap him and so in late 1991 he secretly fled to Sudan.

In Sudan bin Laden used his experience and contacts in the construction industry to help the government organize and fund large domestic projects. During this time anti-American incidents occurred in Somalia and South Yemen. Both involved people who had been trained in Afghanistan. However, bin Laden's direct connection to these incidents has not been proven. Nor did he involve himself in Sudan's civil war. Nonetheless, the Saudi regime had him classified as an enemy of the state and, in 1992, froze his assets. In 1994 they withdrew his citizenship. In 1996, feeling that he had become an embarrassment to the Sudanese government, he returned to Afghanistan where he eventually came under the protection of the Taliban government.

Shortly after his return to Afghanistan, the Khobar towers, a U.S. military housing complex in Saudi Arabia, was bombed. There is strong suspicion that bin Laden was involved in the planning and financing of this attack. Also in 1996 bin Laden issued his first "bayan," or public announcement against the United States. In it he issued a warning to the United States to remove its troops from Arabia, otherwise the same fighters who had defeated the Soviets in Afghanistan would wage war on America. By 1998 this threat was being realized. In that year bomb attacks were launched against U.S. embassies in East Africa. In 2001 the U.S. naval vessel *Cole* was attacked in Yemen. Bin Laden was almost certainly involved in these actions.

While American (non-Muslim) troops in the holy land of Arabia were seen as a sacrilege, this was not bin Laden's only grievance against the United States. He regarded U.S. policy in Iraq, Egypt, and Palestine as part of a Western war on Islam. The way bin Laden interpreted U.S. behavior helped shape his worldview and ultimately led to his involvement in the attacks on the World Trade Center and the Pentagon on September 11, 2001. At that point he became, at least in the West, the world's best-known, and most-wanted "terrorist mastermind." The United States has been hunting for him ever since. However, as of 2002, the U.S. government's emphasis on bin Laden has lessened (perhaps because, so far, they have failed to capture him) in favor of seeking out Al-Qaeda cells in general.

Bin Laden gave one post–September 11th interview and this was to the Al-Jazeera TV network. It was recorded on October 21, 2001 and subsequently broadcast by CNN in February 2002. In this interview bin Laden stated that "we will work to continue this battle, God permitting, until victory or until we meet God. . . . If killing those who kill our sons is terrorism, then let history be witness that we are terrorists."

Abbasi Madani (b. 1931)

Abbasi Madani, the founder of the Islamic Salvation Front of Algeria, was born at Sidi Uqbah in southeastern Algeria in 1931. He grew up in Algeria's eastern Biskra region and received an early traditional religious education. He then became involved in the rebellion against French colonial rule and, in 1954, joined the National Liberation Front (FLN), the Algerian movement that waged war against France. Captured during an attack, he spent most of the years of the rebellion in jail.

After Algeria gained its independence from France in 1964, Madani went abroad to complete his education. He spent nearly a decade in England and earned a Ph.D. in the field of comparative education. When he returned to Algeria, he began teaching as part of the Faculty of Humanities at the university in Algiers. Soon he became involved in Islamically oriented reform causes such as the demand for the Arabization of education (replacing French with Arabic as the language of instruction), the end of coeducation, and the banning of alcohol. That is, Madani joined those who were demanding the gradual re-Islamization of Algerian life.

By the 1970s, Algeria's economic situation was worsening. Its foreign debt had grown along with unemployment and a chronic housing shortage. Madani, and others sharing his Islamic outlook, helped establish welfare organizations in the slums of Algiers to help meet neighborhood needs, particularly the vocational training of youth. For Madani, re-Islamization was tied to a strong sense of social and economic justice as well as the promotion of a self-help ethic. To fully realize the country's potential, however, and meet the needs of its people would require the establishment of an Islamic government. Thus, he became politically active and organized protests against the secular government of Algeria. This led to his imprisonment for two years in 1982.

In March of 1989 he assumed the leadership of the Islamic Salvation Front (FIS), an umbrella group of half-a-dozen organizations pressing for Islamic social, political, and religious reform. The Front contested power within the electoral system and was on the verge of winning national elections when, in 1992, the Algerian military took over the government and aborted the process. The FIS was banned and Madani, as well as other leaders of the movement, was arrested. The result has been an on-going civil war in Algeria between the present military dictatorship and an increasingly radical and violent Islamic opposition.

Madani has usually been seen as the leader of the moderate wing of the Islamic Salvation Front. While insistent that Algeria wants and needs an Islamic government and the institution of Shariah law, he also speaks of the need for a common sense, noncoercive application of Islamic principles. He claims to be willing to "go slow" and find "a middle way" that would not end up oppressing Algeria's large and mostly westernized middle and upper classes. On the other hand, his opinion on such sensitive matters as women's rights seems to be very conservative. No matter what Madani's true feelings, it is impossible to know how he might have operated as ruler of Algeria. The FIS that he led was, by his own admission, a "pluralistic" organization representing many voices, some of which were much more strident than his. With his arrest, and the driving of the Islamic revivalist movement underground, the Algerian regime has allowed a much more violent rebel leadership to come to the fore. Madani remains in prison. Whether his brand of "moderate" Islamization can now work in Algeria is in doubt.

Sayyid Abu'l-A'la Mawdudi (1903–1979)

Abu'l-A'la Mawdudi, one of the most respected and widely read of Islamic fundamentalist thinkers, was born into an upper class Muslim family on September 25, 1903 in Aurangabad, southern India. His family traced its lineage back to the Sufi saints of the Chishti order, some of whom had originally brought Islam to India. The family also had a history of serving the Muslim rulers of the various Indian states prior to the British conquest. This heritage made Mawdudi naturally hostile to imperialism. The family atmosphere in which Mawdudi grew up was religious and ascetic. He was initially educated in a classically religious style and then was sent to school to learn modern subjects, particularly the sciences. At age sixteen, due to his father's death, he withdrew from school but continued to avidly study on his own. As a trade, he took up journalism.

Early in his life, Mawdudi adopted the cause of Indian nationalism and worked to mobilize Indian Muslims to support Indian independence. Simultaneously, his outlook became more religious, and in 1926 he received a certificate in religious training which formally made him one of the ulama. However, he never pursued this vocation. His increasing religious orientation caused him to break with the general anti-imperialist alliance of the Hindu-led independence movement and to focus on Muslim interests. He would eventually advocate a separate homeland for Indian Muslims. While he affirmed his position in a flood of persuasive and exceptionally well-written works, as well as various journals that he came to edit, he knew that just writing alone would not accomplish his aims. Thus, he founded a political organization known as the Jama'at-i Islami (the Islamic party) in 1941.

Mawdudi believed that the two principal Western ideologies, capitalism and socialism, were moral and social failures and could be successfully supplanted by Islam. The struggle to do this should be the object of all Muslim social action and, in fact, the true route to salvation for the believing Muslim. This effort would inevitably culminate in the formation of an Islamic state, the reforms of which would bring to pass a perfect society. For Mawdudi, the inevitability of this process would be self-evident to educated Muslims. As he described it, the Islamic state would have some aspects of Western states, such as a legislature, independent judiciary, constitution, and the like. It would in fact be a harmonious "theo-democracy" because all citizens would agree on basic policy as a function of their Islamic faith. Contentious issues such as women's and minority rights would solve themselves within the context of the just society established by adherence to the Quran and Shariah law.

Thus, unlike the case of Iran, where the founding of the Islamic state preceded the re-Islamization of society, Mawdudi's state required the prior re-Islamization of the populace. And this was one of the chief goals of Jama'at-i Islami. However, as it turned out, the party dedicated itself to the conversion of a small intellectual elite, particularly Muslim students, who could gain influence and control within important sectors of society. After the creation of Pakistan, the Islamic party guided by Mawdudi entered the political arena and pressed for the re-Islamization of the country's laws and customs. It came into conflict with the state under those governments that were secularist minded, and Mawdudi was arrested a number of times. But under those Pakistani regimes that were more traditionally minded, such as the military government of General Muhammad Zia'l-Haq (1977–1988), the party gained great influence and its members held high government posts.

In the end, however, Mawdudi's party never did particularly well at the polls. One can take from this that the re-Islamization of the Pakistani people, at least as defined by Mawdudi's vision of society, is still not accomplished. Nevertheless, Mawdudi's emphasis on education and persuasion as a prerequisite to the Islamic state offers an alternative to the Iranian model, while his willingness to ally with other Islamically minded groups such as elements of the Pakistani military probably offers a precedent others might follow as well.

Abu'l-A'la Mawdudi was a superior intellect with a great talent for clear and precise written prose. This ability, along with his organizational skill and charismatic leadership style, makes him an inspirational source for Islamic movements throughout the Muslim world. Mawdudi died of natural causes on September 22, 1979 in Buffalo, New York where he had gone for medical treatment.

Sayyid Qutb (1906–1966)

Sayyid Qutb, a leading Egyptian fundamentalist theoretician, was born on October 9, 1906 into a family of moderate means living in the village of Musha in upper Egypt. He was sent to Cairo for an education that was of largely Western orientation. He eventually became a teacher and later an inspector of schools. Beginning in the 1930s, he wrote on social, political, and religious subjects as well as producing literary criticism. It is upon his written work that Qutb's reputation stands.

Qutb served with Egypt's Ministry of Education until 1953. From 1948 to 1950 that ministry sent him as a representative to the United States. There he experienced racism and America's general anti-Arab attitudes, especially in relation to the evolving Arab-Israeli conflict. Together with his anti-British sentiments, these experiences produced a general feeling that the West represented a hostile and dangerous political and cultural enemy of Islam.

During the 1930s and 1940s, Egypt was involved in a struggle to free itself from British imperial control, and this effort too shaped Qubt's outlook much as it had that of Hasan al-Banna. It was Qutb's view that imperialism had brought about the moral decline of the Egyptian people, and so Qutb's early social writings represent an analysis of this situation. In exploring this problem, he came to the conclusion that many Muslims had fallen into a state of "jahiliyya" or ignorance, much like that which had existed in Arabia prior to the coming of the prophet Muhammad. The West, itself a "jahiliyya" society, had contributed to this corruption of the Muslim peoples. The solution for Egypt and other Muslim lands must be a moral revival grounded on an Islamic ethic. His analysis eventually moved him from the moral salvation of the individual to that of the community as a whole. In a series of books dealing with Islam and such topics as social justice, capitalism, and world peace, Qutb asserted that Muslims could find in their religion the answer to all the community's social, economic, and political problems. Key to this revival were faith in the Quranic prescription for society and a willingness to turn theory into practice. Qutb asserted the need for enlightened Muslims to act in order to save their society.

With this activist orientation, it is not surprising that Qutb came to find his organizational home with the Society of the Muslim Brothers. He officially joined the organization in 1952 and soon headed its Section for the Propagation of the Call and Publishing. As the Brothers came into conflict with the Egyptian regime of Gamal Abdel Nasser, Qutb suffered the consequences. He was arrested in 1954 and reportedly tortured. In 1955 he was sentenced to fifteen years at hard labor.

While in jail he continued to write, and, surprisingly, most of his works were allowed to be published. His final book, Ma'alim fi al-Tariq or Signposts on the Road, came out in 1964. In this book, he asserted that a new society, in harmony with nature and human nature, could be had by properly interpreting the Quran and the model set by Muhammad and the rightfully guided Caliphs. This being the case, Muslims were under an obligation to struggle against the forces of "jahiliyya" that now controlled their society. Egyptian officials used the book in 1965 to bring Qutb to trial on charges of treason. He was executed in the summer of 1966 and thus became a martyr to the cause of Islamic reform.

Qutb's writings continue to inspire Islamists who feel the need for confrontational action in the face of what they perceive as corrupt and un-Islamic regimes, backed and influenced by Western power and culture.

Those Islamists who are more cautious as to how they seek change either keep a certain distance from Qutb's message or interpret it as directed to the individual's personal transformation rather than as a call to political and social revolution. There seems little doubt, however, that Qutb's own understanding of a Muslim's obligation in the world entailed both personal and communal struggle to realize a "perfect" Muslim society.

Shaikh Omar Abd al-Rahman (b. 1938)

Omar Abd al-Rahman, the spiritual leader of the radical Islamic Group (Gam'a Islamiya) of Egypt, was born in 1938 into a poor family in the village of al-Jamaliyah in lower Egypt. He was accidentally blinded at ten months of age and also suffers from diabetes and a heart condition. His following and fame stem more from his personal status as a handicapped person with the will to stand up against authority than from any inherent charisma, oratorical skills, or original thinking.

Educated at Cairo University and al-Azhar University, al-Rahman became both a cleric and teacher. He has taught at the University of Asyut, an Egyptian industrial city (1973–1977), as well as in Saudi Arabia (1977–1980). In the 1970s he emerged as a vocal critic of the Egyptian government and was soon identified as the spiritual guide of a small clandestine group known as Gam'a Islamiya (the Islamic Group or Community). His followers were implicated in the assassination of President Sadat in 1981. Rahman has been arrested several times in Egypt but has always been acquitted or otherwise released.

Like Hasan Turabi, Rahman does not present a systematic theory of Islamic rule. He focuses on the present-day injustice and immorality of society and government, and condemns it for its "un-Islamic" ways. He calls for the establishment of an Islamic government and the cultural and moral re-Islamization of Egyptian society, even if this requires the use of violent resistance and revolution. He is known for his hostility to Egyptian Christians and the West.

Despite this orientation, he chose to immigrate to the United States in 1990 and use his residence in New Jersey as a base for a campaign against the Egyptian government. The reasons for this choice are unclear. He may have been consciously imitating Khomeini who eventually chose Paris as a venue from which to fight the Shah of Iran. He may have believed that raising funds and issuing propaganda would be relatively easy from the United States. Or he may have wished to organize a community of exiled ex-mujahidin fighters (those who fight for the faith of Islam or "soldiers of God") from the war in Afghanistan who are now living in the United

States. He knew many of these men from his past trips to Pakistan during the Afghan war. Probably a combination of these factors prompted his move.

While in the United States he gathered a considerable following among Egyptian and other expatriots of Islamic fundamentalist persuasion. Some of these figures were implicated and later convicted of the World Trade Center bombing of February 1993. Rahman was also implicated as having encouraged the conspirators by leading them to believe that such an act was religiously justified. He was therefore charged as a co-conspirator and convicted of the bombing for which he is now in prison. Despite his present isolation from the Egyptian scene, he is still influential among small groups of Egyptian "anarcho-Islamists" who see him as a martyr and spiritual inspiration in an on-going war with the secular-minded, westernized Egyptian ruling elite.

Musa al-Sadr (1928–1978?)

Musa al-Sadr, one of Lebanon's most revered Islamic fundamentalist figures, was born in Qum, Iran, in 1928 into a family of well-established Shi'ite clerics whose ancestral roots were in Lebanon. He attended the primary and secondary schools in the city of his birth and then went to university in Teheran where he studied law and political economy. In the end, however, he made a career in religion. In 1960 he moved to Tyre, Lebanon, to become the senior Shi'ite religious authority for that city.

In Lebanon Sadr quickly gained a reputation on several levels. He became known as a political activist by insisting that Islam was a faith of action. Its message for the Lebanese Shi'ites, traditionally discriminated against by both Christians and Sunni Muslims, was that they could act to overcome their disabilities. Here Sadr also drew on Shi'ite historical images of struggle and martyrdom to inspire his people. At the same time, he gained the reputation of a compassionate and pragmatic man who was willing to make reasonable compromises with forces he could not otherwise overcome. He sought to negotiate with other groups in Lebanon for peace and development, while insisting on the rights of the Shi'ite community.

Musa al-Sadr seemed to understand that an Islamic state was an impossibility within the Lebanese context. What was not impossible, but rather in his opinion a necessity, was the conceptualizing of Islam as a politically involved movement dedicated to social justice. Here he was in tune with Ali Shariati, whom he much admired. In his efforts to improve the plight of the Shi'ites of Lebanon, Sadr founded a popular movement known as Harakat al-Mahrumin, or the Movement of the Deprived. This movement acted as a powerful interest lobby for improvements in public services and security for the Shi'ite population. It also sought to limit the power of the political bosses (the za'ims) who thrived within the traditional patronage-based village society of the region.

Sadr's political influence rose steadily throughout the 1960s and early 1970s but was eclipsed by the outbreak of the Lebanese civil war in 1975. Though his movement would, out of necessity, create its own militia (the Lebanese Resistance Detachments, better known by the acronym AMAL, arabic for "hope"), Sadr was not a man of war. The passions and irrational forces released in the civil strife completely overwhelmed his efforts. Nonetheless, Lebanese Shi'ites of all stripes acknowledge his legacy. He was the one who pushed them to abandon a politically passive lifestyle and see their religion as a guide to action.

In August of 1978 Musa al-Sadr disappeared while on a visit to Libya. It is assumed that he was killed by the government of Mu'ammar Qadhafi for reasons that remain unexplained.

Ali Shariati (1933–1977)
Ali Shariati, one of Iran's leading Islamic fundamentalist intellectuals, was born in Mazinan, Iran, a village near the city of Mashhad on November 24, 1933. His father, Muhammad-Taqi Shariati, was a progressive-minded Shi'ite cleric who took to wearing Western dress and preached the compatibility of modern life with Islamic teachings. His son was much influenced by his father's point of view and initially studied Persian and Western literature. The mix of the two cultures produced a crisis of faith in the teenage Shariati, which he eventually resolved through a study of Shi'ite mysticism. However, he never lost his progressive orientation and soon, along with his father, was a member of a group known as Nehzat-e Khoda Parastan-e Socialist, or the Movement of God-Worshiping Socialists. Unlike Muhammad Baqer as-Sadr, Shariati was convinced that much of socialist practice was compatible with Islam. Indeed, one of Shariati's heroes and the man he claimed to model his own life on, was Abu Zar, a companion of the prophet Muhammad who was a forceful proponent of equalitarianism and the just distribution of wealth.

In the early 1950s, Shariati supported the nationalist government of Mossadeq. The latter's move to nationalize Iranian oil brought about a U.S.-sponsored coup. This action further turned Shariati against the capitalist system exemplified by the United States. In 1958 he left Iran and went to study in Paris. Shariati developed a love-hate relationship with

Paris and, through the city, with the West as a whole. For example, he openly acknowledged the intellectual maturation process he underwent under the mentorship of many Western scholars, while for him, the West seemed to be the epitome of materialism and immorality. His time in Paris was also one of political activity: he wrote in support of Algerian independence from France and against the Shah's regime in Iran.

Returning to Iran in 1964, Shariati was immediately arrested and held for a month and a half. Only in 1967 did the government finally allow him to accept a university teaching position, and then only at the remote University of Mashhad. However, Shariati quickly established a reputation as a charismatic and provocative teacher. He had set himself the goal of creating a cadre of progressive Islamic intellectuals who were both willing to struggle against the Shah's dictatorship and able to address the masses in their own Islamic idiom. To this end he published a book entitled Eslamshenasi, or Islamology, in 1969. In this work, he makes a distinction between his vision of an original, genuine Islam that promotes science, intellectual freedom, democracy, and a socialist-style economic system, and the current obscurist and passive Islam offered by the conservative ulama. It was the obligation of all true Muslims to take up the original version.

As time went on, Shariati became more confrontational. His lectures were often attended by students who would later join revolutionary groups seeking the violent overthrow of the regime. He was hated by both the Shah's government and the clerical establishment, and his writings were banned. He went into hiding in 1972 but surrendered to the government after the Iranian secret police took his father and brother-in-law hostage. After eighteen months in prison, much of it in solitary confinement, he was released. Under close surveillance and subject to a smear campaign by the government and ulama, Shariati slipped out of Iran in 1977 and went to London. But the Shah's regime did not want him abroad and free to speak and write, and so once more they took members of his family hostage. This time it was his wife and six-year-old daughter. Soon thereafter, on June 21, 1977, Shariati was found dead in Southampton, England, ostensibly of a heart attack.

Ali Shariati was one of the most prolific and original of the modern Islamic fundamentalists. His collected works run to thirty-five volumes. For him, Islam demanded a social activist commitment which he found distinctly lacking among the conservative Muslims of his day. Because he also believed that Islam was compatible with modern and progressive thought, he developed a philosophy that melded religion with the ethics of socialism. Many Iranian intellectuals, alienated by the more religiously rigid outlook of men like Khomeini, rallied to Shariati's thought and example. His charisma and bravery helped mobilize resistance to the Shah; in the demonstrations that eventually brought down the regime, Shariati's picture was carried by thousands.

Ayatollah Muhammad Kazem Shariatmadari (1899–1986)

Ayatollah Shariatmadari, an important figure in the 1979 Iranian Revolution, was born in Tabriz, Iran, in 1899 and educated in both law and religion in the holy cities of Qum (in Iran) and Najaf (in Iraq). He made a career in religion and steadily rose through the ranks of the Muslim Shi'ite clerical hierarchy. He was near the top of that hierarchy by the late 1950s and early 1960s. One of his chief competitors for leadership was Ayatollah Khomeini. The two contrast greatly not only in their approach to politics, but also in their personality. Shariatmadari, unlike Khomeini, was known as a warm person with a tolerant outlook.

Shariatmadari was also an Iranian nationalist who was critical of the Shah as a leader who had overstepped his authority and become a dictator. At first, however, he was willing to save the Shah his crown through reforms that would create a constitutional monarchy. Within that constitution the ulama were to have oversight of the laws and legal system. Later, as the Shah became more oppressive and the revolutionary movement against him began, Shariatmadari abandoned the idea of a constitutional monarchy in favor of a republican form of government.

Shariatmadari wanted to see Iran reformed along the lines of Islamic principles, but, unlike Khomeini and more like Rashid al-Ghannoushi of Tunisia, he favored a liberal and flexible approach to the problem of social renewal. Shariatmadari was not afraid of assimilating Western concepts and supported the institutionalization of democratic procedures, a multiparty system, and tolerant laws toward minorities. He would have restricted the role of the ulama to an oversight function with veto power over laws. While he wished to see the implementation of Shariah law, he preached a flexible and moderate approach to its use. It is therefore not surprising that Shariatmadari drew his following from liberal and moderate opponents of the Shah, both among the ulama and laypeople.

As the revolution against the Shah evolved, Shariatmadari formed his own political party, the Islamic People's party. However, the party had little success. His moderate and tolerant positions ran counter to the growing radical mood of the country. Nonetheless, his group soon constituted the major Islamic opposition to Khomeini. For instance, he condemned the takeover of the American embassy, for which he was castigated and accused of being "pro-U.S." Once Khomeini had consolidated power, Shariatmadari was placed under house arrest. Only his great reputation as a religious sage saved him from harsher punishment. He lapsed into silence in about 1980, not wanting to encourage civil war.

Hasan'Abdallah al-Turabi (b. 1932)

Hasan al-Turabi, the present Islamic fundamentalist ruler of Sudan, was born in Kasala, Sudan, in 1932 and received an early and thorough Islamic education. He then went to the University of Khartoum where he graduated with a degree in law. He did post-graduate studies in both England and France and speaks the language of both countries fluently. On his return to the Sudan in the mid-1960s, he joined the law faculty of the University of Khartoum and became a member of the Sudanese parliament.

Turabi also joined and revitalized the Sudanese Muslim Brotherhood. His thinking at this stage reflected a desire not only to promote the re-Islamization of Sudanese society leading to an Islamic state, but also to combine resurgent Islam with the notion of Arab self-awareness and anticolonialism. In 1964 he led the Brotherhood into a new coalition party called the Islamic Charter Front, which strove to combat the rising influence of leftist ideologies in Sudan.

In 1969 Sudan was taken over by a military regime led by General Ja'far Numairi. Eventually, Numairi instituted a policy of "national reconciliation" and invited the cooperation of opposition civilian parties. Turabi was one of the few to take up this offer. Turabi's cooperation was facilitated by Numairi's apparent willingness to institute Islamic laws and policies. It also may have indicated a strategy on Turabi's part to cooperate with any force that would allow positioning members of his own party into power. Thus, depending on how one reads Turabi's personality and tactics, he is either a sincere Islamist or a Machiavellian opportunist. In any case, Turabi cooperated with the Numairi dictatorship, serving for a time as his close adviser on Islamic matters and the regime's attorney general.

By the 1970s Sudan's economic situation was deteriorating and the government's foreign debt was growing. This condition was exacerbated by the outbreak of civil war in the south of the country. Here Christian and pagan elements of the population resisted the imposition of Islamic law as well as on-going economic exploitation. To rally support, and underpin his dictatorial powers with a religious rationale, Numairi declared the Sudan an "Islamic republic" in 1983 and officially imposed Shariah law throughout the country.

Despite Numairi's turn toward Islam, he distrusted the assertive Turabi and eventually replaced him with a more subservient attorney general. In March of 1985, the regime moved against the Muslim Brotherhood, and Turabi was briefly jailed. Then, in April of that same year, Numairi was overthrown in yet another military coup. This led to the formation of a predominantly civilian cabinet that led the country for the next four years. Turabi, released from prison, formed a new organization called the Islamic National Front. Government leadership during this transitional phase proved ineffectual in the face of economic problems and continuing civil war. What remained consistent, however, was the government's clinging to Islamic policies, particularly the use of Islamic law.

In 1989, a third military coup did away with civilian rule and established a Revolutionary Council for National Salvation. At present, the major influences behind this military regime are Hasan al-Turabi and his Islamic National Front. Besides the strict enforcement of Islamic laws and morality, there seems to be little to Turabi's Islamism. He seems content to rule through a simple military dictatorship that behaves in a violent and oppressive way. Turabi's apparent ruthlessness also calls into question any insight into the Islamic principles of social justice. Nonetheless, Turabi stands behind one of today's self-proclaimed Islamic governments.

Sheikh Muhammad ibn abd al-Wahhab (1703–1792)

Shiekh al-Wahhab was the founder of the religious reform movement that eventually resulted in the Islamic state of Saudi Arabia. He was born in 1703 at Uyaina, a town no longer in existence, in the Najd region of Arabia. He received a religious education, studying for a time at Medina. He then traveled widely, visiting and studying in places such as Syria, Iraq, Kurdistan, and Persia. When he returned to Arabia he began preaching a puritan form of Islam that called for a return to the basics of Islam as prescribed in the Quran and hadiths.

In about the year 1744 he settled in Dariyah, Arabia and there became the spiritual guide to the house of Saud. The Saud clan at this time was a group of local notables seeking to expand their influence and authority. Wahhab thus struck up a "marriage of convenience" with the clan leader Muhammad ibn Saud. Wahhab and his followers would support the Saud family's efforts at expansion, and the Saud would in turn spread Wahhab's puritan version of Islam.

In the West the followers of that version of Islam are now known as Wahhabis, but historically they have called themselves Mowahhidin or unitarians. This term stems from the first principle of their vision of Islam—the absolute oneness of God. Some of the other important principles Wahhab preached are:

1. A return to the original teachings of Islam as put forth in the Quran and hadiths.
2. The need to unite faith and action.
3. A forbidding of all nonorthodox views and practices. This led Wahhab to wage a life-long campaign against such practices as saint worship and pilgrimages to tombs and shrines to seek the intervention of the saints and idols.
4. The creation of a Muslim state which would be based exclusively on the practice of religious law. To the extent that the Sauds extended their authority in Arabia, something approximating an Islamic state was established.

Muhammad ibn abd al-Wahhab created a movement that did more than lead to today's Saudi Arabia. Wahhabi influence has spread throughout the Muslim world if only through the exposure to this brand of Islam by the millions of pilgrims who go each year to Mecca. Wahhab taught that true Muslims must be concerned about politics and the nature of the state. If their rulers failed to behave as good Muslims, if they failed to create a state in which Shariah law was instituted, then the believing Muslim had the religious obligation to replace that ruler and his un-Islamic government. Even if Wahhab's particular puritan brand of Islam is not the goal of all of today's Muslim reformers, his message of political activism and the melding of faith and action has certainly taken root.

Shaykh Ahmad Yasin (b. 1936)

Shaykh Ahmad Yasin, the founder of the militant Palestinian Islamic fundamentalist group Hamas, was born in the village of Jora in the northern part of the Gaza Strip in 1936. His father was a farmer and moderate landowner who died when Yasin was only five. The family was religious, and Yasin's upbringing and education was a traditional Muslim one.

In 1948 the family was forced to flee Jora because of the first Arab-Israeli war. They took up residence in a refugee camp. The trauma of dispossession and flight had a lasting impact on the young Yasin, and he found both solace and hope in the Muslim faith. He joined the Gaza branch of the Society of the Muslim Brothers and became convinced that only an Islamic revival could lay the basis for the retaking of Palestine from the Israelis and the revival of Palestinian society.

In 1952, at the age of sixteen, Yasin broke his back in an accident that left him partially paralyzed. This misfortune only deepened his religious faith. Following his hospitalization, he found work as a teacher of religion and Arabic language. He also sought to spread Islamic awareness through meetings and discussion groups at the various Gaza mosques. His activities at this time were basically religious and not very political.

In 1967, however, Israel occupied the Gaza Strip. Yasin and his associates in the Muslim Brotherhood adopted a nonprovocative stance, seeking to gradually build a basis for resistance to occupation around religious faith and solidarity. It was the PLO that carried on the armed struggle at this time. While Yasin admired the PLO's efforts, he disapproved of their secular ideology. Yasin and the Muslim Brothers remained outside of the mainstream Palestinian resistance movement.

In the 1970s the PLO suffered a number of setbacks that saw some of its popular support move to the Palestinian Islamic camp. Yasin took advantage of this opening, and, as the PLO's ability to act as a representative and protector of the Palestinians waned, the Islamists would seek to fill the resulting void. At this time, Yasin and his colleagues were calling for the eventual establishment of an Islamic state in all of Palestine. They also now argued that the use of violence was legitimate to "remove oppression and corruption and establish justice." The Iranian Revolution of 1979 seemed to provide proof that these positions were correct. Generous financial aid from Saudi Arabia and other Gulf states allowed the Islamists to expand their activities.

In 1973 Yasin established the Islamic Center in the city of Gaza. It became the headquarters for a growing Islamic infrastructure that included religious, social, economic, educational, and health-related organizations. By the 1980s, it was one of the Gaza Strip's most powerful and influential institutions. Slowly but surely, it was helping to inject an Islamic point of view into the Palestinian national consciousness. As the Center's influence grew, so did that of Yasin, and this caused him to shift to a more aggressive form of action. For example, in 1983 he decided to create two paramilitary organizations. One, Al-Majd, was assigned the task of identifying and punishing those who behaved in overtly anti-Islamic ways, such as drug dealers and prostitutes, but also those who collaborated with the Israelis. The other group, Al-Mujahidum, was assigned the role of carrying out specific military operations against Israel.

As these activities evolved, Yasin's ability and charisma became evident. He proved himself highly intelligent and, despite his handicap, a tireless worker. He became a popular arbiter and mediator of disputes in a Gaza community where the only official legal structure was controlled by the Israeli occupiers. Soon he was a true community leader of immense popularity. His activities inevitably brought him to the attention of the Israelis who arrested him in 1983. He was charged with creating an Islamic organization dedicated to the destruction of Israel and sentenced to thirteen years in prison. However, after ten months he was released in a prisoner exchange.

Then, in 1987, the Palestinian Intifada, or popular uprising, began. Yasin quickly moved to position the Islamic movement at the forefront of the revolt, thus demonstrating a connection between religion and national resistance. To this end he founded Hamas, or the Islamic Resistance Movement, as a separate organization from the Muslim Brotherhood and Islamic Center. In this way, if the revolt failed, the Muslim Brothers could deny any direct involvement. If it succeeded, however, they could claim credit by associating themselves with Hamas.

Yasin declared that the establishment of Hamas was "his duty as a human being, as a Muslim, as an Arab, and as a Palestinian." Like Muhammad Husayn Fadlallah and the Hezbollah, Yasin did not feel that those who "for decades had been suffering under the yoke of intruding and oppressive occupation" had any obligation to fight according to the rules set forth by the enemy. Thus, the actions of Hamas were sometimes terroristic.

The war waged by Hamas combined militancy and religion, moral righteousness and patriotism, all with the promise of personal salvation through action and martyrdom as well as national salvation. Thus, whatever bad press Hamas received in the West, its struggle provided a great psychological lift to many Palestinians and won new recruits for the Islamic camp. In 1989 Yasin was once more arrested and this time sentenced to fifteen years in prison. His imprisonment seemed only to increase his popularity with the Palestinian people, many of whom now consider him a national hero. Due to his failing health, Yasin was released from prison in Israel and deported to Jordan in September of 1997.

Primary Documents of Islamic Fundamentalism

The first part of this document section presents excerpts from the Quran and hadith. These sources are considered by believing Muslims to represent the word of God (the Quran) and the word or example of the prophet Muhammad (hadith). They therefore carry the force of law and are interpreted and enforced as such by Muslim states. In those following documents expressing the views of recognized Muslim fundamentalist thinkers are found representative ideas and concepts that help influence today's Islamic fundamentalist worldview. These are the views of important individuals, but they do not carry the force of law and are accepted or rejected by Muslims according to circumstances. Readers are encouraged to compare these ideas with those that shape Western society and norms to achieve an understanding of the differences in outlook that exist between the two cultures.

The following excerpts are from the Quran and hadith. The Quran is the Muslim holy book revealed by Allah (or God) to the prophet Muhammad. The Quran is divided into chapters known as Surahs. The Surahs given below are translations cited from M. H. Shakir, trans., *The Qur'an* (Elmhurst, N.Y.: Tahrike Tarsile Qur'an, Inc., 1990).

The Hadith are documented accounts of the sayings, actions, and approvals of Muhammad or those of his close companions of which he approved. Those cited here are taken from (1) Mulana Muhammad Ali, *A Manual of Hadith* (Lahore, Pakistan: The Ahmadiyya Anjuman Ishaat Islam, no publication date given) and (2) Allama Sir Abdullah Al-Mamun Al-Suhrawardy, *The Sayings of Muhammad* (New York: Citadel Press, 1995). The numbers given after each hadith listed below indicate one of these sources.

Document 1
THE BASIS OF MUSLIM OR SHARIAH LAW

ON WOMEN
Marriage

In most states with Muslim governments, men are allowed to marry up to four wives, although most wed only one. The basis in Muslim law for this custom is found in the following Quranic verses.

Surah IV:3: . . . then marry such women as seem good to you, two and three and four; but if you fear that you will not do justice (between them), then (marry) only one. . . .

Surah IV:129: And you have it not in your power to do justice between wives, even though you may wish (it), but be not disinclined (from one) . . . and if you effect a reconciliation and guard (against evil), then surely Allah is Forgiving, Merciful.

This Surah has been popularly interpreted to mean that it is unlikely that a husband can treat more than one wife equitably, and that it is best to marry only one.

Hadith

—Abu Hurairah reported the Prophet said "The widow shall not be married until she is consulted, and the virgin shall not be married until her consent is obtained." (1)

—Abu Hurairah reported the Prophet said "The most perfect of the believers in faith is the best of them in moral excellence, and the best of you are the kindest to their wives." (1)

Property Rights

Islamic law guarantees women property rights and the right of inheritance. A woman's property is completely under her control and not subject to a husband's or other male relative's use without her permission. In terms of inheritance, men get twice that of women due to their economic responsibilities within the family.

Surah IV:4: And give women their dowries as a free gift, but if they themselves be pleased to give up to you some portion of it, then eat it with enjoyment and with wholesome result.

Surah IV:7: Men shall have a portion of what the parents and the near relatives leave, and women shall have a portion. . . .

Surah IV:11: The male shall have equal of the portion of two females (in inheritance). . . .

Surah IV:34: Men are the maintainers of women because . . . they spend out of their property. . . .

Hadith

—Muhammad said "The rights of women are sacred. See that women are maintained in the rights assigned to them." (2)

Women's Duty Toward Men

Women are generally seen as subservient to men in Islamic culture because men support the family. Islamic laws tend to reflect this judgment based on the following Quranic citation.

Surah IV:34: Men are the maintainers of women because . . . they spend out their property; the good women are therefore obedient, guarding the unseen as Allah has guarded, and (as to) those on whose part you fear desertion, admonish them; then if they obey you, do not see a way against them. . . .

Hadith

—Muhammad said "The best women are the virtuous; they are the most affectionate to infants, and the most careful of their husbands' property." (2)

Dress

In Islamic law both men and women are to dress modestly. The following citation is often used to justify the wearing of the veil or headcovering by Muslim women.

Surah XXIV:30 & 31: Say to the believing men that they cast down their looks and guard their private parts; that is purer for them; surely Allah is aware of what they do. . . . And say to the believing women that they cast down their looks and guard their private parts . . . and let them wear their headcoverings over their bosoms, and not display their ornaments except to their husbands or their fathers, or their sons . . . or the children who have not attained knowledge of what is hidden of women. . . .

Hadith

—A'ishah reported, Asma, daughter of Abu Bakr, came to the Messenger of Allah (Muhammad) and she was wearing thin clothes. The Messenger of Allah turned away his face from her and said: "O Asma! When the woman attains her majority, it is not proper that any part of her body should be seen except this and this." And he pointed to face and his hands. (1)

THE MUSLIM ATTITUDE TOWARD SCIENCE

It is often thought in the West that Muslims are backward because they are suspicious and unaccepting of scientific investigation and advancement. But this is so only in the case of radical traditionalists who fear all change. Such fear, however, has no basis in Islamic teachings. Most educated Muslims welcome scientific pursuits as something endorsed by God and cite the following Quranic passages referring to nature.

Surah XXIV:43, 44 & 45: Do you not see that Allah drives along the clouds, then gathers them together, then piles them up, so that you see the rain coming forth from their midst? . . . Allah turns over the night and the day; most surely there is a lesson in this for those who have sight. . . . And Allah has created from water every living creature; so of them is that which walks upon its belly, and of them is that which walks upon two feet, and of them is that which walks upon four; Allah creates what he pleases; surely Allah has power over all things.

Surah II:29 & 30: He it is Who created for you all that is in the earth. . . . Your lord said to the angels, I am going to place in the earth a khalif (viceregent who, collectively, are mankind). . . .

Hadith

—Anas said, The Messenger of Allah (Muhammad) said "He who goes forth in search of knowledge is in the way of Allah till he returns." (1)

—Anas said, The Messenger of Allah said "The seeking of knowledge is obligatory upon every Muslim." (1)

—Muhammad said "Philosophy is the stray camel of the Faithful, take hold of it wherever ye come across it." (2)

—Muhammad said "Go in quest of knowledge even unto China." (2)

THE CALL FOR MUSLIMS TO BE POLITICALLY ACTIVE

Islamic fundamentalists believe that Muslims should be politically active and strive to create a polity shaped by Muslim law and values. They draw this inspiration not only from the life of the prophet Muhammad, but also from the following Quranic verses.

Surah II:30: (The) Lord said to the angels, I am going to place in the earth a khalif (viceregent). . . .

Surah III:110: You are the best of nations raised up for (the benefit of) men; you enjoin what is right and forbid the wrong and believe in Allah. . . . .

Surah IV:105: Surely we have revealed the Book to you with the truth that you may judge between people by means of that which Allah has taught you; and be not an advocate on behalf of the treacherous.

Surah IV:135: O you who believe! be maintainers of justice. . . .

Surah XLII:38: And those who respond to their Lord and keep up prayer, and their rule is to take counsel among themselves. . . . (This Surah can be read as a call for consultation or shura as a device for governance.)

Hadith

—Ibn Umar reported the Prophet said "To hear and obey (the authorities) is binding, so long as one is not commanded to disobey (God); when one is commanded to disobey (God), he shall not hear and obey." (1)

—Ali said that Muhammad said "Obedience is due only in that which is good." (1)

—Muhammad said "Deliberation in undertakings is pleasing to God." (2)

RELATIONSHIPS BETWEEN MUSLIMS AND NON-MUSLIMS

Muslims take pride in a history of tolerance toward non-Muslims and claim that within the Muslim state non-Muslims would not be oppressed. What does the Quran say about Muslim relations with Jews and Christians? On the one hand, they are recognized as "People of the Book" to whom God has sent revelations and thus are to be treated fairly. They are not to be compelled to convert to Islam.

Surah II:256: There is no compulsion in religion; truly the right way has become distinct from error . . . and Allah is Hearing, Knowing.

Surah V:44: Surely we revealed the Taurat (Torah) in which was guidance and light; with it the prophets who surrendered themselves (to Allah) judged (matters) for those who were Jews and the masters of divine knowledge and the doctors (rabbis) because they were required to guard (part) of the Book of Allah and they were witnesses thereof. . . .

Surah V:46: And we sent after them in their footsteps Isa (Jesus) . . . verifying what was before him of the Taurat (Torah) and We gave him the Injeel (Gospel) in which was guidance and light. . . .

Hadith

—Muhammad said "When the bier of anyone passeth by thee, whether Jew, Christian or Muslim, rise to thy feet." (2)

On the other hand, Christians and Jews are seen as having misinterpreted the revelations sent to them and rejected the prophet Muhammad along with the Quranic revelations.

Surah III:98: Say: O followers of the Book! why do you disbelieve in the communications of Allah? And Allah is witness to what you do.

Surah III:67: Ibrahim (Abraham) was not a Jew nor a Christian but he was (an) upright (man), a Muslim. . . .

Surah V:18: And the Jews and the Christians say: We are the sons of Allah and His beloved ones. Say: Why does He then chastise you for your faults? Nay, you are mortals from among those whom He has created; He forgives whom he pleases and chastises whom he pleases. . . .

Hadith

—Muhammad, speaking of strife, said "It will appear at the time of knowledge leaving the world." Ziad said "O Messenger of God, how will knowledge go from the world, since we read the Kur'an (Quran), and teach it to our children, and our children to theirs; and so on till the last day?" Then Muhammad said, "O Ziad, I supposed you the most learned man of Medinah. Do the Jews and Christians who read the Bible and the Evangel act on them?" (2)

Thus, between Muslims and non-Muslims there is a certain tension. Yet, historically, this tension has generally not turned into forceful oppression or denial of religious rights in Muslim lands. It has, however, tended to restrict the political and civil rights of non-Muslims.

MUSLIM ATTITUDES TOWARD VIOLENCE AND STRUGGLE

Does the Islamic religion promote violence? The answer to this question should be seen in light of the fact that the Quran was set down at a time of strife between Muhammad and the largely hostile population of Mecca, and so there is much in it that reflects that particular struggle between Muslims and unbelievers. Although, as we have seen in Chapter 5, some contemporary Muslim groups have resorted to violence in what they see as a struggle with the enemies of Islam, most Muslim authorities agree that the Quran does not sanction violence except in self-defense or to render punishment under law.

Surah XLII:39 & 41: And those who, when great wrong afflicts them, defend themselves. . . . And whoever defends himself after his being oppressed, these it is against whom there is no way (to blame).

Surah XLII:42: The way (to blame) is only against those who oppress men and revolt in the earth unjustly; these shall have a painful punishment.

Surah V:38 & 39: And (as for) the man who steals and the woman who steals, cut off their hands as a punishment for what they have earned, an exemplary punishment from Allah. . . . But whoever repents after his inequity and reforms . . . turn to him (mercifully); surely Allah is Forgiving, Merciful.

Hadith

—Imaran ibn Husain said the Messenger of Allah (Muhammad) said "A party of my community shall not cease fighting for the Truth—they shall be triumphant over their opponents." (1)

—Abu Hurairah said I heard the Prophet say "By Him in Whose hand is my soul . . . I would not remain behind an army that fights in the way of Allah; and by Him in Whose hand is my soul, I love that I should be killed in the way of Allah then brought to life, then killed again. . . ." (1)

Western notions of an Islamic state are taken from media reports and analyses of such governments as Iran and Sudan. Our picture is mostly one of repression and religious strictness. The Muslim ideal for government is, however, quite different from the picture held in the West. Below, Abu'l-A'la Mawdudi, an influential reformist thinker, gives his interpretation of this ideal. Note the writer's view of Western civilization.

Document 2
ABU'L A'LA MAWDUDI EXPLAINS THE PURPOSE
OF AN ISLAMIC STATE

With certain people it has become a sort of fashion to somehow identify Islam with one or the other system of life in vogue at the time. So at this time also there are people who say that Islam is a democracy, and by this they mean to imply that there is no vast difference between Islam and the democracy in vogue in the West. Some others suggest that Communism is but the latest and revised version of Islam and it is in the fitness of things that Muslims imitate the Communist experiment of Soviet Russia. Still others whisper that Islam has the elements of dictatorship in it and we should revive the cult of "obedience to the Amir" (the leader). All these people, in their misinformed and misguided zeal to serve what they hold to be the cause of Islam, are always at great pains to prove that Islam contains within itself the elements of all types of contemporary social and political thought and action. Most of the people who indulge in this prattle have no clear idea of the Islamic way of life. . . . As a matter of fact, this attitude emerges from an inferiority complex, from the belief that we as Muslims can earn no honour or respect unless we are able to show that our religion resembles the modern creeds and it is in agreement with most of the contemporary ideologies. . . .

FIRST PRINCIPLE OF ISLAMIC POLITICAL THEORY

The belief in the unity (tawhid) and the sovereignty of Allah is the foundation of the social and moral system propounded by the Prophets. It is the very starting point of the Islamic political philosophy. The basic principle of Islam is that human beings must, individually and collectively, surrender all rights of overlordship, legislation and exercizing of authority over others. . . . None is entitled to make laws on his own authority and none is obliged to abide by them. This right vests in Allah alone (the Quran says): "The Authority rests with none but Allah. He commands you not to surrender to any one save Him. This is the right way (of life)."

According to this theory, sovereignty belongs to Allah. He alone is the law-giver. . . . The Prophet himself is subject to God's commands. . . . Other people are required to obey the Prophet because he enunciates not his own but God's commands. . . . Thus the main characteristics of an Islamic state that can be deduced from (this) are as follows:

1. No person, class or group, not even the entire population of the state as a whole, can lay claim to sovereignty. God alone is the real sovereign; all others are merely his subjects;

2. God is the real law-giver and the authority of absolute legislation vests in Him. The believers cannot resort to totally independent legislation nor can they modify any law which God has laid down. . . .

3. An Islamic state must, in all respects, be founded upon the law laid down by God and His Prophet. The government which runs such a state

will be entitled to obedience in its capacity as a political agency set up to enforce the laws of God and only in so far as it acts in that capacity. If it disregards the law revealed by God, its commands will not be binding on the believers.

THE ISLAMIC STATE: ITS NATURE AND CHARACTERISTICS

The preceding discussion makes it clear that Islam . . . is the very antithesis of secular Western democracy. The philosophical foundation of Western democracy is the sovereignty of the people. . . . Law-making is their prerogative and legislation must correspond to the mood and temper of their opinion. . . . This is not the case in Islam.

A more apt name for the Islamic polity would be the "kingdom of God" which is described in English as a "theocracy." But Islamic theocracy is something altogether different from the theocracy of which Europe has had a bitter experience wherein a priestly class, sharply marked off from the rest of the population, exercises unchecked domination and enforces laws of its own making in the name of God, thus virtually imposing its own divinity and godhood upon the common people. . . . Contrary to this, the theocracy built up by Islam is not ruled by any particular religious class but by the whole community of Muslims including the rank and file. The entire Muslim population runs the state in accordance with the Book of God (the Quran) and the practice of His Prophet. If I were permitted to coin a new term, I would describe this system of government as a "theo-democracy," that is to say a divine democratic government, because under it the Muslims have been given a limited popular sovereignty under the suzerainty of God. The executive under this system of government is con-stituted by the general will of the Muslims who have also the right to depose it. All administrative matters and all questions about which no explicit injunction is to be found in the Shariah are settled by the consensus of opinion among the Muslims. Every Muslim who is capable and qual-ified to give a sound opinion on matters of Islamic law is entitled to interpret the law of God when such interpretation becomes necessary. In this sense the Islamic polity is a democracy. But, as has been explained above, it is a theocracy in the sense that where an explicit command of God or His Prophet already exists, no Muslim leader or legislature, or any religious scholar can form an independent judgement, not even all the Muslims of the world put together have any right to make the least alter-ation in it. . . .

God has laid down . . . "divine limits" (consisting of) certain principles, checks and balances and specific injunctions in different spheres of life and activity, and they have been prescribed in order that man may be trained to lead a balanced and moderate life. . . . These limits he is not permitted to overstep and if he does so, the whole scheme of his life will go awry.

Take for example man's economic life. In this sphere God has placed certain restrictions on human freedom. The right to private property has been recognized, but it is qualified by the obligation to pay zakat (poor dues) and the prohibition of interest, gambling and speculation. A specific law of inheritance for the distribution of property among the largest number of surviving relations on the death of its owner has been laid down and certain forms of acquiring, accumulating and spending wealth have been declared unlawful. If people observe these just limits and regulate their affairs within these boundary walls, on the one hand their personal liberty is adquately safeguarded and, on the other, the possibility of class war and domination of one class over another, which begins with capitalist oppression and ends in working-class dictatorship, is safely and conveniently eliminated.

Similarly in the sphere of family life, God has prohibited the unrestricted intermingling of the sexes and has prescribed purdah (separation of men and women), recognized man's guardianship of woman, and clearly defined the rights and duties of husband, wife and children. The laws of divorce and separation have been clearly set forth, conditional polygamy has been permitted and penalties for fornication and false accusations of adultery have been prescribed. He has thus laid down limits which, if observed by man, would stabilize his family life and make it a haven of peace and happiness. There would remain neither that tyranny of male over female which makes family life an inferno of cruelty and oppression, nor that satanic flood of female liberty and licence which threatens to destroy human civilization in the West. . . .

THE PURPOSE OF THE ISLAMIC STATE

The purpose of the state that may be formed on the basis of the Quran and the Sunna has also been laid down by God. The Quran says: "(Muslims are) those who, if We give them power in the land, establish the system of salat (worship) and zakat (poor dues) and enjoin virtue and forbid evil and inequity;" (and elsewhere:) "You are the best community sent forth to mankind; you enjoin the Right conduct and forbid the wrong; and you believe in Allah."

It will readily become manifest to anyone who reflects upon these verses that the purpose of the state visualized by the Holy Quran is not negative but positive. The object of the state is not merely to prevent people from exploiting each other, to safeguard their liberty and to protect its subjects from foreign invasion. It also aims at evolving and developing that well-balanced system of social justice which has been set forth by God in His Holy Book. Its object is to eradicate all forms of evil and to encourage all types of virtue and excellence expressly mentioned by God in the Holy Quran. For this purpose political power will be made use of as and when the occasion demands; all means of propaganda and peaceful persuasion will be employed; the moral education of the people will also be under-taken; and social influence as well as the force of public opinion will be harnessed to the task.

ISLAMIC STATE IS UNIVERSAL AND ALL-EMBRACING

A state of this sort cannot evidently restrict the scope of its activities. . . . It seeks to mold every aspect of life and activity in consonance with its moral norms and programme of social reform. In such a state no one can regard any field of his affairs as personal and private. Considered from this aspect the Islamic state bears a kind of resemblance to the Fascist and Communist states. But you will find later on that, despite its all inclu-siveness, it is something vastly and basically different from the modern totalitarian and authoritarian states. Individual liberty is not suppressed under it nor is there any trace of dictatorship in it. It presents the middle course and embodies the best that the human society has ever evolved. . . .

ISLAMIC STATE IS AN IDEOLOGICAL STATE

Another characteristic of the Islamic state is that it is an ideological state. It is clear from a careful consideration of the Quran and the Sunna that the state in Islam is based on an ideology and its objective is to establish that ideology. The state is an instrument of reform and must act likewise. It is a dictate of this very nature of the Islamic state that such a state should be run only by those who believe in the ideology on which it is based and in the Divine Law which it is assigned to administer. The administrators of the Islamic state must be those whose whole life is de-voted to the observance and enforcement of this Law, who not only agree with its reformatory programme and fully believe in it but thoroughly comprehend its spirit and are acquainted with its details. Islam does not recognize any geographical, linguistic or colour bars in this respect. It puts forward its code of guidance and the scheme of its reform before all men.

Whoever accepts this programme, no matter to what race, nation or country he may belong, can join the community that runs the Islamic state. But those who do not accept it are not entitled to have any hand in shaping the fundamental policy of the state. They can live within the confines of the state as non-Muslim citizens (dhimmis). Specific rights and privileges have been accorded to them in Islamic law. A dhimmi's life, property and honour will be fully protected, and if he is capable of any service, his services will also be made use of. He will not, however, be allowed to influence the basic policy of this ideological state. . . . Here again, we notice some sort of resemblance between the Islamic and the Communist states. . . . Unlike the Communist state, Islam does not impose its social principles on others by force, nor does it confiscate their properties or unleash a reign of terror by mass executions of the people and their transportation to the slave camps of Siberia. Islam does not want to eliminate its minorities, it wants to protect them and give them the freedom to live according to their own culture.

THE THEORY OF THE CALIPHATE AND THE NATURE OF DEMOCRACY IN ISLAM

I will try to give a brief exposition of the composition and structure of the Islamic state. I have already stated that in Islam, God alone is the real sovereign. Keeping this cardinal principle in mind, if we consider the position of those persons who set out to enforce God's law on earth, it is but natural to say that they should be regarded as representatives of the Supreme Ruler. Islam has assigned precisely this very position to them. Accordingly the Holy Quran says: "Allah has promised to those among you who believe and do righteous deeds that He will assuredly make them to succeed (the present rulers) and grant them viceregency in the land just as He made those before them succeed (others)."

The verse illustrates very clearly the Islamic theory of the state. Two fundamental points emerge from it.

1. The first point is that Islam uses the term "viceregency" (khilafa) instead of sovereignty. Since, according to Islam, sovereignty belongs to God alone, anyone who holds power and rules in accordance with the laws of God would undoubtedly be the viceregent of the Supreme Ruler and would not be authorised to exercise any powers other than those delegated to him.

2. The second point stated in the verse is that the power to rule over the earth has been promised to the whole community of believers; it has not been stated that any particular person or class among them will be raised

to that position. From this it follows that all believers are repositories of the Caliphate. . . . The Holy Prophet has said: "Everyone of you is a ruler and everyone is answerable for his subjects." This is the real foundation of democracy in Islam.

The following points emerge from an analysis of this conception of popular viceregency:

A. A society in which everyone is a Caliph of God and an equal participant in this Caliphate, cannot tolerate any class divisions based on distinctions of birth and social position. All men enjoy equal status and position in such a society. The only criterion of superiority in this social order is personal ability and character. This is what has been repeatedly and explicitly asserted by the Holy Prophet: "No one is superior to another except in point of faith and piety. All men are descended from Adam and Adam was made of clay. An Arab has no superiority over a non-Arab nor a non-Arab over an Arab; neither does a white man possess any superiority over a black man nor a black man over a white man, except in point of piety. . . ."

B. In such a society no individual or group of individuals will suffer any disability on account of birth, social status, or profession that may in any way impede the growth or hamper the development of his personality. . . .

C. There is no room in such a society for the dictatorship of any person or group of persons since everyone is a Caliph of God herein. . . . The position of a man who is selected to conduct the affairs of the state is no more than this; that all Muslims . . . delegate their Caliphate to him for administrative purposes. He is answerable to God on the one hand and on the other to the other fellow Caliphs who have delegated their authority to him. Now, if he raises himself to the position of an irresponsible absolute ruler, that is to say a dictator, he assumes the character of a usurper rather than a Caliph, because dictatorship is the negation of popular viceregency. . . . The guidance given by God about every aspect of life will certainly be enforced in its entirety. But an Islamic ruler cannot depart from these instructions and adopt a policy of regimentation on his own. He cannot force people to follow or not to follow a particular profession; to learn or not to learn a special art; or to use or not to use a certain script; to wear or not to wear a certain dress and to educate or not to educate their children in a certain manner. . . . Besides this, another important point is that in Islam every individual is held personally answerable to God. This personal responsibility cannot be shared by anyone else. Hence, an individual enjoys full liberty to choose whichever path he likes and to develop his faculties in any direction that suits his natural gifts. If the leader obstructs him or obstructs the growth of his personality, he will himself be punished by God for this tyranny. That is precisely the reason why there is not the slightest trace of regimentation in the rule of the Holy Prophet and of his Rightly-Guided Caliphs;

D. In such a society every sane and adult Muslim, male and female, is entitled to express his or her opinion, for each one of them is the repository of the Caliphate. God has made this Caliphate conditional, not upon any particular standard of wealth or competence but only upon faith and good conduct. Therefore all Muslims have equal freedom to express their opinions.

Abu'l-A'la Mawdudi, "Political Theory of Islam," in Khurshid Ahmad, ed., *Islam: Its Meaning and Message* (London: The Islamic Foundation, 1988), pp. 147–148, 158–161, 163–170.

> In this essay the Sudanese Islamic leader Hasan al-Turabi explains his ideas on the proper makeup of an Islamic state. Gaps between ideals and practice always exist when it comes to the exercise of power, and many aspects of Islamic Sudan do not match the picture painted below by al-Turabi. Nonetheless, al-Turabi does set forth an accurate view of the ideals inherent in Sunni Islamic state theory.

Document 3
HASAN TURABI EXPLAINS THE MAKEUP OF AN ISLAMIC STATE

INTRODUCTION

Although I have been directly involved in a political process that seeks to establish an Islamic state, I am not going to describe the forms that an Islamic government might take in any particular country. Rather, I will try to describe the universal characteristics of an Islamic state. These derive from the teachings of the Quran as embodied in the political practice of the Prophet Muhammad, and constitute an eternal model that Muslims are bound to adopt as a perfect standard for all time. The diversity of historical circumstances, however, in which they try to apply that ideal introduces a necessary element of relativity and imperfection in the practice of Islam.

An Islamic state cannot be isolated from society, because Islam is a comprehensive, integrated way of life. The division between private and public, the state and society, which is familiar in Western culture, has not been known in Islam. The state is only the political expression of an Islamic society. You cannot have an Islamic state except insofar as you have an Islamic society. Any attempt at establishing a political order for the establishment of a genuine Islamic society would be the superimposition of laws over a reluctant soicety. This is not in the nature of religion; religion is based on sincere conviction and voluntary compliance. Therefore an Islamic state evolves from an Islamic society. In certain areas, progress toward an Islamic society may be frustrated by political suppression. Whenever religious energy is thus suppressed, it builds up and ultimately erupts either in isolated acts of struggle or resistance, which are called terrorist by those in power, or in a revolution. In circumstances where Islam is allowed free expression, social change takes place peacefully and gradually, and the Islamic movement develops programs of Islamization before it takes over the destiny of the state because Islamic thought—like all thought—only flourishes in a social environment of freedom and public consultation (shura).

TAWHID: THE SOURCE OF ALL PRINCIPLES
OF GOVERNANCE

The ideological foundation of an Islamic state lies in the doctrine of tawhid—the unity of Allah and of human life—as a comprehensive and exclusive program of worship. This fundamental principle of belief has many consequences for an Islamic state: first, it is not secular. All public life in Islam is religious, being permeated by the experience of the divine. Its function is to pursue the service of Allah as expressed in a concrete way in the shariah, the religious law. The Christian West has been through an important historical experience of secularization. There have also been certain elements of secularization in the political conduct of Muslims. But the difference between Christianity and Islam is that Muslims are never fully resigned to such practices because the preserved sources of religious guidance (the Quran and the example of the Prophet) constantly remind them of any gap that develops between their ideal and their practice. . . . Once the Muslims . . . become conscious of the fact that public life has moved away from the moral values and norms of religion, they rise to reform their political attitudes and institutions.

Second, an Islamic state is not a nationalistic state because ultimate allegiance is owed to Allah and thereby to the community of all believers—the ummah. One can never stop at any national frontier and say the nation is absolute, an ultimate end in itself. Islam does not allow for limited allegiances either social, ethnic, or territorial. . . . In modern times Muslims have adopted Arab, Turkish or other nationalities as a framework for development, but they were never enthusiastic about it, and always yearned for an open ummah. This does not mean, however, that every Muslim all over the world should necessarily have immediate access to an Islamic state: it does mean that the state would be much more open and less discriminatory in its domestic laws and foreign policies. It would develop institutionalized international links with other Muslim states and would work toward the eventual unity of the ummah and beyond. Ultimately, there is nothing final even about the so-called Muslim world or Muslim nation, because Islam is universal and open to all humanity.

Third, an Islamic state is not an absolute or sovereign entity. It is subject to the higher norms of the shariah that represent the Will of Allah. Politically this rules out all forms of absolutism. Legally it paves the way for the development of constitutional law, a set of norms limiting state powers. . . .

Fourth, an Islamic state is not primordial; the primary institution in Islam is the ummah. The phrase "Islamic state" itself is a misnomer. The state is only the political dimension of the collective endeavor of Muslims. . . .

States come and go; Islamic society can and has existed without the structures of a state for centuries. Of course, society, if able to live religion in its integral, comprehensive manner, would have its political dimension in a government that seeks to fulfill some of the purposes of religious life.

IJMA AND SHURA

The form of an Islamic government is determined by the foregoing principles of tawhid, entailing the freedom, equality, and unity of believers. One can call an Islamic state a republic since the shariah rules out usurpation and succession as grounds of political legitimacy. In early Islam the system of government was called a caliphate (al-khilafah) which emphasized succession to the Prophet and thereby subordination of all power to his Sunnah or way. Whereas the Prophet was appointed by Allah, however, the caliph was freely elected by the people who thereby have precedence over him as a legal authority. The caliph, however, or any similar holder of political power, is subject both to the shariah and the will of his electors. As reflected in Islamic jurisprudence this implies that, save for the express provision of the shariah, consensus (ijma) is mandatory for the resolution of all important public issues.

The caliphate began as an elected consultative institution. Later it degenerated into a hereditary, or usurpatory, authoritarian government. This pseudocaliphate was universally condemned by jurists, though many excused its acts on the grounds of necessity or tolerated them in the interest of stability.

In a large Islamic state, consultation would have to be indirect and undertaken by representatives of the people. This was practiced in early

Islam. . . . In a parallel development ijma, which is the conclusion of a process of consultation, came to mean the consensus of the ulama. This was a practical adaptation of the original popular concept of ijma as the consensus of the community which had resulted from the Muslim expansion. In effect, Muslims were then to be found all over the world, and there was no practical way of consulting everyone in the general ummah in those days. So the ulama posed as representatives of the people and maintained that their consensus was a form of indirect representation, of indirect binding ijma. In different circumstances other formal delegates can lawfully represent the ummah in the process of consultation.

It follows that an Islamic order of government is essentially a form of representative democracy. But this statement requires the following qualification. First an Islamic republic is not strictly speaking a direct government of and by the people; it is a government of the shariah. But, in a substantial sense, it is a popular government since the shura represents the convictions of the people and, therefore, their direct will. This limitation on what a representative body can do is a guarantee of the supremacy of the religious will of the community.

The consultative system of government in Islam is related to and reinforced by similar features of Muslim society since politics is an integral part of all religious life and not simply a separate secular vocation. The fair distribution of political power through shura, whether direct or indirect, is supported by an equally just distribution of economic wealth, so that an Islamic democracy may never degenerate into a system where, because of the concentration of wealth, the rich alone exercise their political rights and determine what is to be decided.

Also, ideally there is no clerical or ulama class, which prevents an elitist or theocratic government. Whether termed a religious (or) . . . theocratic (state) an Islamic state is not a government of the ulama. Knowledge, like power, is distributed in a way that inhibits the development of a distinct, religious hierarchy.

Nor is an Islamic democracy government by the male members of the society. Women played a considerable role in public life during the life of the Prophet; and they contributed to the election of the third caliph. Only afterwards were women denied their rightful place in public life, but this was history departing from the ideal, just like the development of classes based on property, knowledge, or other status. In principle, all believers, rich or poor, noble or humble, learned or ignorant, men or women, are equal before Allah, and they are His viceregents on earth and the holders of His trust.

An Islamic government should be a stable system of government because the people consider it an expression of their religion and therefore
contribute positively to the political process. In their mutual consultations,
they work toward a consensus that unites them. The majority/minority
pattern in politics is not an ideal one in Islam. That is not to say that
decisions have to await a unanimous vote, because this could paralyze a
government. But people can deliberate openly and argue and consult to
ultimately reach a consensus and not simply assert or submit to a majority
opinion.

This raises the question of the party system. Can an Islamic government
have a multiparty system or a single party system? There is no legal bar
to the development of different parties or to the freedom of opinion and
debate. Such was the case in the constitutional practice of the caliph. A
well-developed Islamic society, however, would probably not be conducive
to the growth of rigid parties wherein one stands by one's party whether
it is wrong or right. This is a form of factionalism that can be very oppressive of individual freedom and divisive of the community, and it is
therefore antithetical to a Muslim's ultimate responsibility to Allah and to
ummah. While there may be a multiparty system, an Islamic government
should function more as a consensus-oriented rather than a minority/ma-
jority system with political parties rigidly confronting each other over
decisions. Parties should approach the decision-making process with an
open mind and after a consensus adopt a mutually agreeable policy.

Finally, decisions should not be arrived at lightly. Parliament does not
simply deliberate and come to a conclusion. Any agreement must be an
enlightened decision with conscious reference to the guiding principles of
the shariah. Because of this, the ulama should have a role in the procedure,
not as the ultimate authority determining what the law is, but as advisors
in the shura to enlighten the Muslims as to the options which are open to
them. What do I mean by ulama? The word historically has come to mean
those versed in the legacy of religious (revealed) knowledge (ilm). However, ilm does not mean that alone. It means anyone who knows anything
well enough to relate it to Allah. Because all knowledge is divine and
religious, a chemist, an engineer, an economist, or a jurist are all ulama.
So the ulama in this broad sense, whether they are social or natural sci-
entists, public opinion leaders or philosophers, should enlighten society.
There should be an intensive procedure of hearings, research, and delib-
erations and thus a wider consultation than that which sometimes takes
place now in modern parliaments where bills can be rushed through and
policies resolved on arbitrary passion and prejudice.

LIMITED GOVERNMENT AND HUMAN RIGHTS

What are the functions and frontiers of an Islamic government? . . . Because Islam is comprehensive, one might conclude that an Islamic government, acting for society, is a totalitarian one. In many ways, however, an Islamic government is a very limited government. First, not every aspect of Islam is entrusted to government to enforce. . . . Most aspects of Islamic life are subjective or private and outside the domain of law as applied by governments. Second, and this is a question which depends on history, where society can manage, government has no business interfering. This is similar to a liberal, minimal theory of government. . . .

A modern Islamic government could, subject to the shariah, establish and enforce . . . legal codes. Such codes, as were known to Muslims in the past, did not emanate from the state but from the great jurists like Malik, Abu Hanifah, and Shafi'i. There were seven such operative legal codes throughout the Muslim world. . . . Subject to the shariah and ijma it is up to a Muslim government today to determine its system of public law and economics.

An Islamic government is bound to exercise all powers necessary for providing a minimum of basic conditions of Muslim life. The actual scope of government depends on society. Where society on its own manages to realize social justice, for example, then the government does not need to interfere. In Muslim history, governments were mostly illegitimate and did not or were not allowed to develop a macro-economic policy. Therefore, Muslims addressed questions of social justice within their private dealings. This was done especially through a wide, mutually supportive family system, through extensive charities and endowments, and through a system of private mutual insurance still operative in many parts of Muslim society today. Where this failed for any reason, the government was bound to step in and try to rectify the situation. This holds for other welfare services as well. Society can manage, for example, its own system of private education like that of Muslim Spain which was so widespread that it almost eliminated illiteracy through free education for all. Otherwise, the government is bound and entitled to promote education, health services, and what have you.

What are the frontiers of government vis-à-vis society and the individual? This question has not been posed very accurately in the past. . . . Even though the particular caliph might be a usurper, an authoritarian, and a tyrant, he was not a totalitarian, absolute dictator. Certainly, where his security was threatened, he would impinge on freedom, but otherwise people were left alone.

It is only recently when secularized governments were introduced and established in Muslim lands and the protective shield of the shariah withdrawn and the forms of government regulation expanded, that Muslims really felt the bitter oppression of totalitarian government, and that the issue of fundamental rights and liberties was raised.

The freedom of the individual ultimately emanates from the doctrine of tawhid which requires a self-liberation of man from any worldly authority in order to serve Allah exclusively. Society, including particularly those in power, is inspired by the same principle, and the collective endeavor is not one of hampering the liberty of an individual but of cooperation toward the maximum achievement of this ideal. To promote this cooperation, the freedom of one individual is related to that of the general group. The ultimate common aim of religious life unites the private and the social spheres; and the shariah provides an arbiter between social order and individual freedom.

I do not have to go into the various rights of a man vis-à-vis the state or society in Islam. The individual has the right to his physical existence, general social well-being, reputation, peace, privacy, education, and a decent life. These are rights that the state ought to recognize and guarantee for a better fulfillment of the religious ideals of life. Freedom of religion and of expression should also be guaranteed and encouraged. . . . Actually, these are not pure rights that the individual is free to exercise. He owes it to Allah and to his fellow Muslims to observe these as a social obligation as well. He should contribute to the political solidarity and well-being of the state. If government becomes so alien as to transcend the shariah, he has the right and obligation to revolt. This is the revolutionary element in Islam. A Muslim's ultimate obedience is to Allah alone.

CHECKS AND BALANCES

What about representative institutions in an Islamic government? This depends on the particular historical circumstances. In the period of the Prophet, all the functions of the state were exercised by him as teacher and sovereign. He wisely but informally consulted with his companions. Later this consultative process was developed almost into an indirect representative institution called ahl al-shura or majlis al-shura (consultative consul). The breakdown of the early legitimate political order did not allow the procedures and institutions of shura to crystalize. Today this could very well be formulated through a parliament, a council, or a majlis al-shura. People may directly, through referendum, exercise their consensus or otherwise delegate power to their deputies. There would, however, be certain rules regulating the qualifications of candidates and election campaigns for the choice of deputies or other officers of the state. In Islam, for example, no one is entitled to conduct a campaign for themselves directly or indirectly in the anarchic and demagogic manner of Western electoral campaigns. The presentation of candidates would be monitored by a neutral institution that would explain to the people the options offered in policies and personalities. Factors of relative wealth or access to the communications media are also not allowed to falsify the representative character of deputies. The prevailing criteria of political merit for the purposes of candidature for any political office revolves on moral integrity as well as other relevant considerations. All this would, no doubt, influence the form and spirit of accession to positions of power.

The other central institution in an Islamic government is that which provides both leadership and effective execution of the general will: Caliph, Commander of the Believers, President of the Republic, or Prime Minister. As noted earlier, the word "caliph" was not originally chosen for any specific reason except to denote succession and compliance with the prophetic example of leadership. Most modern and contemporary constitutional theory tends to vest political leadership in one individual and not in a collegiate body—a presidency rather than a council of ministers. But neither a president nor a prime minister can be very powerful and representative of the unity of political purpose so essential to an Islamic polity. Whatever form the executive may take, a leader is always subject both to the shariah and to the ijma formulated under it. He enjoys no special immunities and can therefore be prosecuted or sued for anything he does in his private or public life. This is a fundamental principle of Islamic constitutional law, ensuing from the supremacy of the shariah. . . .

JUDICIAL INSTITUTIONS AND THE SHARIAH

The judiciary, although appointed as part of the administration, plays an extremely important role as a check and balance in an Islamic state. . . . The shariah is the highest revealed law followed by popular laws based on ijma and by executive orders and regulations. Because of this, judges, as the guardians of the shariah, adjudicate in all matters of law. Early Muslims were very keen to provide judges with a generous income to protect them against temptation and to allow them a very large degree of autonomy with broad powers to administer justice. The legal systems of Islam, however, did not know a lawyer's profession. The modern capitalist institution which requires the participation of solicitors and barristers in the administration of justice ultimately works in favor of the rich who can afford the expenses and the delays of justice in a system administered in this way. I realize as a lawyer, myself, that adjudication in a contemporary society is a very complicated, time-consuming process. Judges cannot listen to all the complaints and determine the issues. But such a difficulty was resolved in early Islam by the office of a counsellor to the judge: an assistant who first heard the parties, ascertained the matters in issue, marshalled all the relevant evidence, and researched the law in preparation for a decision by the judge. In an Islamic state there would be a tendency to do away with or to minimize the role of the legal profession by establishing an extended system of legal counsel and assistance especially for the poor.

As far as public law for the administration of an Islamic state or government is concerned, one can draw upon early Islamic history and tradition regarding . . . forms of achieving the political ideals of Islam. . . . Any form or procedure for the organization of public life that can be ultimately related to Allah and put to His service in furtherance of the aims of Islamic governance can be adopted unless expressly excluded by the shariah. . . . Through this process of Islamization, the Muslims were always very open to expansion and change. Thus, Muslims can incorporate any experience whatsoever if not contrary to their ideals. [Early] Muslims took most of their bureaucratic forms from Roman and Persian models. Now, much can be borrowed from contemporary sources, critically appreciated in the light of the shariah values and norms, and integrated into the Islamic framework of government.

INTERNATIONAL RELATIONS

Finally, I come to the inter-state and inter-faith relations of the Muslim state. I have remained quiet about the status of non-Muslims because I did not want to complicate issues. The historical record of Muslims' treatment of Christians and Jews is quite good, especially compared with the history of relations between different religious denominations in the West. . . . These non-Muslims have a guaranteed right to their religious conviction . . . and even to criticize Islam and engage in a dialogue with Muslims. Non-Muslims also have the right to regulate their private life, education, and family life by adopting their own family laws. If there is any rule in the shariah which they think religiously incompatible, they can be absolved from it. . . . It is more than a matter of tolerance and legal immunity. Muslims have a moral obligation to be fair and friendly in their person-to-person conduct toward non-Muslim citizens, and will be answerable to Allah for that. They must treat them with trust, beneficence, and equity. There may be a certain feeling of alienation because the public law generally will be Islamic law. The public law of Islam, however, is one related rationally to justice and to the general good, and even a non-Muslim may appreciate its wisdom and fairness.

As to the inter-state or international relations of a Muslim state. . . . the sanctity of treaty obligations and the vocation of world peace, except in situations of aggression, provide a basis for the development of extensive international relations. . . .

In conclusion, it is important to note that an awareness of the general nature and features of the Islamic state is necessary for an understanding of modern Islam as a resurgent force seeking to make up for a failure to realize Islam fully.

Hasan Turabi, "Principles of Governance, Freedom and Responsibility in Islam," in *The American Journal of Islamic Social Sciences,* Vol. 4, No. 1 (1987), 1–11.

In the United States it is our constitution that sets the criteria for who can serve as president, while a mix of history and shifting values and perceptions set the standards for what constitutes a good leader. What are the criteria Muslim fundamentalists use for these judgments? It is an important question for those who would establish an Islamic state or critique present governments in Muslim lands. Below, the early modern Islamic reformer, al-Afghani, sets forth criteria that are still used by today's Muslim political activists.

The views on Islamic government set forth by Abu'l Mawdudi and Hasan Turabi are largely shaped by the Sunni Muslim tradition. Those of the Ayatollah Khomeini, the founder of Iran's Islamic state, are, on the other hand, a product of the Shi'ite Muslim tradition. Unlike the Sunnis, the Shi'ites have a hierarchically arranged clerical organization with strong leaders. In the selection below, Khomeini explains why Muslims must strive for an Islamic state, and why that state should have a centralized authority known as the jurisprudent.

Document 4
THE NEED FOR AN ISLAMIC STATE AND THE RULE OF THE JURISPRUDENT

DISTINCTION FROM OTHER POLITICAL SYSTEMS

The Islamic government is not similar to the well-known systems of government. It is not a despotic government in which the head of state dictates his opinion and tampers with the lives and property of the people. The prophet . . . and Ali, the Amir of the faithful, and the other Imams [successors of the prophet Muhammad in the Shi'ite tradition] had no power to tamper with people's property or with their lives. The Islamic government is not despotic but constitutional. However, it is not constitutional in the well-known sense of the word, which is represented in the parliamentary system or in the people's councils. It is constitutional in the sense that those in charge of affairs observe a number of conditions and rules underlined in the Quran and in the Sunna and represented in the necessity of observing the system and of applying the dictates and laws of Islam. This is why the Islamic government is the government of divine law. The difference between the Islamic government and the constitutional governments, both monarchic and republican, lies in the fact that the people's representatives or the King's representatives are the ones who codify and legislate, whereas [in the Islamic state] the power of legislation is confined to God. . . .

The Islamic government is the government of the law and God alone is the ruler and the legislator. God's rule is effective among all the people and in the state itself. All individuals—the prophet, his successors and other people—follow that Islam, which descended through revelation and which God had explained through the Quran and through the words of His prophet. . . .

The venerable prophet . . . was appointed ruler on earth by God so that he may rule justly and not follow whims. God addressed the prophet through revelation and told him to convey what was revealed to him to those who would succeed him. The prophet obeyed the dictates of this order and appointed Ali, the Amir of the faithful, as his successor. He was not motivated in this appointment by the fact that Ali was his son-in-law and the fact that Ali had performed weighty and unforgettable services but because God ordered the prophet to do so.

Yes, government in Islam means obeying the law and making it the judge. The powers given to the prophet . . . and to the legitimate rulers after him are powers derived from God. . . . There is no place for opinions and whims in the government of Islam.

The Shari'a and reason require us not to let governments have a free hand. The proof of this is evident. The persistence of governments in their transgressions means obstructing the system and laws of Islam. . . . We are responsible for eliminating the traces of idolatry from our Muslim society and for keeping it away from our life. At the same time, we are responsible for preparing the right atmosphere for bringing up a faithful generation that destroys the thrones of false gods and destroys their illegal powers because corruption and deviation grow on their hands. . . . Under the canopy of [such an illegal government] no faithful and pious person can live abiding by and preserving his faith and piety. Such a person has before him two paths . . . either be forced to commit sinful acts or rebel against and fight the rule of false gods, try to wipe out or at least reduce the impact of such a rule. We only have the second path open to us. . . .

This is a duty that all Muslims wherever they may be are entrusted—a duty to create a victorious and triumphant Islamic political revolution.

NEED FOR ISLAMIC UNITY

On the other hand, colonialism has partitioned our homeland and has turned the Muslims into peoples. When the Ottoman State appeared as a united state, the colonialists sought to fragment it. The Russians, the British and their allies united and fought the Ottomans and then shared the loot, as you all know. We do not deny that most rulers of the Ottoman State lacked ability, competence and qualifications and many of them ruled the people in a despotic monarchic manner. However, the colonialists were afraid that some pious and qualified persons would, with the help of the people, assume leadership of the Ottoman State and (would safeguard) its unity, ability, strength and resources, thus dispersing the hopes and aspirations of the colonialists. This is why as soon as World War I ended, the colonialists partitioned the country into mini-states and made each of these mini-states their agent. Despite this, a number of these mini-states later escaped the grip of colonialism and its agents.

The only means that we possess to unite the Muslim nation, to liberate its lands from the grip of the colonialist and to topple the agent governments of colonialism, is to seek to establish our Islamic government. The efforts of this government will be crowned with success when we become able to destroy the heads of treason . . . who disseminate injustice and corruption on earth.

NEED FOR RESCUING WRONGED AND DEPRIVED

To achieve their unjust economic goals, the colonialists employed the help of their agents in our countries. As a result of this, there are hundreds of millions of starving people who lack the simplest health and educational means. On the other side, there are individuals with excessive wealth and broad corruption. The starving people are in a constant struggle to improve their conditions and to free themselves from the tyranny of the aggressive rulers. Both the ruling minorities and their government agencies are also seeking to extinguish this struggle. On our part, we are entrusted to rescue the deprived and the wronged. We are instructed to help the wronged and to fight the oppressors, as the Amir of the faithful (Ali) instructed his two sons in his will: "Fight the tyrant and aid the wronged." The Muslim ulama are entrusted to fight the greedy exploiters so that society may not have a deprived beggar and, on the other side, someone living in comfort and luxury. . . .

The opinion of the Shi'i concerning the one who is entitled to lead the people is known since the death of the prophet. . . . To the Shi'i the Imam [Ali and his successors] is a virtuous man who knows the laws and implements them justly and who fears nobody's censure in serving God. . . . If [however, in the Imam's absence] a knowledgeable and just jurisprudent [or a group of jurisprudents] undertakes the task of forming the government, then he [or they] will run the social affairs that the prophet used to run and it is the duty of the people to listen to and obey him [or them].

This ruler will have as much control over running the people's administration, welfare and policy as the prophet and Amir of the faithful had despite the special virtues and traits that distinguished the prophet and the Imam. Their virtues did not entitle them to contradict the instructions of the Shari'a or to dominate people with disregard to God's order. God has given the actual Islamic government that is supposed to be formed . . . the same powers that he gave the prophet and the Amir of the faithful in regard to ruling, justice and the settlement of disputes, the appointment of provincial rulers and officers, the collection of taxes and the development of the country. All that there is to the matter is that the appointment of the ruler at present depends on (finding) someone who has both knowledge and justice.

THE RULE OF THE JURISPRUDENT (VILAYAT I-FAQIH)

Nobody should imagine that the fitness of the jurisprudent for rule raises him to the status of prophecy or of Imams because our discussion here is not concerned with status and rank but with the actual task. [This] means governing the people, running the state and applying the laws of the Shari'a. . . . It is a practical task of extreme significance.

The rule of the jurisprudent is a . . . matter dictated by the Shari'a, [in the same manner] as the Shari'a considers one of us a trustee over minors. The task of a trustee over an entire people is not different from that of the trustee over minors. . . .

If a just jurisprudent . . . is appointed, would he establish restrictions in a manner different from that in which they were established in the days of the prophet or of the Amir of the faithful? Did the prophet punish the unmarried fornicator more than one hundred lashes? Does the jurisprudent have to reduce the number to prove that there is a difference between him and the prophet? No, because the ruler, be he a prophet, an Imam or a just jurisprudent, is nothing but an executor of God's order and will.

The prophet collected taxes: The one-fifth tax, the alms tax on the Christians and the Jews and the land tax. Is there a difference between what the prophet and the Imam collected and what the present-day jurisprudent should collect?

God made the prophet the ruler of all the faithful. . . . The jurisprudent has the same rule and governance. Therefore, the jurisprudents must work separately or collectively to set up a legitimate government that establishes the strictures, protects the borders and establishes order. If competence for this task is confined to one person, then this would be his duty to do so . . . otherwise the duty is shared equally.

The jurisprudent has been appointed by God to rule and the jurisprudent must act as much as possible in accordance with his assignment. He must collect the alms tax, the one-fifth tax, the land tax and the tax from Christians and Jews . . . so that he may spend all this in the interest of the Muslims. If he can, he must implement the divine strictures. [A] temporary inability to form a strong and complete government does not at all mean that we should retreat. Dealing with the needs of the Muslims and implementing among them whatever laws are possible is [our] duty. . . .

Ayatollah Ruhollah Khomeini, "Islamic Government," translated and published by *The Joint Publications Research Service* (Arlington, Va.: National Technical Information Service [a branch of the U.S. Department of Commerce], 1979), pp. 17–18, 21–22.

Nationalism is the product of Europe's nation-building process, and it was only with the spread of European imperialism in the nineteenth century that this concept of state organization became accepted worldwide. Many Islamic fundamentalists, therefore, identify a link between nationalism and imperialism and interpret nationalism as a device used by the West to divide the Muslim world and open it up for exploitation. They see Islam as a transnational ideology that is superior to nationalism as an organizing principle. Below, Hasan al-Banna, the founder of Egypt's Society of the Muslim Brothers, gives such an analysis, and explains how the Society offers a revitalized Islam as a curative for the "disease" of Western nationalism.

Document 5
THE ISLAMIC VIEW OF NATIONALISM AND IMPERIALISM

OUR ISLAM

Listen, Brother! Our mission is one described most comprehensively by the term "Islamic." . . . We believe that Islam is an all-embracing concept which regulates every aspect of life . . . and prescribing for it a solid and rigorous order. . . . Some people mistakenly understand by Islam something restricted to certain types of religious observances or spiritual exercises, and confine themselves and their understanding to these narrow areas. . . .

But we understand Islam . . . very broadly and comprehensively as regulating the affairs of men in this world and the next. We do not make this claim out of presumption . . . rather it is based solely on our understanding of the Book of God [Quran] and the biographies of the first Muslims. If the reader wishes to understand the mission of the Muslim Brotherhood . . . let him take up his Quran and rid himself of whimsy and prejudgment.

PATRIOTISM

People are at times seduced by the appeal of patriotism, at other times by that of nationalism, especially in the East, where the Eastern peoples are aware of the abuses of the West toward them, abuses that have done injury to their dignity, their honor, and their independence, as well as commandeered their wealth and shed their blood; and where these peoples suffer under the Western yolk which has been forced upon them. Hence they are trying to free themselves from it with whatever strength, resistance, opposition, and endurance they are capable of summoning up. The tongues of their leaders have been given free rein, a stream of newspapers has gushed forth, their writers have written, their orators have made speeches, and their broadcasters have broadcast, all in the name of patriotism and the majesty of nationalism.

This is good and fine. But it is neither good nor fine that when you try to acquaint the Eastern people—they being Muslim—with the fact that this is to be found in Islam in a state more complete, more pure, more lofty, and more exalted than anything that can be found in the utterances of Westerners and the books of Europeans, they reject it and persist in imitating these latter blindly, claiming that Islam belongs in one category and this ideology in another. . . .

This mistaken notion has been a danger for the Eastern peoples from every standpoint, and with this notion I would now like to turn to the attitude of the Muslim Brotherhood and their mission, insofar as they deal with the idea of patriotism. . . . [For] if by it the propagandists mean love of this land, attachment to it, sentiment toward it . . . something anchored in the very nature of the soul . . . it is prescribed in Islam. . . .

The bone of contention between us and them [the propagandists influenced by the West] is that we define patriotism according to the standard of credal belief, while they define it according to territorial borders and geographical boundaries. For every region in which there is a Muslim . . . is a fatherland in our opinion, possessing its own inviolability and sanctity, and demanding love, sincerity, and earnest effort for the sake of its welfare. All Muslims in these geographically determined countries are our people and our brethren: we are concerned about them, and we share their feelings and sensibilities. Propagandists for patriotism alone are not like this, since all that interests them is what concerns a specific and narrowly delimited region of the earth. This practical difference shows forth clearly whenever any one of the nations desires to aggrandize itself at the expense of any other one, for we do not approve of this taking place at the expense of any Islamic country. We seek power only that we may all share in it together. . . .

NATIONALISM

And now I shall speak to you about our attitude toward the principle of nationalism. If, by what they [the propagandists] vaunt as the principle of nationalism, they mean that [our sons] should follow in the footsteps of their ancestors on the ladder of glory and grandeur; that they should emulate them in their faculties of exceptional ability and resolution; that they should take them as a good example to follow, and that the grandeur of the forefathers is something their descendants may boast of, and through which they may discover bravery and magnanimity . . . then it is a worthy, fine goal which we encourage and advocate. Does our apparatus for awakening the ardor of the present generation exist for any other reason than to spur them on through the glories of those gone before? Perhaps a clear directive for this may be seen in what the Apostle of God [Muhammad] said: "Men are treasure-troves: the best of them in pagan times are the best of them in Islam, if they but knew."

Or if they [the propagandists] mean by nationalism that a man's kin and his nation are the most deserving out of all mankind of his benevolence and devotion, and the most worthy of his favor and zealous striving (jihad)—then it is the truth, for who does not think that his people are the most deserving of mankind of his zealous efforts, when he has sprung from them and has grown up among them?

If what is intended by nationalism is that all of us are put to the test and held accountable to work and strive assiduously, it is up to every collectivity to realize the goal from its own vantage point until we converge, God willing, in the forecourt of victory, and then this division will have been a good thing indeed! . . .

All this and the like comprised by the concept of nationalism is fine and wonderful: Islam does not reject it—Islam being our criterion—but in fact, our hearts are open to receive it, and we urge all to accept it.

If, however, what is meant by nationalism is . . . racial self-aggrandizement to a degree which leads to the disparagement of other races, aggression against them, and their victimization for the sake of the nation's glory . . . as claimed by every nation which preaches its superiority over all others—then this too is a reprehensible idea. It has no share in humanitarianism, and means that the human race will liquidate itself for the sake of a delusion with no basis in fact and embodying not the slightest good. . . .

Brother, know and learn that nations, in terms of their strength, weakness, youth, old age, health, and sickness, are like human individuals, without exception. For even as you look at a human being, strong, sound, and enjoying good health, lo and behold, you will see him seized with illness and beleaguered by maladies. Ailments and pains undermine his strong constitution, and he continues to complain and groan until God's mercy . . . overtakes him in the form of a skilled physician and well-trained specialist who knows the locus of the complaint and diagnoses it expertly . . . and working with dedication to cure it. . . . Imagine exactly the same situation with respect to nations: the changes of time confront them with threats to their very existence, breaking apart their solid structure while disease infiltrates the surface appearance of their strength. It continues to work away at them without interruption until it wreaks its damage upon them, and they turn out sickly and weak, the covetous eyeing them with greed, and the spoilers robbing them. . . . They can only be cured by these means: knowledge of the locus of the ailment, endurance to put up with the pain of the treatment, and an expert who will undertake it until God realizes his goal through his hands, and he brings his cure to a successful conclusion.

Experience has taught us, and events have given us to know, that the disease afflicting these Eastern nations assumes a variety of aspects and has many symptoms. It has done harm to every expression of their lives, for they have been assailed on the political side by imperialist aggression on the part of their enemies, and by factionalism, rivalry, division, and disunity on the part of their sons. They have been assailed on the economic side by the propagation of usurious practices throughout all their social classes, and the exploitation of their resources and natural treasures by foreign companies. They have been afflicted on the intellectual side by anarchy, defection, and heresy which destroy their religious beliefs and overthrow the ideals within their sons' breasts. They have been assailed on the sociological side by licentiousness of manners and mores, and through the sloughing off of the restraints of the humanitarian virtues they inherited from their . . . ancestors; while through imitation of the West, the viper's venom creeps insidiously into their affairs, poisoning their blood and sullying the purity of their well-being. They have been assailed through the workings of a positive law which does not restrain the criminal, chastise the assailant, or repel the unjust; nor does it even for one day take the place of the divinely revealed laws which the Creator of creation . . . has set down. They have been assailed also through anarchy in their policy of education and training, which stands in the way of effectively guiding their present generation, the men of their future and those who will be responsible for bringing about their resurgence. They have been assailed on the spiritual side by a death-dealing despair, a murderous apathy, a shameful cowardice, an ignoble humility, an all-pervading impotence, a niggardliness and an egocentricity which prevent people from making any effort, preclude self-sacrifice, and thrust the nation from the ranks of earnest strivers into those of triflers and gamesters. What hope is there for a nation against which all these factors, in their strongest manifestations and most extreme forms, have been conjoined for the assault—imperialism and factionalism, usury and heresy and licentiousness, anarchy in education and legislation, foreign companies, despair and niggardliness, impotence and cowardice, and admiration for the enemy, an admiration which prompts one to imitate him in everything he does, especially his evil acts. One of these diseases alone is sufficient to kill off numerous proud nations, and how much more now that it has been spread about among all, in every nation without exception? If it were not for the resistance, imperviousness, hardihood, and strength of the Eastern nations whose enemies have been contending with them from the remote past . . . if it were not for these qualities, their traces would have been long ago swept away and wiped out of existence. But God and the believers will not tolerate this.

Brother, this is the diagnoses which the Brotherhood make of the ailments of the umma, and this is what they are doing in order to cure it of them and to restore to it its lost health and strength.

HOPES AND FEELINGS

Brother, I would like you to know, before I talk to you about these means, that we do not despair of ourselves, that we hope for a great good, and that we believe that only such despair stands between us and success. For if hope grows strong within us, we shall arrive at this great good, God willing, and therefore we do not despair. . . .

The Muslim Brotherhood do not believe in a nationalism containing these ideas or their like, nor do they advocate Pharaoism, Arabism, Phoenicianism, or Syrianism, or employ any of those epithets by which peoples are held up to insult. But they do believe in what the Apostle of God . . . said: "God has removed from you the arrogance of paganism and the vaunting of your ancestry—mankind springs from Adam, and Adam springs from dust. The Arab has no superiority over the non-Arab except by virtue of his piety." How splendid this is, how fine and just! Mankind are of Adam, and therefore they are equals, and people vie with one another in their works, and it is their duty to be rivals in doing good—two firm pillars, which, if human life were only built upon them, would lift mankind up to the highest heavens! Mankind . . . are brethren and it is their duty to cooperate with one another, to keep the peace among themselves, to deal mercifully with one another, to guide one another toward the good and to vie with one another in performing good works. . . . Have you ever seen . . . a teaching more excellent than this?

Nevertheless, we are not denying that various nations have their own distinct qualities and particular moral characters, for we know that every people has its own quality and its own share of excellence and moral fiber, and we know too that in this respect the various peoples differ from one another. . . . We believe that in these respects Arabdom possesses the fullest and most abundant share, but this does not mean that its peoples should seize upon these characteristics as a pretext for aggression. Rather should they adopt them as a means of realizing the foremost task for which every people is responsible—the renaissance of humanity. Probably we will not find in all of history any one of the peoples of this earth who have grasped this concept as fully as did that Arabian phalanx consisting of the Companions of the Apostle of God (May God bless and save him).

THE BOND OF CREDAL DOCTRINE

Now that we have learned all this . . . know that the Muslim Brotherhood regard mankind as divided into two camps vis-à-vis themselves: one, believing as they believe, in God's religion and His Book, and in the mission of His Apostle and what he brought with him. These are attached to us by the most hallowed of bonds, the bonds of credal doctrine, which is to us holier than the bond of blood or of soil. These are our closest relatives among the peoples—we feel sympathy toward them, we work on their behalf, we defend them and we sacrifice ourselves and our wealth for them in whatever land they may be, or from whatever origin they may spring. As for other people with whom we do not yet share this bond, we will be at peace with them as long as they refrain from aggression against us. We believe, however, that a bond does exist between us and them—the bond of our mission—and that it is our duty to invite them to what we adhere to because it is the best that humanity has to offer, and to employ such ways and means to succeed in this mission as our faith has designated for that end. As for those of them who show hostility toward us, we repel their aggression by the most virtuous means through which such hostility may be repelled. If you wish to hear this authenticated by the Book of God, listen!

1. "The believers are none other than brothers; therefore make peace between your two brothers." (Quran 49:10)

2. "God does not forbid you to deal with those who have not fought against you in religion, and have not expelled you from your homes, that you should treat them with kindness and justice, for indeed, God loves the just. He forbids you only those who fought against you in religion, and expelled you from your homes, and helped expel you, that you should take them as friends." (Quran 60:8–9)

Perhaps through this I have revealed to you an aspect of our mission which will not leave it ambiguous or enigmatic in your mind. And perhaps after this, you will know what kind of organization the Muslim Brotherhood is.

Charles Wendell, trans. and ed., *Five Tracts of Hasan al-Banna (1906–1949),* (Berkeley: University of California Press, 1978), pp. 46–47, 51–52, 54–56, 60–62.

In the West, one of the least known aspects of Islamic thinking has to do with economics. Most Westerners assume that Muslims adhere to the same capitalist ideas that shape their own marketplace. After all, trade and business activities of all kinds are pervasive throughout Muslim lands. However, Islamic fundamentalists and other devout Muslims look at business differently than do most Western capitalists (and socialists too). Like much else in the Muslim worldview, ideas about economic behavior are shaped by religious teachings. Below,

Khalid Ishaque, a former member of Pakistan's Islamic Ideology Council, offers his views of some of the religious influences that shape a
Muslim's approach to economics.

Document 6
WHAT HAS ISLAM TO SAY ABOUT ECONOMICS?

WESTERN THEORY AND MODELS

In the West . . . human activity in the economic field is primarily directed
towards individual gain. It was formerly widely believed that competi-
tiveness generated by each individual's drive for personal gain would
somehow bring about an overall harmony of interests and mutual gain.
The West is only now discovering that this is not wholly true. Without
moral or legal restraints the big fish tend to eat up the small ones. The
path recommended and often willingly chosen (i.e., following Western
models of development), is not a road to salvation for the Third World,
especially in the case of the Muslim part of the Third World which does
not share the worldview of the capitalist or the socialist. The problem of
under-development has to be tackled within the framework of its Islamic
commitment, a commitment not confined merely to some aspects of worship, but to a total life-view in which economic activity has a definite
place and purpose. Not enough importance is given by the foreign advisers
or by the existing ruling elites to the fact that there is a radical difference
between the vision of a good and successful life in the worldview of Islam
and that of the capitalist or the socialist world. In the former it consists
of fulfilling one's covenant with Allah and of living out the worldly life
in terms of divine guidance as preparation for a more beautiful life await-
ing mankind. The First (capitalist) and the Second (socialist) worlds have
an essentially materialistic and earthly worldview. The total picture of the
good life painted with a mix of hues provided by Freud's vision of sexual
man and Marx's vision of an economic man does not coincide with that
which Islam portrays.

THE NEW TASK

To be able to utilize all the resources available to the Muslim community, several types of action shall have to be taken simultaneously and on
several fronts.

Disabusing the Muslim Mind About Imported Economic Models

The first task is to disabuse the Muslim of the necessity of adopting
one or the other of the two models projected by the First and the Second

Worlds. Both are basically materialistic, have priorities basically different from those of Islam . . . and continue to have aspects which permit whole-sale exploitation. . . . In both cases oligarchies run the society and knowing no control or criterion higher than their will, they exploit and oppress without even feeling guilty. There is nothing inevitable about these models as both stand discredited and exposed. The Muslims are and should feel free to devise their own models for solving their problems.

Our second task is to introduce the Muslims to Islam's distinctive ap-proach to the whole range of economic activity. It is the only ideology whose dimensions cover the life in this world as well as hereafter. Islam alone teaches man how to lead a moral and meaningful life in poverty and in wealth; it provides a motivational pattern to an individual for a spiri-tually meaningful commitment of his life and his worldly possessions. . . . [The] charting of our future will demand consideration of not merely the economic and political factors, but also the spiritual and moral factors without which politics becomes a game of oppression and economics a hunt by exploiters. Socio-economic injustices are the first object of attack under an Islamic commitment.

QURANIC PRINCIPLES OF ECONOMIC ACTIVITY
Participation in Economic Activity

According to the Quran, participation in economically creative activity is obligatory for every Muslim (Quran, 62:10). Muslims are also expected to work hard (Quran, 73:20). The Jews sought fulfillment of God's blessing in worldly life, and Christians went to the other extreme by propagating asceticism. Islam in unequivocal terms affirmed the fundamental and ab-solute precedence of life hereafter over worldly life (Quran, 4:77); [but also] expected Muslims to use the good things of life (Quran, 24:60, 7:31) and to be grateful to God for his blessings . . . because Allah increases His blessings for those who are grateful (Quran, 14:7). The blessing in worldly things is abused when a man squanders his wealth (Quran, 17:26–27), or exalts and makes a wanton public display thereof (Quran, 28:72); therefore waste and wanton display in contrast to moderate display within the family circle to increase the beauty and charm of life (Quran, 24:31) is prohibited. The importance of this principle becomes clear when one realizes that . . . [one of the] strongest criticism[s] against capitalism is in regard to its wastefulness, i.e., both the non-utility of a large number of items produced and also their inequitable distribution and use. One person wallows in ostentatious high living and another barely survives in a con-dition of extreme poverty and deprivation. Criticism can [also] be levelled against the socialist system . . . because . . . once a person has earned his wage he can do with it what he likes. Waste of hard earned wages on alcoholism is a special problem of Russian society.

According to the Quran everyone is entitled to a share in what he earns (Quran, 4:32); no one is permitted to withhold all that he earns (Quran, 104:2). He is required to use it in the categories prescribed by Allah (Quran, 28:78) but is prohibited from using it for wanton public display (Quran, 28:79). . . . Throughout the Quran there is repeated mention of the punishment the wealthy ones invite by hoarding their wealth, and not using it in a manner which would save them in the hereafter (Quran, 28:77; 104:2).

Duty to Produce More Than One's Needs

Economic activity is not to be confined to earning or producing enough to meet one's personal needs only. Muslims are expected to produce more because they cannot participate in the process of purification [spiritual improvement] through providing security to others (zakat or alms tax) unless they produce more than what they themselves consume. The most recommended use of fairly earned wealth is to apply it to procuring of all means to fulfill a Muslim's covenant with Allah. A Muslim is under a covenant to struggle for establishment of Islamic order with his life and all worldly belongings (Quran, 9:111). This too would become impossible if individuals only produced enough for personal needs. This of course does not mean that for those who have no wealth there is no compensation with Allah. They can improve the quality of social life [in noneconomic ways] even without surplus economic resources.

The duty to produce carries further implications of which due note must be taken. In the production of goods Muslims must give priority to those things which are good and wholesome and help to improve the quality of life. Goods for mere display or for titillating artificially created wants would have very low social priority. The goods whose use is unlawful or prohibited may not be produced at all. Under no circumstances should production be by means which are disapproved because in such circumstances even if there is appearance of an immediate gain . . . in reality there is a loss which is not immediately apparent (Quran, 30:30).

The importance of these principles becomes obvious when we realize that one of the major faults of the economic order of the First World is over production of goods which merely whet the appetite by creating a passing fancy and do little to add to the real quality of life. Every day media of all kinds keep inflicting advertisements for cigarettes, wine, clothes, and innumerable consumer items for which markets are artificially created and for projection of these wares, a specious culture is created and inflicted. In the end not all the consumer items reach everyone. A good many go completely to waste. In the process a great many social priorities remain unattended. The individual produced in such a society is morally indifferent and spiritually famished.

The Quran prohibits wagering transactions [speculation and gambling]. In a wagering transaction the winner makes an undeserved gain and the loser suffers an undeserved loss, without both parties being involved in any process of producing more. Such transactions constitute a clear abuse of wealth. . . . [They] cause envy, rancour and enmity (Quran, 5:90) and destroy dignity and the necessity of productive labor. Through them people acquire power to command more goods and services without participating in any exercise of adding to the sum total of socially available goods.

The Quran explicitly prohibits usury (riba) (Quran, 3:130) because of its evil effects on human society. . . . Ultimately, usury assures unearned incomes, and converts business into exploitative bargains (Quran, 2:275) and by and large develops a style of production wherein business transactions do not benefit both parties . . . (Quran 4:16).

The Quran insists that Muslims must not block wealth but must constantly spend it though with wisdom (Quran, 9:34) and moderation (Quran, 17:29), and keeping in view the permitted uses of wealth (Quran, 9:35). The full implications of this command do not become apparent at first glance and stand in need of some explication.

Participation in economically productive activity is the duty of every man and woman. The Prophet . . . is reported to have said that hateful in the eyes of Allah is one who does nothing. The individual's savings represent the surplus generated over and above what is consumed in the process of production. Part of this surplus is reserved by the shariah for the benefit of those who, due to some permanent disability or temporary incapacity, cannot look after their own needs or those of their dependents. This part is contributed and collected by the mandate of Divine Law and is known as the zakat. As far as the rest of the savings is concerned, this too needs to be thrown back into the process of production in the form of capital, to further social productivity. Islam seeks maximum use of capital, total utilization of manpower. Severe chastisement is promised to those who withhold socially available capital by storing it up in the form of gold and silver [money] (Quran, 9:34).

Gold and silver by themselves are at best universally accepted symbols to command services or to buy goods, and by themselves do not carry any intrinsic value to provide direct satisfaction of human needs. So long as the savings in individual accounts are . . . available as capital for the community, the problem of chronic shortage of capital may not often arise. For example, a man "A" works and from his wages he saves a hundred rupees. This amount he puts in a bank. The bank, as his agent, invests it in a joint venture with someone else, say "B." From the surplus generated the bank and "B" make provision to return the original sum, the bank takes part of the profits made in the joint venture with "B," and "B" deposits say fifty rupees as savings from part of the profit that accrued to him. Now say the bank enters into another joint venture with "C" utilizing the amount of rupees deposited by "A" and "B" and makes further profit and generates further savings by "C." In this way the sum total of socially available goods and services increases without destroying the capacity of "A" and "B" to call [on] certain [wealth] to which they are entitled by virtue of their savings. The profits of [the bank would, in part, be distributed to all] depositors [by being] calculated [into their] annual savings. The transaction would then be different from an ordinary banking transaction wherein the lender gets his interest at a predetermined rate irrespective of the benefit which may or may not accrue to the borrower. . . . In joint ventures [undertaken on Muslim principles] both parties risk profit or loss. . . .

There are many factors which operate to [define] profit. The Quranic injunction of equality, and the Prophet's command that in all transactions both parties must profit, and the other principles already referred to above have a direct bearing on the question of the quantum of profit permissible to a Muslim. Until quite recently the First World economists used to say that profit is as much as anyone is willing to pay minus the cost, and often justified it by saying that the competitive market fixes the margin. We know now that there is no absolutely free competitive market like that the academic economists visualize, and that there are too many factors which prevent the market from reaching a fair equilibrium. The Prophet . . . is reported to have prohibited making of profit on articles of absolute need like food-grains though he refused to fix prices in spite of requests. On other items he required the believers to make reasonable profits to assure full benefits of each transaction to all contracting parties. The Islamic social framework, insisting as it does on nurturing social confidence, would provide the requisite field for successful operation of these principles.

Quranic principles operate in the numerous patterns of economic arrangements in such a way as to preclude exploitation. They seek to assure that within the limits set by shariah, each party shall receive due benefit for its contribution, industry, work, entrepreneurial skill, [and] inventiveness. Those who contribute more shall receive more (Quran, 53:32). There will remain certain inequalities . . . but they will not hurt the group because strict controls regulate the uses of wealth. Those who have more wealth have more responsibilities, and more to account for.

The Quran recognizes the difference between man and man in terms of intelligence, health, strength and morality. It also recognizes the fact that some work harder than others and some work more intelligently and consistently for better objectives. Some work only to get the good things of this life and some use their worldly life as a means for betterment of the real life of hereafter. Some save their earnings and others squander them. Recognizing all these differences, the Quran affirms the principle of just requittal by declaring that: "There is naught for man but what he strives for" (Quran, 53:39). . . .

In short, therefore, the Quran makes it clear that principles of just requittal require that the wages of sin and virtue all be reckoned and paid to each according to the labor he puts in. Any egalitarian philosophy which destroys or even fails to recognize the qualitative differences between a good man and a knave, a hard worker and a waster, is totally unacceptable to Islam. . . . The answer provided by Islam . . . does not seek to establish social justice by steam-rolling all into a state of unmerited equality. . . . The transfer of legal ownership of means of production to government instead of individuals does not ipso facto establish the equality that is sought. Even in the government-owned farm or factory there is the manager who commands and oppresses like the owner that he replaces. Human dignity and freedom are as effectively choked under the new arrangement as they were under the old; perhaps they are even more effectively and irretrievably lost, because the new master is a member of a vast bureaucracy infinitely more powerful and power-drunk than the . . . capitalist that he replaces. Islam protects the individual not on the basis of hatred or class-war, but in a manner infinitely surer, wiser and more human.

At this stage it might be useful to refer to Islam's attitude toward private property. We have already referred to the fact that the first addressee of Quran is the individual. He is called upon to achieve salvation and ultimate fulfillment by living up to the terms of his covenant with Allah irrespective of the performance of other members of the community. . . . Islamic individualism is irreconcilable with the collectivism and moral relativity of socialist thought. The distinctive characteristics that the concept of private property has in an Islamic society must be understood in this context. In Islam no person has an absolute right to his property to use it as he will, except perhaps in the sense that he can use it for some purpose that has been accepted as lawful by the Quran. It is not the property which is in itself the source of trouble but it is the misuse of the property which causes unhappiness and unrest. . . . The Prophet . . . was extremely careful in suppressing ostentatiousness and wanton display of wealth. He constantly warned the community that wealth was one means amongst others whereby to win one's laurels in the life hereafter. All things created were for use of man in his spiritual journey. . . .

But whereas the believers are called upon to lawfully earn what they can, they are simultaneously placed under a duty to spend what they have earned in the path of Allah, i.e., for that which is laudable, approved or permitted by the Divine Book and the Holy Prophet. The hoarders of wealth have been promised the most severe punishment. The Quran declares: "Woe to every back-biter, slanderer, who amasses wealth and counts it time after time. He thinks that his wealth makes him immortal, Nay, he shall be cast into crushing punishment" (194:2–6).

It is for this reason that we notice that many of the companions of the Messenger of Allah . . . left no wealth worth mention in spite of the vast amount that came to their share as income or as war booty. It is well known that during Umar bin Abdul Aziz's reign there was a shortage not of the bountiful but of the needy.

Islam's way to social justice is the establishment of a brotherhood of believers, thereby destroying tyranny without destroying legitimate differences. In this brotherhood each individual is duty-bound to work for self-support and to help the other, even though each one works for whatever he aspires for. Islam recognizes that ambition for self-development and advancement, for progress and salvation, is the mainspring of an individual's efforts. It puts these urges and ambitions into a constructive channel. It does not prevent a man from acquiring or enjoying the just and lawful produce of his labor, but insists that what is earned be spent in a manner prescribed or approved by Allah. . . .

It is part of Quranic justice that it does not permit the concentration of capital or of wealth. It refuses to approve hoarding of wealth. It promises a grievous chastisement for hoarders of gold and silver. It directs us to look at the glorious examples of the companions of the Holy Prophet who have left us a brilliant trail to follow. . . .

Khalid M. Ishaque, "The Islamic Approach to Economic Development" in John L. Esposito, ed., *Voices of Resurgent Islam* (New York: Oxford University Press, 1983), pp. 268–276.

Many in the West believe that the religious teachings of Islam are oppressive toward women. To some extent, this opinion is the result of confusing Islamic teachings with local customs and traditions, many of which predate Islam, that are restrictive of women's rights. Often men, including religious leaders, reared in these traditions will inter-pret religion in their light. Thus Islam, like any other religious or secular ideology, is open to interpretation and distortion as it is fil-tered through local culture. In the piece below, Gamal A. Badawi, a Muslim commentator on social issues, argues that Islam, properly interpreted, is not oppressive toward women.

Document 7
WHAT DOES ISLAM SAY ABOUT THE STATUS OF WOMEN?

The status of women in society is neither a new issue nor is it a fully settled one. The position of Islam on this issue has been among the sub-jects presented to the Western reader with the least objectivity. This paper is intended to provide a brief and authentic exposition of what Islam stands for in this regard. The teachings of Islam are based essentially on the Quran (God's revelation) and Hadith (elaborations by Prophet Muham-mad). The Quran and Hadith, properly and unbiasedly understood, provide the basic source of authentication for any position or view which is at-tributed to Islam. . . .

THE SPIRITUAL ASPECT

The Quran provides clear-cut evidence that woman is completely equated with man in the sight of God in terms of her rights and respon-sibilities. The Quran states: "Every soul will be (held) in pledge for its deeds (Quran, 74:38). . . .

Woman according to the Quran is not blamed for Adam's first mistake. Both were jointly wrong in their disobedience to God, both repented, and both were forgiven (Quran, 2:36–37; 7:20–24).

In terms of religious obligations, such as Daily Prayers, Fasting, Poor-Due and Pilgrimage, woman is no different from man. In some cases, indeed, woman has certain advantages over man. For example, the woman is exempted from the daily prayers and from fasting during her menstrual periods and [for] forty days after childbirth. She is also exempted of fast-ing during pregnancy and when she is nursing her baby if there is any threat to her health or her baby's. If the missed fasting is obligatory (during the month of Ramadan), she can make up for the missed days whenever she can. . . . Women used to go to the mosque during the days of the

Prophet, [but now] attendance at the Friday congregational prayers is optional for them while it is mandatory for men (on Friday).

This is clearly a tender touch of Islamic teachings for they are considerate of the fact that a woman may be nursing her baby or caring for him, and thus may be unable to go out to the mosque at the time of the prayers. They also take into account the physiological and psychological changes associated with her natural female functions.

THE SOCIAL ASPECT

As a Child and an Adolescent

Despite the social acceptance of female infanticide among some Arabian tribes [at the time of the Prophet Muhammad], the Quran forbade this custom, and considered it a crime like any other murder. . . .

Among the sayings of Prophet Muhammad in this regard [is] the following: "Whosoever has a daughter and he does not bury her alive, does not insult her, and does not favour his son over her, God will enter him into Paradise."

As a Wife

The Quran clearly indicates that marriage is sharing between the halves of the society, and that its objectives, besides perpetuating human life, are emotional wellbeing and spiritual harmony. Its bases are love and mercy. Among the most impressive verses in the Quran about marriage is the following: "And among His signs is this: That He created mates for you from yourselves that you may find rest, peace of mind in them, and He ordained between you love and mercy, Lo, herein indeed are signs for people who reflect" (Quran, 30:21).

According to Islamic Law, women cannot be forced to marry anyone without their consent. Ibn Abbas reported that a girl came to the Messenger of God, Muhammad, and she reported that her father had forced her to marry without her consent. The Messenger of God gave her the choice (between accepting the marriage or invalidating it). In another version [of this story] the girl said: "Actually I accept this marriage but I wanted to let women know that parents have no right (to force a husband on them)."

Besides all other provisions for her protection at the time of marriage, it was specifically decreed that woman has the full right to her Mahr, a marriage gift, which is presented to her by her husband and is included in the nuptial contract, and that such ownership does not transfer to her father or husband. The concept of Mahr in Islam is neither an actual or symbolic price for the woman, as was the case in certain cultures, but rather it is a gift symbolizing love and affection.

The rules for married life in Islam are clear and in harmony with upright human nature. In consideration of the physiological and psychological make-up of man and woman, both have equal rights and claims on one another, except for one responsibility, that of leadership. This is a matter which is natural in any collective life and which is consistent with the nature of man. The Quran thus states: "And they (women) have right similar to those (of men) [though in certain situations] men are a degree above them" (Quran, 2:229). Such a degree [has to do with] Qiwama (maintenance and protection). This refers to that natural difference between the sexes which entitles the weaker sex to protection. It implies no superiority or advantage before the law. Yet, man's role of leadership in relation to his family does not mean the husband's dictatorship over his wife. Islam emphasizes the importance of taking counsel and mutual agreement in family decisions. . . .

Over and above her basic rights as a wife comes the right which is emphasized by the Quran and is strongly recommended by the Prophet; kind treatment and companionship. The Quran states: "But consort with them in kindness, for if you hate them it may happen that you hate a thing wherein God has placed much good" (Quran, 4:19).

As the woman's right to decide about her marriage is recognized, so also her right to seek an end for an unsuccessful marriage is recognized. To provide for the stability of the family, however, and in order to protect it from a hasty decision under temporary emotional stress, certain steps and waiting periods should be observed by men and women seeking divorce. Considering the relatively more emotional nature of women, a good reason for asking for divorce should be brought before the judge. Like the man, however, the woman can divorce her husband without resorting to the court, if the nuptial contract allows that. . . .

As a Mother

Islam considers kindness to parents next to the worship of God. "Your Lord has decreed that you worship none save Him, and that you be kind to your parents" (Quran, 17:23). . . . A famous saying of the Prophet is "Paradise is at the feet of mothers," [and] "It is the generous (in character) who is good to women, and it is the wicked who insults them."

THE ECONOMIC ASPECT

Islam decreed a right of which woman was deprived . . . the right of independent ownership. According to Islamic Law, woman's right to her money, real estate, or other properties is fully acknowledged. This right undergoes no change whether she is single or married. She retains her full rights to buy, sell, mortgage or lease any or all her properties. It is nowhere suggested in the law that a woman is a minor simply because she is a female. It is also noteworthy that such right applies to her properties before marriage as well as to whatever she acquires thereafter.

With regard to the woman's right to seek employment, it should be stated first that Islam regards her role in society as a mother and wife as the most sacred and essential one. Neither maids nor babysitters can possibly take the mother's place as the educator of an upright, complex-free, and carefully reared child. Such a noble and vital role, which largely shapes the future of nations, cannot be regarded as "idleness."

However, there is no decree in Islam which forbids women from seeking employment whenever there is a necessity for it, especially in positions which fit her nature and in which society needs her most. Examples of these professions are nursing, teaching (especially for children), and medicine. Moreover, there is no restriction on benefitting from woman's exceptional talent in any field. Even for the position of a judge, [where there] may be a tendency to doubt the woman's fitness for the post due to her more emotional nature, we find early Muslim scholars such as Abu-Hanifa and al-Tabari holding there is nothing wrong with it.

In addition, Islam restored to women the right of inheritance. . . . Her share is completely hers and no one can make any claim on it, including her father and her husband. . . . Her share in most cases is one-half of the man's share, with no implication that she is worth half a man! It would seem grossly inconsistent after the overwhelming evidence of woman's equitable treatment in Islam . . . to make such an inference. This variation in inheritance rights is only consistent with the variations in financial responsibilities of man and woman according to Islamic Law. Man in Islam is fully responsible for the maintenance of his wife, his children, and in some cases of his needy relatives, especially the females. This responsibility is neither waived nor reduced because of his wife's wealth or because of her access to any personal income gained from work, rent profit, or any other legal means.

Woman, on the other hand, is far more secure financially and is far less burdened with any claims on her possessions. Her possessions before marriage do not transfer to her husband and she even keeps her maiden name. She has no obligation to spend on her family out of such properties or out of her income after marriage. If she is divorced, she may get an alimony from her ex-husband. . . .

THE POLITICAL ASPECT

Any fair investigation of the teachings of Islam or into the history of Islamic civilization will surely find clear evidence of woman's equality with man in what we call today "political rights." This includes the right of election as well as the nomination to political offices. It also includes woman's right to participate in public affairs. Both in the Quran and in Islamic history we find examples of women who participated in serious discussions and argued even with the Prophet himself (see Quran, 58:1 and 60:10–12).

During the Caliphate of Umar Ibn al-Khattab, a woman argued with him in the mosque, proved her point, and caused him to declare in the presence of people: "A woman is right and Umar is wrong."

Although not mentioned in the Quran, one Hadith of the Prophet is interpreted to make woman ineligible for the position of head of state. The Hadith referred to is roughly translated: "A people will not prosper if they let a woman be their leader." This limitation, however, has nothing to do with the dignity of woman or with her rights. It is rather, related to the natural differences in the biological and psychological make-up of men and women.

According to Islam, the head of the state is no mere figurehead. He leads people in the prayers, especially on Fridays and festivities; he is continuously engaged in the process of decision making pertaining to security and well being of his people. This demanding position, or any similar one, such as the Commander of the Army, is generally inconsistent with the physiological and psychological make-up of woman. It is a medical fact that during monthly periods and pregnancies, women undergo various physiological and psychological changes. Such changes may occur during an emergency situation, thus affecting her decision. . . .

Even in modern times, and in the most developed countries, it is rare to find a woman in the position of a head of state acting as more than a figurehead, a woman commander of the armed services, or even a proportionate number of women representatives in parliaments, or similar bodies. One cannot possibly ascribe this to backwardness of various nations or to any constitutional limitation on woman's right to be in such positions. . . . It is more logical to explain the present situation in terms of the natural . . . differences between men and women, a difference which does not imply any "supremacy" of one over the other. The difference implies rather the "complementary" roles of both the sexes in life.

CONCLUSION

In [this] paper, the status of women in Islam is briefly discussed. Emphasis . . . is placed on the original and authentic sources of Islam. This represents the standard according to which . . . adherence of Muslims [to teaching on this subject] can be judged. It is also a fact that during some of [the Muslim world's] moments of decline, such teachings were not strictly adhered to by many people who professed to be Muslims.

Such deviations were unfairly exaggerated by some writers, and the worst of these were superficially taken to represent the teachings of Islam to the Western reader without taking the trouble to make any original and unbiased study of the authentic sources. . . . Even with such deviations three facts are worth mentioning:

1. The history of Muslims is rich with women of great achievements in all walks of life from as early as the seventh century (CE).

2. It is impossible for anyone to justify any mistreatment of woman by any decree or rule embodied in the Islamic Law, nor could anyone dare to cancel, reduce or distort the clearcut legal rights of women given in Islamic Law.

3. Throughout history, the reputation, chastity and maternal role of Muslim women were objects of admiration by impartial observers.

It is worthwhile to state that the status of women reached during the present era was not achieved due to the kindness of men or due to natural progress. It was rather achieved through a long struggle and sacrifice on woman's part and only when society needed her contribution and work, more especially during the two world wars, and due to the escalation of technological change.

In the case of Islam such compassionate and dignified status was decreed, not because it reflects the environment of the seventh century, nor under the threat or pressure of women and their organization, but rather because of its intrinsic truthfulness.

If this indicates anything, it would demonstrate the divine origin of the Quran and the truthfulness of the message of Islam, which, unlike human philosophies and ideologies . . . established such humane principles as neither grew obsolete during the course of time . . . nor can become obsolete in the future. After all, this is the message of the All-Wise and All-Knowing God whose wisdom and knowledge are far beyond . . . human thought and progress.

Gamal A. Badawi, "Woman in Islam," in Khurshid Ahmad, ed., *Islam: Its Meaning and Message* (London: The Islamic Foundation, 1988), pp. 135–144.

Muslim fundamentalists find inspiration in the examples, guidelines, and values of the Quran and hadiths. Many of their critics claim that this produces a very narrow worldview with a rigid set of rules taken from a literal reading of the Muslim holy book and the behavioral patterns of a man (Muhammad) who lived centuries ago in a very different world. However, while a few fundamentalists may take this narrow approach, most do not. Below, Ali Shariati, an Iranian Muslim thinker who attempted to meld Islamic teaching and modern social and economic ideas (see the description of his life in the biography section of this book), demonstrates a creative and adaptive approach to reading the Quran.

Document 8
CAN A MUSLIM READ THE QURAN CREATIVELY?

The duty of today's [Muslim] intellectual is to recognize and know Islam as a school of thought that gives life to man, individual and society, and that is entrusted with the mission of the future guidance of mankind. He should regard this duty as an individual and personal one, and whatever be his field of study, he should cast a fresh glance at the religion of Islam and its great personages from the viewpoint of whatever may be his [interest]. . . . For Islam has so many different dimensions and varying aspects that everyone can discover a fresh and exact vantage point for viewing it within his field of study. . . .

My field is the sociology of religion. . . . [And] one of the facts I encountered in my study of Islam and the Quran was the existence of scientific theories of history and sociology peculiar to the custom and work of the Prophet. . . . What I mean is . . . namely, that I extracted from the Quran a whole series of new topics and themes relating to history, sociology and the human sciences. The Quran itself, or Islam itself, was the source of the ideas. . . . and when I later checked them against history and sociology, I found them to be fully correct.

There are several important topics in the human sciences that I discovered with the aid of the Quran that have not yet been discussed by these sciences. One is the topic of migration. . . . From the tone in which the Quran discussed emigration and migrants, from the life of the Prophet, and, in general, from the concept of migration held in early Islam, I came to realize that migration, despite what Muslims imagine, is not merely a historical event.

The understanding that Muslims have of the hijra is that a number of the Companions [of Muhammad] migrated from Mecca . . . to Medina on the orders of the Prophet. They imagine that migration has the general sense in history of the movement of a primitive or semi-civilized people

from one place to another, as a result of geographical or political factors.
. . . But from the tone in which migration is discussed in the Quran, I
came to perceive that migration is a profound philosophical and social
principle. Then, turning my attention to history, I realized that migration
is an infinitely glorious principle, and that it constitutes a totally fresh
topic, one by no means as simple as history and historians have made it
out to be. Even the philosophers of history have not paid attention to the
question of migration as it truly deserves, for migration has been the
primary factor in the rise of civilization throughout history. . . .

All the civilizations in the world—from the most recent, the civilization
in America, to the most ancient that we know of, the civilization of Su-
mer—came into being on the heels of a migration. In each case, a primitive
people remained primitive as long as it stayed in its own land, and attained
civilization after undertaking a migration and establishing itself in a new
land. All civilizations are, then, born of the migrations of primitive peoples.

There are numerous subjects and topics that I came to understand in
this way. Islam and the Quran, in proportion to my own degree of knowledge of them, helped me to understand questions of history and sociology
in a better, fresher and more precise fashion. I thus came to realize that
through applying the special terms of the Quran, it is possible to discover
numerous topics even in the most modern of sciences, the human sciences.

The subject I now wish to discuss . . . is the greatest dilemma of both
sociology and history: the search for the basic factor in the change and
development of societies. What is the basic factor that causes a society
suddenly to change and develop, or suddenly to decay and decline; the
factor that sometimes causes a society to make a positive leap forward; to
change totally its character, its spirit, its aim and its form, in the course
of one or two centuries; and to change completely the individual and social
relationships obtaining in it? . . . The question constantly raised is this:
What is the motor of history? . . . The various schools of sociology part
company at this point, each one devoting attention to a particular factor.

Certain schools do not believe at all in history, but regard it as nothing
more than a worthless collection of narrations from the past. . . . [These
schools] say that the changes, advancements, declines, and revolutions
that take place in nations all come into existence as the result of accident.
For example, suddenly the Arabs attacked Iran; by chance, Iran was defeated and later the Iranians became Muslim. By chance, Ghengiz Khan
attacked Iran; it so happened that Iran's government was weak at that time,
so that it was defeated. The Mongols entered Iran, so that the Mongol
culture and way of life became intermingled with the Irano-Islamic way

of life, and certain change took place. Similarly, the First and Second World Wars also broke out by accident; it was possible that they should not have taken place. In short, this school regards everything as the outcome of chance.

Another group is composed of the materialists and those who believe in historical determinism. They believe that history and society, from the very beginning down to the present, are like a tree, devoid of any volition. In its origin it was a seed. Then it emerged from the seed, appeared above the ground, put forth roots, stems, branches and leaves and grew into a great tree, compelled to yield fruit, to wither in winter, to blossom again in spring, to attain perfection and finally to decay. This group believes that human societies traverse a long life throughout history in accordance with determining factors and laws that play in human society exactly the same role as the laws of nature in the natural realm.

According to this belief, individuals can have no effect on the fate of their societies, and society is a natural phenomenon that develops according to natural factors and laws.

The third group consists of those who worship heroes and personalities. It includes the fascists and Nazis, as well as great scholars like Carlyle, who also wrote a biography of the Prophet of Islam, and Emerson, and the like. This group believes that laws are no more than a tool in the hands of powerful individuals. . . . Average and sub-average persons, equally, have no share in the changing of society; they too are like tools for others to use. The only fundamental factor in the reform or advancement of society, or the cause of its downfall, is the powerful personality. . . .

In the view of this group . . . the happiness or wretchedness of societies does not, then, depend on the masses of the people, nor is it caused by inevitable laws of environment and society, nor is it the result of mere accident; it depends solely on great personalities who every now and then appear in societies in order to change [their] destiny . . . and sometimes that of mankind. . . .

The opinion also exists that the people, the generality of society, do play a role in determining their destiny; but no school of thought, not even democracy in its ancient or modern forms, claims that the masses are the fundamental factor in social development and change. Democratic schools of thought believe that the best form of government is that in which the people participate; but from the time of Athenian democracy down to the present, none of these schools has believed that the broad masses of the people are the decisive factor in social change and development. The most democratic sociologists, then, even while believing that the best form of government and of administrative and social organization is that in which the people participate by casting their votes and electing the government, do not regard the "people" as the basic factor of social change. . . . Instead, they regard determinism, great personalities, the elite, mere chance or divine will as the decisive factor. . . .

In Islam and the Quran, none of the foregoing theories is to be found. Now from the point of view of Islam, the Prophet is the greatest of all personalities; and if Islam were to believe in the role of the Prophet as the fundamental factor in social change and development, it would have to recognize all the prophets, and especially the Prophet Muhammad, as constituting the fundamental factor. We see, however, that this is not the case. The mission and the characteristics of the Prophet are clearly set forth in the Quran, and they consist of the conveying of a message. He is . . . a warner and a bearer of glad tidings. And when the Prophet is disturbed by the fact that the people do not respond and he cannot guide them as he would wish, God repeatedly explains to him that his mission consists only of conveying the message, of inspiring fear in men and giving them glad tidings, of showing them the path; he is not in any way responsible for their decline or advancement, for it is the people themselves who are responsible.

In the Quran, the Prophet is not recognized as the active cause of fundamental change and development in human history. He is depicted rather as [one] whose duty is to show men the . . . path of the truth. His mission is then completed, and men are free either to choose the truth or to reject it, either to be guided or to be misguided.

"Accident" also has no decisive role to play in Islam, for all things are in the hand of God, so that accident, in the sense of an event coming into being without any cause or ultimate purpose, is inconceivable, whether in nature or in human society. . . .

The conclusion we deduce from the Quran is, then, that Islam does not consider the fundamental factor in social change and development to be personality, or accident, or overwhelming and immutable laws.

In general, those addressed by . . . every religion, every prophet . . . constitute the fundamental and effective factor of social change. . . . It is for this reason that we see throughout the Quran an address being made to al-nas, i.e., the people; it is al-nas who are accountable for their deeds . . . in short, the whole responsibility for society and history is borne by al-nas.

The word al-nas is an extremely valuable one, for which there exist a number of equivalents and synonyms. But the . . . word that [best] resembles it . . . is the word "mass."

In sociology, the masses comprise the whole people taken together as an entity without concern for class distinctions that exist among them or distinguishing properties that set one group apart from another. "Mass" means, therefore, the people as such. . . .

From this we deduce the following conclusion: Islam is the first school of social thought that recognizes the masses as the basis, the fundamental and conscious factor in determining history and society—not the elect as Nietzsche thought, not the aristocracy and nobility as Plato claimed, not great personalities as Carlyle and Emerson believed, not those of pure blood as Alexis Carrel imagined, not the priests or the intellectuals, but the masses. . . .

None of the privileges and distinctions assumed by these [thinkers] exist in Islam. The only fundamental factor in social change and development is the people. . . .

Ali Shariati, "Approaches to the Understanding of Islam," from Hamid Algar, trans., *On the Sociology of Islam* (Berkeley, Calif.: Mizan Press, 1979), pp. 42–49.

Document 9
ISLAMIC FUNDAMENTALIST VIEWS OF MAJOR CONTEMPORARY EVENTS

THE 1979 AMERICAN HOSTAGE CRISIS IN IRAN

In October 1979 the American government allowed the exiled Shah of Iran, who was dying of cancer, to enter the United States for medical treatment. The government did so despite an awareness that there might be Iranian retaliation for such an act. From the American point of view, the Shah was an old and reliable ally who had been forced from his country by a radical Islamic revolution. Letting him come to the United States was seen as a humanitarian gesture to a long-time friend. However, from the point of view of the Islamic revolutionaries in Iran, the American gesture only served to confirm U.S. complicity in what they perceived as decades of dictatorial and corrupt rule. The Iranian response to the American decision to admit the Shah came in early November when radical students took over the American Embassy in Tehran. Fifty-two American embassy personnel were held hostage. The United States, in turn, froze billions of dollars of Iranian assets and applied selective restrictions on Iranian citizens (mostly students) in this country.

While not all Islamic fundamentalists approved of hostage taking as a tactic, most agreed that Western actions and policies in the Muslim world had long generated angry feelings that now fueled the hostage crisis of 1979. Below, official Iranian government documents make clear the Islamic Republic's view of both the crisis and the U.S. role in Iran.

[Document 371] Message from the Leader of the Revolution and Founder of the Islamic Republic of Iran (Imam Khomeini) to the Pilgrims of Beytollah al-Haram, September 12, 1980.

Iranian Conditions for the Release of American Hostages:

I have said several times that the hostage taking by the fighting, committed Muslim students was the natural reaction to the damages that have been inflicted on our nation by the United States. On the return of the deposed Shah's wealth and the cancellation of all the U.S. claims against Iran, a guarantee of no U.S. military and political interventions in Iran and the freeing of all our investments, the hostages will be set free. Of course I have given this duty to the Islamic Consultative Assembly so that it may decide on any course of action that it deems beneficial to the interest of the nation. The hostages have been treated well in Iran, yet the United States and its satellites have not spared any effort to fabricate falsehoods in this field. While the United States and Britain have inflicted on our dear sons [Iranians resident in those countries] the worst insults . . . no official body or international organization . . . has condemned the United States and Britain for taking these savage actions.

[Document 373] Report of the Iranian Special Commission to the Islamic Consultative Assembly, Approved November 2, 1980.

Iranian Conditions for Release of the Hostages:

In the name of God, the compassionate, the merciful: The special commission investigating the issue of the American spies submits the following proposals to the Islamic Consultative Assembly, according to the guidelines of the Imam:

1. Since, in the past, the American Government has always interfered in various ways in Iran's political and military affairs, she should make a pledge and a promise that from now on she will in no way interfere, either directly or indirectly, politically or militarily, in the affairs of the Islamic Republic of Iran.

2. Unfreeze all of our assets. . . .

3. Abrogation and cancellation of all economic and financial decisions and measures against the Islamic Republic of Iran. . . .

4. Return of the assets of the cursed Shah, while officially recognizing the measures taken by Iran and their effectiveness in asserting its sovereignty in confiscating the assets of the cursed Shah and his close relatives, whose assets, according to Iranian laws belong to the Iranian nation. . . .

According to this recommendation, the Islamic Republic Government will release all 52 U.S. criminals in return for the fulfillment of these conditions by the U.S. Government. . . .

The Islamic Republic Government is required to enforce this recommendation, after ratification by the Islamic Majlis, taking into account the Islamic [Republic's] independence and the general policy of [allying the country with] neither east nor west. Should the U.S. Government fail to comply with all or some of the conditions, then the judicial system, in accordance with its required duty, will carry out its duty and punish the criminals.

American Foreign Policy Basic Documents 1977–1980, Published by the Department of State, Bureau of Public Affairs, Office of Historian, Washington, D.C., 1983.

THE PERSIAN GULF WAR

In August of 1990 Iraqi troops invaded and occupied Kuwait. This was much more than a local war between Arab states because Kuwait was an important supplier of oil to the West and an immediate neighbor of Saudi Arabia, the world's major producer of petroleum, and an ally of the United States. Most of the Western powers, and a good number of Arab countries as well, came together in a coalition to confront Iraq and force it to retreat from Kuwait. In January of 1991 American and allied forces launched a major air and ground campaign against Iraq.

Islamic fundamentalists approached these events with mixed feelings. On the one hand, they did not approve of Iraq's aggressive actions and supported Arab efforts to settle the conflict through negotiation. On the other hand, they were appalled and frightened by the influx of thousands of non-Muslim troops into Saudi Arabia, the country that is home to the holy cities of Mecca and Medina. In the comments on the Persian Gulf war by Islamic fundamentalists given below, this ambivalence comes through.

The war which had been expected ever since the expiration of the UN Security Council deadline began early this morning when U.S., British, French and Saudi airplanes conducted a fierce bombardment of various targets in Iraq. In this way, a regrettable war, which can cause irrevocable losses and damage to the people of the region, began.

. . . Within the framework of its principled policy, the Islamic Republic of Iran constantly called on Iraq to terminate its occupation of Kuwait, while condemning the presence of foreign forces in the region.

. . . The stance of the Islamic Republic of Iran was reiterated by various personalities and associations, and the repercussions of a devastating war in the region was constantly stressed. In any case, following the expiration of the Security Council deadline, there was no doubt about the inevitability of the war. . . .

Foreign Broadcast Information Service (of the U.S. Government), Daily Report, Near East and South Asia. FBIS-NES-91-012, 17 January 1991, p. 45—Tehran Radio Commentary.

The war is going on in a region inhabited by Muslims. The richest resources of the Muslim people are in this region. The damage inflicted, ultimately, is a loss for Muslims and is against their national and Islamic interests. . . .

All through the Persian Gulf crisis, our country tried to make the Iraqi Government understand that it had started a dangerous game and would have no alternative but to retreat from Kuwait and end its aggression. At the same time, the Islamic Republic of Iran tried, in the international arena, to point out that the danger posed by the presence of countless multinational forces would not serve the interests of the people of the region in any way, and would even threaten their existence and independence. . . .

Foreign radios, in their propaganda of the past few months, have instilled the idea that they are pursuing some humane objectives and that their main objective is to restore Kuwait's sovereignty and independence. This claim is a deceitful cover for their partially vague objectives and intentions for the region's future and the imposition of their aggressive policies. . . .

The current propaganda of the foreign radios demonstrates one-sided reporting of the news. . . . In view of our experience with Western propaganda, one cannot trust or rely on their statements at all. . . . We therefore instruct those who possibly listen to these radios that they receive the news censored and that these radios are officially prevented from reporting everything.

FBIS-NES-91-013, 18 January 1991, p. 54—Tehran Radio Warns of Western "Propaganda" in Gulf War.

Shaykh Sa'id Sha'ban, leader of the Islamic Unification Movement, has said: "In spite of U.S. President George Bush's statements, which confirm his determination to carry on with the air raids to destroy what is left of Iraq, many Arabs and the world have remained silent over this ugly crime that is being committed against an Arab and Muslim people, who are being massacred without any denunciation being heard."

He added: "By staying neutral on an issue of the magnitude of this crime, which will make us lose Iraq after we have lost Palestine, means we are becoming partners in realizing the Israeli dream, when Baghdad falls and when the Atlantic alliance settles in the heart of the Muslim world."

FBIS-NES-91-035, 21 February 1991, p. 5—Arabic Broadcast Service, Al-Nahar, Beirut. Islamic Unification Leader Criticizes Neutrality.

ISRAEL AND ZIONISM

All Islamic fundamentalists support the Palestinian right of self-determination. They see Israel as a Western colonial outpost in the heartland of the Muslim world and thus oppose it and the Zionist ideology that is the basis of the Israeli state. Most are careful, however, to explain that this opposition is not anti-Semitism or hostility to the human rights of Jews. In the two brief comments below by Islamic fundamentalists, the outlines of this opposition are made clear.

Islam is not opposed to Judaism but regards it as the religion of God. . . . Zionism [however] is designed to transform Palestine into a Jewish State. . . . It stopped at nothing in this effort, including . . . forced eviction of Palestinian[s] . . . from lands which they had inherited from their ancestors through the millennia.

For its crimes against . . . the Palestinians, against the individual Arabs of the surrounding countries as well as the ummah, Islam condemns Zionism. . . .

Therefore, the Islamic position leaves no chance for the Zionist state but to be dismantled and destroyed. . . . However, [this] does not necessarily mean the destruction of Jewish lives and property. . . . Islam commands the Muslims . . . never to go beyond the termination of injustice. . . . Islam further recommends pardon, mercy and forgiveness. . . .

Once the Zionist state, its army and other public institutions are destroyed, the problem of what to do with its population would have to be faced. . . . The solution is for the Jews . . . to be given the right to dwell wherever they wish. . . . If, for reasons of religious attachment, they wish to live in those areas of the Muslim world associated with their history . . . they ought to be entitled to do so by virtue of the respect Islam pays to the Prophets of God and the necessary sympathy and love for those that honor the prophetic tradition. . . .

Ismail R. al Faruqi, "Islam and Zionism," in John L. Esposito, ed., *Voices of Resurgent Islam* (New York: Oxford University Press, 1983), pp. 261–263.

Sheikh Ibrahim al-Quqa [a leader of Hamas] points out that the Intifada [the 1987–1991 Palestinian rebellion against Israeli occupation of the West Bank and Gaza Strip] . . . was born as a result of the interactions that had accumulated in the Islamic mentality and psyche inside the Occupied Territories. Al-Quqa summarized these interactions as follows:

• The true and profound Islamic consciousness, created by the Islamic mosques, pulpits, centers and institutions, and the strong Islamic groupings in the universities and colleges of occupied Palestine.

• The Muslim generation that is committed to its religion after a long alienation where it counted on earthly flags that were eclipsed by the 1967 defeat. [The 1967 Arab-Israeli war]

• The repressive practices by the Israeli occupation authorities, which came to us bearing the hatred of history, the complex of Nazism, and the thirst for blood in revenge. . . .

• The bankruptcy, negativism, and the end of the road to which the (Palestinian) organizations came; these organizations which raised non-Islamic slogans, abandoned the jihad and the determination to liberate all of Palestine.

Sheikh Ibrahim al-Quqa . . . states that the Intifada is "a phase, and a prelude to a more serious process of getting rid of the nightmare of the Zionist presence on this land."

Ziad Abu-Amr, *Islamic Fundamentalism in the West Bank and Gaza* (Bloomington: Indiana University Press, 1994),

THE SEPTEMBER 11, 2001, TERRORIST ATTACKS

On September 11, 2001, terrorists hijacked four American airliners and successfully crashed three of them into the two World Trade Center towers in New York City and the Pentagon outside of Washington, D.C. The man who is seen as responsible for these attacks is Osama bin Laden, a wealthy Saudi-born Islamic fundamentalist radical. Below is part of a statement issued by bin Laden in August of 1996 "declaring war" on the United States. Also presented here are comments from the Arab press shortly after the September 11 attacks.

DECLARATION OF WAR AGAINST THE AMERICANS
OCCUPYING THE LAND OF THE TWO HOLY PLACES—A
MESSAGE FROM USAMA BIN LADEN UNTO HIS MUSLIM
BRETHREN ALL OVER THE WORLD GENERALLY AND IN
THE ARAB PENINSULA SPECIFICALLY

Praise be to Allah, we seek His help and ask his pardon. . . . O you who believe be careful of your duty to Allah and speak the right word; He will put your deeds into a right state for you, and forgive your faults; and who ever obeys Allah and his Apostle, he indeed achieves a mighty success.

It should not be hidden from you that the people of Islam have suffered from aggression, iniquity and injustice imposed on them by the Zionist Crusader's alliance and their collaborators; to the extent that the Muslims' blood became the cheapest and their wealth as loot in the hands of their enemies. Their blood was spilled in Palestine and Iraq. The horrifying pictures of Qana in Lebanon are still fresh in our memory. . . . All of this the world watched and heard, and not only didn't respond to these atrocities, but also with a clear conspiracy between the USA and its allies, and under the cover of the iniquitous United Nations, the dispossessed people were even prevented from obtaining arms to defend themselves.

The people of Islam awakened and realized that they are the main target for the aggression of the Zionist Crusader's alliance. All false claims and propaganda about "human rights" were hammered down and exposed by the massacres that took place against the Muslims in every part of the world. The latest and greatest of these aggressions . . . is the occupation of the Land of the two Holy Places, the foundation of the house of Islam, the place of the revelation, the source of the message and the place of the noble Ka'ba, the Qiblah of all Muslims, by the armies of the American crusaders and their allies. . . .

We, myself and my group, have suffered some of this injustice ourselves. We have been prevented from addressing the Muslims. We have been pursued in Pakistan, Sudan and Afghanistan. Hence, this long absence on my part. But by the grace of Allah, a safe base is now available in the high Hindukush mountains in Khurasan where, by the grace of Allah, the largest infidel military force of the world [the Soviet Union in Afghanistan] was destroyed. The myth of the superpower was withered in front of the Mujahiden cries of Allah Akbar [God is greater]. . . . From here today we begin the work, talking and discussing the ways of correcting what has happened to the Islamic world in general, and the Land of the two Holy Places in particular.

In that land [Saudi Arabia] injustice has affected the people of industry and agriculture. It affects the people of the rural and urban areas. The situation . . . has become like a huge volcano at the verge of eruption that would destroy the Kufr [infidels who hide or cover the truth] and the corruption at its sources. The explosions at Riyadh and Al Khobar [attacks on U.S. military installations] are warnings of this volcanic eruption emerging as a result of the severe oppression, suffering, excessive iniquity, humiliation, and poverty.

The inability of the regime to protect the country, and allowing the enemy of the Ummah [Muslim community], the American Crusader forces, to occupy the land for the longest years [is a sign of its corruption]. The crusader forces became the main cause of our disastrous condition, particularly the economic aspect, due to our [Saudi] unjustified heavy spending in order to help support these forces. [Poor conditions are also] a result of the policy imposed . . . in the oil industry where production is restricted or expanded and prices are fixed to suit the American economy, ignoring the economy of our own country. Expensive deals were imposed on the country to buy arms. People are asking what is the justification for the very existence of a regime [that behaves in this fashion].

Quick efforts were made by individuals and by different groups of the society to contain the situation and to prevent danger. They advised the government both privately and openly. . . . The advocates of correction and reform were very keen on using peaceful means in order to protect the unity of the country and to prevent blood shed. Why is it then that the regime closed all peaceful routes and pushed the people toward armed actions? That was soon the only choice left for them to implement righteousness and justice. To whose benefit does prince Sultan and prince Nayeff push the country into a civil war that will destroy everything? . . . No doubt that this is the policy of the American-Israeli alliance as they are the first to benefit from this situation.

Clearly, after Belief there is no more important duty than pushing the American enemy out of the Holy Land. . . . There is no other duty after Belief than fighting the enemy who is corrupting life and religion. . . . If it is not possible to push back the enemy except by the collective movement of the Muslim people, then there is a duty on the Muslims to ignore the minor differences among themselves. The ill effect of ignoring these differences, at a given period of time, is much less than the ill effect of the occupation of Muslim lands by the main Kufr [infidel].

To My Muslim brothers of the world I say, your brothers in Palestine and in the Land of the two Holy Places are calling upon your help and asking you to take part in fighting against the enemy, your enemy, the

Americans and the Israelis. They are asking you to do whatever you can to expel the enemy. . . .

I say to you [the American leadership] that these [Muslim] youths love death as you love life. They inherit dignity, pride, courage, generosity, truthfulness, and sacrifice from father to father. They are most delivering and steadfast in war. . . . These values are approved and completed by Islam as stated by the messenger of Allah. [We] reject humiliation.

The Azzam foundation Web site, azzam/html/articlesdeclaration.htm. The document can also be obtained through the Web site of the Joyner Library of East Carolina University, http://www.lib.ecu.edu/govdoc/terrorism.html#binladn.

ARAB PRESS COMMENTS ON THE SEPTEMBER 11, 2001, ATTACKS AND THEIR AFTERMATH

The war in Afghanistan against the former Soviet Union gave international legitimacy to the military wing of political Islam. . . . The Arab world over the past three years has witnessed a number of confrontations with the "Islamicist" movement, the most famous being the assassination of Anwar al-Sadat. . . . [Arab] regimes relied on security measures, arrests, military and secret courts, and assassinations to tackle the movement. At the same time they made major concessions, thus exerting as much effort in adopting the ideas and propaganda of the movement as they did in containing and liquidating it. It was as if violent ideas were in no way responsible for extremism and violence. Furthermore, the regimes tried to tackle this movement with restrictions on public liberty and the silencing of other voices in society, oblivious of the need for democracy and freedom of expression, the building of state institutions, economic reform and a campaign against corruption.

No doubt political regimes in the Arab world have now realized their past mistakes. Adopting the idea of extremism and [at the same time] attacking its symbols delayed the occurrence of the catastrophe [but] did not remedy the problem. Instead, it created a new generation of extremists. What is needed in the immediate future is a campaign against extremist thought that produces terrorism, while reinforcing freedom and democracy.

Daud al-Hiryan, "Who Is Responsible for the Extremism?" published in the Arabic daily *al-Hayat* on October 13, 2001 (translation by Middle East Economic Survey, www.mees.com).

The Americans these days are asking: "Why do they hate us?" Just as many Arabs are asking: "Why do they insult us and hold us in contempt?"

Each side addresses the other in language which lacks mutual understanding. . . . At this extremely dangerous and sensitive time, perhaps [we have] an appropriate opportunity to answer a number of other questions, among them: why have American-Arab relations been afflicted by this gulf between them despite the fact that they have so many shared interests? To say that the American-Israeli relationship is conducted at the expense of the rights of the Arabs is not the only answer, although it is central to the issue. The failed and revengeful American policy against Iraq is not the only answer either. . . . America will not win the battles of this war if they are based on the military, intelligence and financial aspect of it, rather than the political one. No matter how much American tells the peoples in the Arab and Islamic worlds that it is not a war against the Arabs and the Muslims, the words will have no effect unless America changes its policies. And in order to change its [American] policies . . . grassroots Arab participation will be necessary from a number of sectors—from governments, the silent majority, the active minority, the religious community and the media [to send a message to the American government]. The decision is Arab as much as American. The question is, what do we want? What is the will of the Arab majority—and not just the minority who have made it abundantly clear that damage and destruction, and boycotting others and isolating themselves from today's world is the preferred choice.

Ms. Raghda Dargham, "America Will Profit from the War if It Amends Its Policies" published in the Arabic daily *al-Hayat* on October 12, 2001 (translation by Middle East Economic Survey, *www.mees.com*).

The United States has begun its military and financial war against terrorism. Those implicated in the criminal acts carried out in New York, sadly, were Muslims, as Usama bin Laden revealed in his televised speech when he described them as "a vanguard of holy warriors" who had become martyrs. There is another war that should get under way in every Arab and Islamic land. This is not a military or security war, nor is our aim to arrest adherents to various streams of political Islam or prevent them from expressing their opinions within the law. Rather the war is against the presentation of Islam to our young people and children as an extremist religion. . . . The war against terrorism . . . requires an appropriate and proper foundation, with human rights and freedom of expression at its core. We need to establish humane conditions for our youth in which there is no unemployment, poverty and inequality of opportunity. And we need to propagate the idea of tolerance and accepting the views of others. Terrorism exists and no religion can stop it. . . . There is no religion for terrorism and extremism, but there is an environment in which terrorism grows and is nurtured. Our duty is to eliminate the environment of terrorism and drain its wells by protecting our youth from the idea of immoderation and extremism and by creating a healthy climate for human existence which does not allow terrorism to survive.

Ahmad al-Rub'i, "Their War . . . and Our War Against Terrorism," published in the Arabic daily Asharq al-Awsat on October 9, 2001 (translation by Middle East Economic Survey, *www.mees.com*).

In my speech I focused on four points. With respect to our expressions of deep sadness about the killing of 6,000 innocent American civilians, we should not forget the killing of a million innocent Iraqi children who have died because of the embargo, and the tens of thousands of innocent Palestinians who have fallen victim to the occupation. Secondly, while politicians have called for an international alliance against terrorism, it is more appropriate that people of conscience should call for an equivalent international alliance against oppression and hatred. Thirdly, Mr. Berlusconi [the Italian Prime Minister who asserted on September 26, 2001 that Western civilization was superior to Islamic civilization] should be thanked for what he said about Islamic civilization, not because we agree with his remarks, but because they revealed what was beneath the surface and articulated the true feelings of the majority of politicians and intellectuals in the Western world—feelings rooted in superiority over and loathing of Islam and Muslims. This is a state of affairs that warns us of the need to heed the role of the prevailing culture in the West in encouraging bigotry and sweeping hatred towards us among its people. Fourthly, I do not see any significant difference between the views of bin Laden and Mr. Berlusconi, because they are both the victims of mistaken perceptions and stand together in the same square of hatred. The former hates the West and fights it with weapons, while the latter hates Islam and uses the arrows of his public pronouncements to confront it.

Fahmi Huwaidi referring to a speech he gave at a recent meeting on Christianity and Islam in Rome, published in *al-Watan* on October 9, 2001 (translation by Middle East Economic Survey, *www.mees.com*).

Glossary of Selected Terms

ISLAMIC FUNDAMENTALIST ORGANIZATIONS

Below are listed some of the more well-known Islamic fundamentalist groups that actively pursue the goal of an Islamic state. It is to be noted that the vast majority of those who see themselves as Islamic fundamentalists do not belong to the more militant and sometimes violent organizations. There are thousands of Islamic welfare and civic organizations that are not politically active but still consider themselves fundamentalist in their interpretation of the Muslim faith.

Al-Qaeda (the Base or the Firm Base). An organization of mujahedin fighters (resistance fighters who in this case see themselves as "warriors for God") established by Usama bin Laden in the 1980s. It is made up mainly of Arab veterans of the war in Afghanistan against the Soviet Union. Toward the end of the Afghan war (1989), al-Qaeda cells were established in many Middle Eastern countries. Their aim was to fight for a "purer form of Islam." After the Gulf War (1991) al-Qaeda concentrated particularly on Saudi Arabia and the United States. The main issue was the retention of American military forces in the "holy land" of Arabia. Subsequently, al-Qaeda attacked a series of American targets including military barracks, embassies, the U.S. naval ship *Cole*, and finally the World Trade Center and the Pentagon. This last attack triggered the U.S. war against the Taliban government of Afghanistan in late 2001 because it harbored Usama bin Laden and the al-Qaeda leadership.

Hamas (also known as the Islamic Resistance Movement). A militant Palestinian Islamic fundamentalist organization, founded in 1987 just after the outbreak of the Palestinian rebellion known as the Intifada. Growing out of the older and more moderate Muslim Brotherhood in the Gaza Strip, it denounced any compromise with the Israelis and called for transformation of all of Palestine into an Islamic state. Hamas engages in some social and economic welfare work as well as maintaining a clandestine military wing. This wing is responsible for numerous attacks on Israeli occupation forces as well as civilians. The organization is also the main opposition group contesting the power of the Palestine National Authority of Yasir Arafat.

Hezbollah (the Party of God). The major Shi'ite Islamic fundamentalist organization of Lebanon. It was begun in the early 1980s with the help of Iranian Shi'ite volunteers then active in Lebanon and established itself as a social service organization running clinics, hospitals, schools, and food cooperatives. Today it continues with much of this activity. Its military wing participated in the Lebanese civil war and was involved in the taking of Western hostages, car bombings, and other violent acts. It also fought against the Israeli invasion of Lebanon and continues to resist Israeli occupation of a "buffer zone" strip of southern Lebanon. Today, Hezbollah's political wing functions as a legal political party within the Lebanese democratic system.

Islamic Action Front. The major Islamic fundamentalist organization of Jordan. In Jordan, social welfare and religious groups are not allowed to present themselves as political parties; consequently, the Front only carries on political activity. It is, however, informally associated with the Jordanian Muslim Brotherhood. The Front fields political candidates in Jordanian elections and, working within the system, pressures for the re-Islamization of the Jordanian state and society. It has opposed the Israeli-Jordanian peace treaty.

Islamic Group (also known as Gam'a Islamiya). One of the more militant Egyptian Islamic fundamentalist organizations. Founded in the early 1970s, it draws its membership mostly from poor villages, urban slums, and students. The organization claims Shaikh Umar Abd al-Rahman as its spiritual guide. A social service-oriented operation known as the Da'wa (or Call) is affiliated with the Islamic Group. The Islamic Group has been implicated in attacks on Egyptian government personnel and others and is thus considered an illegal organization.

Islamic Jihad (also known as New Jihad). Another militant Egyptian Islamic fundamentalist organization considered illegal because of its violent attacks on the Egyptian state. Its members are thought to have been involved in the assassination of Anwar Sadat. Islamic Jihad recruits from students and the professional classes.

Islamic National Front. The major Islamic fundamentalist party of Sudan. For more information on the Islamic National Front, see the biography of its leader, Hasan 'Abdallah al-Turabi.

Islamic Salvation Front (FIS). The now suppressed major Islamic fundamentalist movement of Algeria. For more information on the FIS, see the biography of its leader, Abbasi Madani.

Islamic Tendency Movement (also known as MTI and the Islamic Tunisian Renaissance Organization). The now suppressed major Islamic fundamentalist movement of Tunisia. For more information on the MTI, see the biography of its leader, Rashid al-Ghannoushi.

Islamic Welfare Party (also known as Refah). The major Islamic fundamentalist party of Turkey. Turkey is an officially secular state with democratic practices. In recent years, however, the Islamic Welfare party has made major electoral gains due to its effective grassroots organizing and to the popular frustration over economic and social problems. While the party seeks the reintroduction of Islamic practices into public life (law, education, dress, the media), it cannot risk threatening the democratic process without inviting military intervention. Nonetheless, Refah proved strong enough in the 1996 Turkish national elections to be able to form a coalition government.

Jama'at-i Islami (also known as the Islamic party). The major Islamic fundamentalist party of Pakistan. For more information on the Jama'at-i Islami, see the biography of its leader, Sayyid Abu'l-A'la Mawdudi.

Muslim Brotherhoods. Almost every country of the Muslim world has an active Muslim Brotherhood more or less fashioned on the original organization founded in Egypt by Hasan al-Banna. In most cases, these Brotherhoods, though espousing the re-Islamization of their states and societies, are politically discrete and seek, as far as possible, to work within the established political systems. Their activities are often focused on social/economic welfare projects and issues.

The Taliban. The most militarily successful of the Islamic fundamentalist organizations of Afghanistan. Reportedly founded by devout Islamic students during the long Afghan civil war, the group emerged as a military force in 1995–1996. Until the U.S. attack on Afghanistan in 2001, the Taliban controlled a good part of the country, including the capital of Kabul. The Taliban were very strict and conservative in their application of Islamic law and have drawn much criticism in the West for their refusal to allow women access to either the job market or public education.

TERMS AND NAMES

Ali. The prophet Muhammad's cousin and son-in-law as well as the fourth Caliph. Shi'ite Muslims believe that Ali was the only rightful, and God-ordained, heir to Muhammad's worldly authority.

Allah. The Muslim name for God. Allah is the same God as that of Jews and Christians.

Amir. A Muslim ruler or governor.

Ayatollah. A Shi'ite religious and legal authority of high rank.

Caliph. (Khalifa). Viceregent or heir of Muhammad as worldly leader of the Islamic community.

C.E. Common Era. The date designation used by Muslims and Jews in the place of A.D. (Anno Domini).

Chador. See Veil.

Dhimmi. Non-Muslim citizens of a Muslim state. Such citizens were subject to a special "poll" tax and designated as a "protected group."

Hadith. A report of the prophet Muhammad's words or actions, or those of his close companions of which he approved. Such reports must be documented through a chain of witnesses judged historically reliable. So judged, such a report, or hadith, becomes a valid basis for Muslim law.

Hakim. Judge and administrator. The worldly position Muhammad held at Medina.

Hijab. See Veil.

Hijrah. The movement (emigration) of Muhammad and his followers from Mecca to Medina where he established the first Islamic state. This occurred in 622 C.E., but it is from this date that Muslims begin the counting of their calendar.

Ijma. Consensus of opinion among either the overall community of Muslims or the Muslim ulama. Such consensus can be a basis for religious law.

Ijtihad. Independent judgment exercised on matters of religion or religious law not specifically detailed in the Quran.

Imam. A religio-political leader of the Shi'ite Muslim community. Traditionally, an Imam is a descendant of Muhammad through the line of Ali.

Intifada. The Palestinian rebellion of the late 1980s against Israeli occupation of the West Bank and Gaza Strip. The Intifada gave rise to the militant Palestinian Islamic fundamentalist group known as Hamas.

Islam. The religion of the Muslims which declares the existence of one almighty God who revealed Himself to humankind through a series of prophets, the last and final one being Muhammad. To Muhammad, God gave His final revelation, the Quran. Islam literally means submission to God.

Islamic Fundamentalism. A Western term used to designate contemporary Islamic movements that advocate a strict observance of Islamic law and values, and the institutionalization of these through the establishment of an Islamic state. Also known as Islamic revivalism, Islamic activism, and political Islam.

Islamic Modernists. A movement of Islamic reformers active at the end of the nineteenth and the beginning of the twentieth centuries. They advocated the reform of Muslim society through a modern reinterpretation of Muslim teachings and values. This would dovetail with the Islamization of certain aspects of Western ways and institutions.

Jahiliyya. The state of ignorance that Arabia was in before Muhammed's revelation and the introduction of Islam. Today's Islamic fundamentalists use the term to describe the un-Islamic behavior of contemporary society.

Jihad. Literally to strive or struggle to follow the precepts of Islam. This can entail war waged in defense of the faith, but more commonly it means the daily effort an individual makes to live the life of a righteous Muslim. In the West, however, the word has taken on the meaning of fanatical warfare.

Jurisprudent (vilayat-i-faqih). The highest state office in the Islamic Republic of Iran. The post was first held by the Ayatollah Khomeini.

Koran. See Quran.

Majles. A parliament or advisory council; the name of the legislative body in the Islamic Republic of Iran.

Mosque. Muslim house of worship. As in the West with churches and synagogues, mosques also often serve as community centers.

Mujahedin. A resistance fighter. Those adhering to Islamic fundamentalist causes see themselves as "warriors for God." In the West the term is increasingly associated with armed Islamic militants.

Mullah. A religious leader. The term is most widely used in Iran.

Muslim. Literally translated, the term means one who submits to God's will; any follower of the religion of Islam.

Pahlavi. The name of the ancient language of pre-Islamic Persia. The last ruling family of Iran (1925–1979) took this term as its dynastic name.

Prophet, The. Muhammad who, in the Islamic faith, is the receiver of Allah's, or God's, final revelation.

Purdah. A Persian term meaning the separation of women from men, as well as the modest dress of women.

Quran. The Muslim holy book (often spelled Koran in English translation) in which is written Allah's, or God's, final revelation. The Quran is the main source of Muslim religious, or Shariah, law.

Shah. The title taken by the former kings of Persia and Iran.

Shariah. The body of Muslim law based primarily on the Quran and the documented sayings and actions of the prophet Muhammad (hadith). Shariah law also can be formulated using the techniques of analogy, consensus, and legal opinion that flow from and are consistent with the Quran and hadiths.

Shi'ite (Shi'a or Shi'i). A minority branch of Islam in which the members believe that, following the death of Muhammad, leadership of the Muslim community should have gone to Ali. Shi'ites believe that their rightful leader is now the Imam, who is descended from Ali, and in whose absence the community is best led by religious leaders known as Ayatollahs.

Shura. An advisory council. In Islamic political theory, the shura can be the basis for a parliament or legislature.

Sufism. Islamic mysticism. Islamic mystics (Sufis) and those attracted to such pursuits are often organized in Sufi Orders. Historically, such groups have done much to integrate local traditions and beliefs into the religion of Islam.

Sometimes this has incurred the resistance and hostility of more orthodox ulama.

Sunna. The behavior and practice of the prophet Muhammad. Particular documented reports of such practice are known as hadiths. The Sunna is one of the main sources of Islamic law.

Sunni. The majority branch of Islam. Sunnis accept the legitimacy of the Caliphs who immediately succeeded Muhammad. They see themselves as true followers of Muhammad's way, or path (his Sunna).

Tawhid. The oneness of God or God's absolute unity; by extension, God's sovereignty over the Islamic community or state. Thus, God's laws (Shariah) are the only basis for law and values in the Islamic state.

Ulama. The collective term used to designate Muslim scholars, jurists, and clerics. The singular form of the word is alim.

Ummah. The Islamic community. The term is used not only for a local or national community, but also for the community of Muslims worldwide.

Veil (Hijab or Chador). The scarf or headcovering worn in public by Muslim women. This may take a more or less elaborate form, sometimes covering just the hair while at other times also covering most of the face, shoulders, and breasts. The chador of Iran constitutes a loose-fitting robe covering most of the body.

Wahhabi. The austere Islamic sect founded by Muhammad ibn Abd al-Wahhab in the eighteenth century. It is now the dominant sect of Islam in Saudi Arabia.

Zakat. An annual charity tax for the aid of the needy. It usually stands at 2.5 percent of one's wealth. All Muslims are called upon to pay the zakat or give to charity in one form or another. The zakat has been made a formal tax in countries with Islamic governments.

Annotated Bibliography

BOOKS

Abrahamian, Ervand. *Iran Between Two Revolutions.* Princeton, N.J.: Princeton University Press, 1982. A comprehensive study of the historical and sociopolitical background of the 1979 revolution that ushered in the Islamic Republic of Iran. After a short chapter on the nineteenth century, the author picks up the story with the "constitutional" revolution of 1906 and traces the political history of Iran through to 1979.

Abu-Amr, Ziad. *Islamic Fundamentalism in the West Bank and Gaza: Muslim Brotherhood and Islamic Jihad.* Bloomington: Indiana University Press, 1994. A study of Islamic fundamentalism within the context of Israeli occupation of the Gaza Strip. The author demonstrates how the Intifada (the Palestinian rebellion of the late 1980s against the occupation) enhanced the standing and membership of the Palestinian Islamic movement. The book also demonstrates clearly the tactical differences among fundamentalists.

Abul Jobain, Ahmad, and Ahmed Bin Yousef, eds. *The Politics of Islamic Resurgence: Through Western Eyes.* North Springfield, Va.: United Association for Studies and Research, Inc., 1992. A bibliographic survey that lists books and articles on the "Islamic resurgence" written by Western authors. Three essays by Muslim writers commenting on Western perceptions of Islam precedes the list.

Algar, Hamid, trans. and ed. *Islam and Revolution: Writings and Declarations of Iman Khomeini.* Berkeley, Calif.: Mizan Press, 1981. A rendering into English of some of Khomeini's more important pronouncements. The contents are well edited, and esoteric Shi'ite terms and concepts are adequately explained.

Appleby, R. Scott, ed. *Spokesmen for the Despised: Fundamentalist Leaders of the Middle East.* Chicago: University of Chicago Press, 1997. A collection of essays on the many religious orthodox movements and their leaders in the Middle East, offering a comparative perspective on religion and politics in the region.

Bakhash, Shaul. *The Reign of the Ayatollahs: Iran and the Islamic Revolution.* London: Tauris, 1985. A good historical account of what occurred in Iran in the years following the Islamic revolution. The book provides insights into the personalities behind the various factions as well as the tactics and maneuverings that led to the formation of Iran's Islamic government.

Bodansky, Yossef. *Bin Laden: The Man Who Declared War on America.* New York: Prima Publishing, 1999. A biography of Usama bin Laden focusing on his radicalization and growing hostility toward the United States. The book includes a wealth of facts as well as undocumented speculation.

Esposito, John. *Islam and Politics.* Syracuse, N.Y.: Syracuse University Press, 1991. An analysis of the impact of Islamic revivalism on the concepts of society, statecraft, nationalism, and other aspects of politics as practiced in the modern Muslim world. The book also takes up the ideas of influential contemporary Muslim thinkers such as Qutb, Mawdudi, Shariati, and Khomeini.

Esposito, John. *The Islamic Threat: Myth or Reality?* New York: Oxford University Press, 1992. A discussion of the various present-day Islamic organizations, followed by a consideration of whether Islamic activism is really a threat to the West, or whether its goals are truly incompatible with Western social or political norms. The author's approach is one of empathy toward Islam, and he is here, at least in part, trying to respond to those who try to paint Islamic activists as enemies of Western civilization.

Esposito, John. *The Straight Path.* New York: Oxford University Press, 1988. A general introductory work on Islam as both a religion and a sociopolitical worldview. Along the way, the book effectively debunks the Western stereotype of Islam as a violent and aggressive ideology.

Esposito, John, ed. *Voices of Resurgent Islam.* New York: Oxford University Press, 1983. A work divided into two sections. The first offers selected essays by non-Muslim experts who analyze the positions taken by influential Islamic thinkers such as Qutb, Iqbal, and Shariati. In a separate section, Muslim thinkers present their ideas on topics such as the state, social change, democracy, and economics.

Esposito, John, and John Donohue, eds. *Islam in Transition: Muslim Perspectives.* New York: Oxford University Press, 1982. A broad range of essays, written by noted thinkers from throughout the Islamic world, on subjects of concern to reformist-minded Muslims. Topics range from law to economics, women's rights issues, and family planning

Fernea, Elizabeth Warnock, ed. *Women and the Family in the Middle East.* Austin: University of Texas Press, 1985. A series of life histories, supplemented by other documents and original sources. It attempts to depict the changing nature of women's lives, particularly in the Arab Muslim world. Topics covered include health, law, violence, and education.

Fuller, Graham, and Ian Lesser. *A Sense of Siege: The Geopolitics of Islam and the West.* (A Rand Study). Boulder, Colo.: Westview Press, 1995. A well-balanced and insightful work that explores the roots of Western fears of an Islamic revival, as well as similar fears felt by the Muslim East toward the West.

Gerges, Fawaz A. *America and Political Islam: Clash of Cultures or Clash of Interests?* New York and London: Cambridge University Press, 1999. The book focuses on U.S. policy making toward the Middle East and the impact of Islamic Fundamentalism on that process. Fair but critical, the work highlights the inability of American policy makers to understand the Muslim world on its own terms.

Gilsenan, Michael. *Recognizing Islam: Religion and Society in the Modern World.* New York: Pantheon Books, 1983. An examination of Islam as it shapes society in various communities around the Muslim world. The work provides a sense of the variety of Muslim experience, thus undercutting the myth of a monolithic Islamic world. Also taken up are the varying Muslim reactions to the impact of Western culture.

Haddad, Yvonne Yazbeck, and Wadi Z. Haddad, eds. *Christian-Muslim Encounters.* New Brunswick, N.J.: Transaction Books, 1996. A series of essays by prominent Islamic and Western scholars on the ways Muslims and Christians have encountered and engaged one another over time, with attention to recent interpolitical, intersocial, and intereconomic concerns.

Haddad, Yvonne, Byron Haines, and Ellison Findly, eds. *The Islamic Impact.* Syracuse, N.Y.: Syracuse University Press, 1984. A collection of ten clearly written essays looking at Islam's impact on such areas as politics, education, law, art, women's issues, and economics.

Hunter, Shireen T., ed. *The Politics of Islamic Revivalism: Diversity and Unity.* Bloomington: Indiana University Press, 1988. A collection of essays on the activities and influence of Islamic movements broken down by country. The work covers not only the core countries of the Middle East, but also West Africa, Pakistan, Malaysia, and Indonesia.

Ismael, Tareq Y., and Jacqueline E. Ismael. *Government and Politics in Islam.* New York: St. Martin's Press, 1985. A relatively short work (177 pp.) that looks at the impact of resurgent Islamic forces on the politics of the modern Muslim world.

Lawrence, Bruce B. *Shattering the Myth: Islam Beyond Violence.* Princeton, N.J.: Princeton University Press, 1998. This book emphasizes the complex, transnational character of the Muslim religion, and argues that it is too diverse and multifaceted to be neatly categorized, or stereotyped.

Lewis, Bernard. *Islam and the West.* New York: Oxford University Press, 1993. A collection of essays by a noted scholar, examining such subjects as Western perceptions of Islam historically and in light of recent geopolitical interests, the misinterpretation of Islamic/Arabic concepts and terms, the tensions between religious and secular concepts of the state and Islam, and the "demonology" of militant Muslim fundamentalism.

Lewis, Bernard. *What Went Wrong? Western Impact and Middle East Response.* New York: Oxford University Press, 2002. In this book Lewis explores Muslim attitudes to the West and the cultural and political impact on their world. He argues that the Muslim society has a responsibility to let go its "rage" and renew its civilization in ways compatible with the modern age.

Mayer, Ann Elizabeth. *Islam and Human Rights.* 2nd ed. Boulder, Colo.: Westview Press, 1995. A comparative study of Islamic notions of human rights set against the Western-based standards that now underlay international law. The author draws on the writings of many Islamic fundamentalists as well as the experience of such countries as Iran and Sudan.

Mernissi, Fatima. *Beyond the Veil: Male-Female Dynamics in Modern Muslim Society.* 2nd ed. Bloomington: Indiana University Press, 1987. A famous work that looks at the gender relationships and sexual attitudes of Muslim men and women. These are then connected to the Islamic law and mores prevailing in the Muslim world. The introduction to the second edition discusses the situation Muslim women find themselves in given the rise of Islamic revivalist movements.

Milani, Mohsen M. *The Making of Iran's Islamic Revolution: From Monarchy to Islamic Republic.* 2nd ed. Boulder, Colo.: Westview Press, 1994. This work offers a brief history of twentieth-century Iran with the specific aim of understanding the revolution of 1979. It also examines events that followed the fall of the Shah and the competition for power among the varying radical and moderate factions that made up the revolutionary movement.

Miller, Judith. *God Has Ninety-Nine Names.* New York: Simon and Schuster, 1996. A book written by the Cairo Bureau Chief of the New York Times and a reporter in the Middle East of many years. It constitutes a country-by-country account of the author's interviews with, and impressions of, Islamic leaders and their movements.

Mitchell, Richard P. *The Society of the Muslim Brothers.* New York: Oxford University Press, 1993 ed. The best and most detailed English-language study of the Egyptian Muslim Brothers. The author traces the brotherhood from its founding through the mid-1950s. He also weaves into the history of the Society a brief biography of its founder, Hasan al-Banna.

Mottahedeh, Roy. *The Mantle of the Prophet: Religion and Politics in Iran.* New York: Pantheon Books, 1985. An excellent work that uses the construction of the life of a fictional Iranian Mullah as a literary device to trace out the history of Iran in the twentieth century. In the process, the country's Shi'ite religious tradition and values are explained and the rise of the ulama to power is explored.

Nasr, Sayyed Hossein. *Islam and the Plight of Modern Man.* London: Longman, 1975. A well-written book that gives an in-depth look into the dilemmas faced by the modern, believing Muslim. It describes the tension created by faith in a Muslim worldview confronted by the allures of Western materialism.

Pinto, Maria do Ceu. *Political Islam and the United States.* Reading UK: Ithaca Press, 1999. This book describes the debate over how to respond to Islamic Fundamentalism going on in the United States. It explains how Islamic Fundamentalism has come to be identified as a major security threat by many in the government and how such an interpretation also reflects the views of powerful interest groups.

Piscatori, James P. *Islam in a World of Nation-States.* New York: Cambridge University Press, 1986. An examination of modern nationalism juxtaposed with the traditional Islamic belief in the transnational nature of the Muslim community. The author argues that the organizational structure of the modern nation-state is here to stay. Therefore, over time, Islamic political values can and will be adapted to it, even while Muslim states promote cultural and religious links.

Rahnema, Ali, ed. *Pioneers of Islamic Revival.* London: Zed Books, 1994. An offering of biographical essays on ten major Islamic reformers including

Hasan al-Banna and Ayatollah Khomeini. Well-written and researched, these essays give insight into the upbringing and social background of some of the men behind the on-going Islamic resurgence.

Rashid, Ahmed. *Taliban.* New Haven, Connecticut: Yale University Press, 2000. This book by a reporter who has spent years in the Pakistan and Afghanistan region is a detailed description of the rise of the Taliban movement. It also explains Taliban behavior on such questions as women's rights.

Said, Edward. *Covering Islam: How the Media and the Experts Determine How We See the Rest of the World.* New York: Pantheon Books, 1981. A revealing analysis of the biases and stereotypes that pervade media coverage and "expert" opinions on events in the Muslim world. The author spends much time on coverage of Iran and, in the end, demonstrates that the simplistic and partial nature of what we are told about Islam is driven by deeply rooted prejudices and interest-oriented politics.

Shaheen, Jack G. *Arab and Muslim Stereotyping in American Popular Culture.* Washington, D.C.: Georgetown University Center for Muslim–Christian Understanding, 1997. A short (80 pages) outline of the stereotyping of Arabs and Muslims in American movies, television, and news print and programming. The book also describes incidents where such stereotyping has been challenged.

Shaheen, Jack G. *Reel Bad Arabs: How Hollywood Vilifies a People.* Northhampton, Mass.: Interlink Publishing Group, 2001. An encyclopedic look at how Hollywood films have portrayed Arabs. In this 592-page effort the author has considered almost every American film that has included Arabs as part of the script. The result helps the reader understand how films have played a major role in defaming the Arab character, and therefore have much to do with the distorted image Americans have of Arabs today.

Sidahmed, Abdel Salam, and Anoushiravan Ehteshami, eds. *Islamic Fundamentalism.* Boulder, Colo.: Westview Press, 1996. A series of essays on contemporary Islamic movements. After a general discussion of the Islamic worldview, the book proceeds to case studies of Islamic movements in Algeria, Egypt, Iran, Pakistan, and other places. The work ends with a comparative essay on Algeria and Iran.

Sisk, Timothy D. *Islam and Democracy.* Washington, D.C.: United States Institute of Peace Press, 1992. This small work (72 pp.) discusses the repoliticization of Islam now occurring and juxtaposes it with "the global wave of democratization in the late twentieth century." It then considers the question of whether Islam is compatible with democracy, examining the stance of Islamic movements in various countries in the process.

Stowasser, Barbara Freyer, ed. *The Islamic Impulse.* Washington, D.C.: Center for Contemporary Arab Studies, 1987. A series of papers analyzing Islamic fundamentalism from two different perspectives—first from a secular perspective, covering topics such as Islam and nationalism, capitalism, and political power; then from the Islamic reformist perspective, covering such topics as criminal justice, constitutionalism, women and the family, and the Muslim critique of the status quo.

Suleiman, Michael. *The Arabs in the Mind of America.* Brattleboro, Vt.: Amana Books, 1988. A revealing consideration of American attitudes toward Muslims. The author has particularly concentrated on an examination of high school textbooks to determine the prevailing stereotypes of Arabs held by Americans.

Taylor, Alan R. *The Islamic Question in Middle East Politics.* Boulder, Colo.: Westview Press, 1988. An excellent exploration of the problems that have confronted the Middle East in the twentieth century and the various indigenous responses made to these challenges. Particular attention is paid to Islamic modernism and Islamic fundamentalism, or what the author calls "neofundamentalism." A detailed analysis of the Iranian Revolution is also given.

Wendell, Charles, trans. and annotator. *Five Tracts of Hasan Al-Banna (1906–1949).* Berkeley, Calif.: University of California Press, 1978. A translation of five of Hasan al-Banna's essays covering topics such as "Our Mission" and "On Jihad."

Winters, Paul A., ed. *Islam: Opposing Viewpoints.* San Diego, Calif.: Greenhaven Press, 1995. A series of essays arranged by chapter so as to argue two sides of an issue. Various issues relevant to the phenomenon of modern Islamic fundamentalism are offered such as "Can Democracy Coexist with Islam?" and "What Is the Status of Women Under Islam?" Designed to promote thought and discussion, this book is an excellent classroom tool.

Zakaria, Rafiq. *The Struggle Within Islam.* London: Penguin Books, 1989. A descriptive analysis of the origins and evolution of Islamic fundamentalism. The work covers not only the Middle East, but also Africa and India. The author deals topically with such issues as nationalism and the Islamic response to socialism and communism. The last one-third of the book is comprised of appendices that include a detailed chronology of events from Muhammad's birth in 570 to the 1980s.

INTERNET SOURCES OF INFORMATION

Information about Islam and Islamic movements on the Internet is available from AWAIR, Arab World and Islamic Resources and School Services. This is a nonprofit organization dedicated to education about Arab and Muslim culture. It offers a guide to a large variety of books, audio tapes, and curriculum aids for teachers. AWAIR can be accessed at *http://www.telegraphave.com/gui/awairproductinfo.html*. General information about Islam and the Middle East can be obtained from the Center for Middle Eastern Studies Web site at *http://w#arizona.edu/-cmesua/*. The site is maintained by the University of Arizona's Center for Middle Eastern Studies; and also the Center for Middle Eastern and Islamic Studies Web site at *http://www.dur.ac.uk/-dme0www/*. The site is maintained by the University of Durham in England.

FILMS (VHS)

The Arabs: A Living History—In the Shadow of the West. Landmark Films. Falls Church, Va. (50 minutes). Written by historian Edward Said. Among the issues that have enhanced the popularity of Islamic fundamentalism is the intractable problem of Palestinian-Israeli violence. The film *In the Shadow of the West,* written and narrated by Professor Edward Said of Columbia University, explores this conflict within a larger context of East-West history. While this film does not touch directly on Islamic fundamentalism, it gives the viewer a good sense of how Islamists view the Arab-Israeli conflict and thus why they are moved to active opposition to Israel.

The Arabs: Between Two Worlds. Landmark Films. Falls Church, Va. (58 minutes). Written by the anthropologist Abdallah Hammoudi. This film follows the life of an upper middle-class Moroccan man from childhood to maturity. His life as a child is a traditional one, but upon maturity he becomes exposed to Western life and culture. The film examines the resulting dilemmas and the man's efforts to meld the two influences.

Covered. Produced and directed by Tania Kamal-Edin. A Her Way Production, 1995. (50 minutes). An examination of the trend among women in many parts of the Muslim world to return to Islamic styles of dress. The social, cultural, and religious influences that encourage this phenomenon are explored in a wide range of interviews and analysis.

The Fundamental Question. Landmark Films. Falls Church, Va. A First Take Production, Produced and Directed by Ahmed Ajamal, 1994. (75 minutes). A description and history of modern Islamic activism in many

Muslim countries. It takes the viewer to Pakistan, Afghanistan, Egypt, Algeria, Tunisia, Jordan, and Turkey. Through interviews with both Islamist activists and their critics, the film examines the questions of fundamentalist Islam and democracy, women's issues, poverty, the law, and the issue of violence. The film draws a distinction between violent Islamic fringe groups (that grab most of the publicity given Islamic activism in the West) and the vast majority of Islamic moderates and reformers.

The Islamic Conversations series from Films for the Humanities, Inc. Princeton, N.J. (30 minutes each). A series of films discussing issues both relevant to the world of Islam and of concern to Western observers. Titles include: The Islamic State; Authority and Change; Islam and Christianity; Women and Islam; and Islam and Pluralism. The format of each film consists of a conversation between the interviewer and an expert on the subject who is him or herself a Muslim of note.

We Are God's Soldiers. Al-Quds Distribution. Normal, Ill. (53 minutes). Film made by Hanna Musleh. An exploration of the lives and outlooks of two brothers belonging to activist movements in the Gaza Strip. The film offers a picture of how Islamic fundamentalists have been influenced by the existence and actions of the state of Israel. It demonstrates that while Muslims oppose Israel and its occupation of Arab land, they do not always agree on how that opposition should be expressed.

Index

About the Author

LAWRENCE DAVIDSON is Professor of History at West Chester University in West Chester, Pennsylvania, where he teaches Middle East history. His latest book is titled *America's Palestine: Popular and Official Perceptions from Balfour to Israeli Statehood.*